Casenote® *Legal Briefs*

BUSINESS ORGANIZATIONS

Keyed to Courses Using

Allen and Kraakman's
Commentaries and Cases on the Law of Business Organization
Fifth Edition

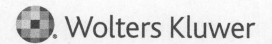

Copyright © 2017 CCH Incorporated. All Rights Reserved.

Published by Wolters Kluwer in New York.

Wolters Kluwer Legal & Regulatory US serves customers worldwide with
CCH, Aspen Publishers, and Kluwer Law International products.
(www.WKLegaledu.com)

To contact Customer Service, e-mail customer.service@wolterskluwer.com,
call 1-800-234-1660, fax 1-800-901-9075, or mail correspondence to:

Wolters Kluwer
Attn: Order Department
P.O. Box 990
Frederick, MD 21705

Printed in the United States of America.

1 2 3 4 5 6 7 8 9 0

ISBN 978-1-4548-8313-5

About Wolters Kluwer Legal & Regulatory US

Wolters Kluwer Legal & Regulatory US delivers expert content and solutions in the areas of law, corporate compliance, health compliance, reimbursement, and legal education. Its practical solutions help customers successfully navigate the demands of a changing environment to drive their daily activities, enhance decision quality and inspire confident outcomes.

Serving customers worldwide, its legal and regulatory portfolio includes products under the Aspen Publishers, CCH Incorporated, Kluwer Law International, ftwilliam.com and MediRegs names. They are regarded as exceptional and trusted resources for general legal and practice-specific knowledge, compliance and risk management, dynamic workflow solutions, and expert commentary.

Format for the Casenote® Legal Brief

Nature of Case: This section identifies the form of action (e.g., breach of contract, negligence, battery), the type of proceeding (e.g., demurrer, appeal from trial court's jury instructions), or the relief sought (e.g., damages, injunction, criminal sanctions).

Fact Summary: This is included to refresh your memory and can be used as a quick reminder of the facts.

Rule of Law: Summarizes the general principle of law that the case illustrates. It may be used for instant recall of the court's holding and for classroom discussion or home review.

Facts: This section contains all relevant facts of the case, including the contentions of the parties and the lower court holdings. It is written in a logical order to give the student a clear understanding of the case. The plaintiff and defendant are identified by their proper names throughout and are always labeled with a (P) or (D).

Palsgraf v. Long Island R.R. Co.

Injured bystander (P) v. Railroad company (D)

N.Y. Ct. App., 248 N.Y. 339, 162 N.E. 99 (1928).

NATURE OF CASE: Appeal from judgment affirming verdict for plaintiff seeking damages for personal injury.

FACT SUMMARY: Helen Palsgraf (P) was injured on R.R.'s (D) train platform when R.R.'s (D) guard helped a passenger aboard a moving train, causing his package to fall on the tracks. The package contained fireworks which exploded, creating a shock that tipped a scale onto Palsgraf (P).

🏛 RULE OF LAW
The risk reasonably to be perceived defines the duty to be obeyed.

FACTS: Helen Palsgraf (P) purchased a ticket to Rockaway Beach from R.R. (D) and was waiting on the train platform. As she waited, two men ran to catch a train that was pulling out from the platform. The first man jumped aboard, but the second man, who appeared as if he might fall, was helped aboard by the guard on the train who had kept the door open so they could jump aboard. A guard on the platform also helped by pushing him onto the train. The man was carrying a package wrapped in newspaper. In the process, the man dropped his package, which fell on the tracks. The package contained fireworks and exploded. The shock of the explosion was apparently of great enough strength to tip over some scales at the other end of the platform, which fell on Palsgraf (P) and injured her. A jury awarded her damages, and R.R. (D) appealed.

ISSUE: Does the risk reasonably to be perceived define the duty to be obeyed?

HOLDING AND DECISION: (Cardozo, C.J.) Yes. The risk reasonably to be perceived defines the duty to be obeyed. If there is no foreseeable hazard to the injured party as the result of a seemingly innocent act, the act does not become a tort because it happened to be a wrong as to another. If the wrong was not willful, the plaintiff must show that the act as to her had such great and apparent possibilities of danger as to entitle her to protection. Negligence in the abstract is not enough upon which to base liability. Negligence is a relative concept, evolving out of the common law doctrine of trespass on the case. To establish liability, the defendant must owe a legal duty of reasonable care to the injured party. A cause of action in tort will lie where harm,

though unintended, could have been averted or avoided by observance of such a duty. The scope of the duty is limited by the range of danger that a reasonable person could foresee. In this case, there was nothing to suggest from the appearance of the parcel or otherwise that the parcel contained fireworks. The guard could not reasonably have had any warning of a threat to Palsgraf (P), and R.R. (D) therefore cannot be held liable. Judgment is reversed in favor of R.R. (D).

DISSENT: (Andrews, J.) The concept that there is no negligence unless R.R. (D) owes a legal duty to take care as to Palsgraf (P) herself is too narrow. Everyone owes to the world at large the duty of refraining from those acts that may unreasonably threaten the safety of others. If the guard's action was negligent as to those nearby, it was also negligent as to those outside what might be termed the "danger zone." For Palsgraf (P) to recover, R.R.'s (D) negligence must have been the proximate cause of her injury, a question of fact for the jury.

ANALYSIS
The majority defined the limit of the defendant's liability in terms of the danger that a reasonable person in defendant's situation would have perceived. The dissent argued that the limitation should not be placed on liability, but rather on damages. Judge Andrews suggested that only injuries that would not have happened but for R.R.'s (D) negligence should be compensable. Both the majority and dissent recognized the policy-driven need to limit liability for negligent acts, seeking, in the words of Judge Andrews, to define a framework "that will be practical and in keeping with the general understanding of mankind." The Restatement (Second) of Torts has accepted Judge Cardozo's view.

Quicknotes

FORESEEABILITY A reasonable expectation that change is the probable result of certain acts or omissions.

NEGLIGENCE Conduct falling below the standard of care that a reasonable person would demonstrate under similar conditions.

PROXIMATE CAUSE The natural sequence of events without which an injury would not have been sustained.

Party ID: Quick identification of the relationship between the parties.

Concurrence/Dissent: All concurrences and dissents are briefed whenever they are included by the casebook editor.

Analysis: This last paragraph gives you a broad understanding of where the case "fits in" with other cases in the section of the book and with the entire course. It is a hornbook-style discussion indicating whether the case is a majority or minority opinion and comparing the principal case with other cases in the casebook. It may also provide analysis from restatements, uniform codes, and law review articles. The analysis will prove to be invaluable to classroom discussion.

Issue: The issue is a concise question that brings out the essence of the opinion as it relates to the section of the casebook in which the case appears. Both substantive and procedural issues are included if relevant to the decision.

Holding and Decision: This section offers a clear and in-depth discussion of the rule of the case and the court's rationale. It is written in easy-to-understand language and answers the issue presented by applying the law to the facts of the case. When relevant, it includes a thorough discussion of the exceptions to the case as listed by the court, any major cites to the other cases on point, and the names of the judges who wrote the decisions.

Quicknotes: Conveniently defines legal terms found in the case and summarizes the nature of any statutes, codes, or rules referred to in the text.

Wolters Kluwer Legal & Regulatory US is proud to offer *Casenote® Legal Briefs*—continuing thirty years of publishing America's best-selling legal briefs.

Casenote® Legal Briefs are designed to help you save time when briefing assigned cases. Organized under convenient headings, they show you how to abstract the basic facts and holdings from the text of the actual opinions handed down by the courts. Used as part of a rigorous study regimen, they can help you spend more time analyzing and critiquing points of law than on copying bits and pieces of judicial opinions into your notebook or outline.

Casenote® Legal Briefs should never be used as a substitute for assigned casebook readings. They work best when read as a follow-up to reviewing the underlying opinions themselves. Students who try to avoid reading and digesting the judicial opinions in their casebooks or online sources will end up shortchanging themselves in the long run. The ability to absorb, critique, and restate the dynamic and complex elements of case law decisions is crucial to your success in law school and beyond. It cannot be developed vicariously.

Casenote® Legal Briefs represents but one of the many offerings in Legal Education's Study Aid Timeline, which includes:

- *Casenote® Legal Briefs*
- *Emanuel® Law Outlines*
- Emanuel® *Law in a Flash* Flash Cards
- Emanuel® *CrunchTime®* Series

Each of these series is designed to provide you with easy-to-understand explanations of complex points of law. Each volume offers guidance on the principles of legal analysis and, consulted regularly, will hone your ability to spot relevant issues. We have titles that will help you prepare for class, prepare for your exams, and enhance your general comprehension of the law along the way.

To find out more about our law school tools for success, visit us at *www.WKLegaledu.com* or email us at *legaledu@wolterskluwer.com*. We'll be happy to assist you.

How to Brief a Case

A. Decide on a Format and Stick to It

Structure is essential to a good brief. It enables you to arrange systematically the related parts that are scattered throughout most cases, thus making manageable and understandable what might otherwise seem to be an endless and unfathomable sea of information. There are, of course, an unlimited number of formats that can be utilized. However, it is best to find one that suits your needs and stick to it. Consistency breeds both efficiency and the security that when called upon you will know where to look in your brief for the information you are asked to give.

Any format, as long as it presents the essential elements of a case in an organized fashion, can be used. Experience, however, has led *Casenote® Legal Briefs* to develop and utilize the following format because of its logical flow and universal applicability.

NATURE OF CASE: This is a brief statement of the legal character and procedural status of the case (e.g., "Appeal of a burglary conviction").

There are many different alternatives open to a litigant dissatisfied with a court ruling. The key to determining which one has been used is to discover *who is asking this court for what.*

This first entry in the brief should be kept as *short as possible.* Use the court's terminology if you understand it. But since jurisdictions vary as to the titles of pleadings, the best entry is the one that addresses who wants what in this proceeding, not the one that sounds most like the court's language.

RULE OF LAW: A statement of the general principle of law that the case illustrates (e.g., "An acceptance that varies any term of the offer is considered a rejection and counteroffer").

Determining the rule of law of a case is a procedure similar to determining the issue of the case. Avoid being fooled by red herrings; there may be a few rules of law mentioned in the case excerpt, but usually only one is *the* rule with which the casebook editor is concerned. The techniques used to locate the issue, described below, may also be utilized to find the rule of law. Generally, your best guide is simply the chapter heading. It is a clue to the point the casebook editor seeks to make and should be kept in mind when reading every case in the respective section.

FACTS: A synopsis of only the essential facts of the case, i.e., those bearing upon or leading up to the issue.

The facts entry should be a short statement of the events and transactions that led one party to initiate legal proceedings against another in the first place. While some cases conveniently state the salient facts at the beginning of the decision, in other instances they will have to be culled from hiding places throughout the text, even from concurring and dissenting opinions. Some of the "facts" will often be in dispute and should be so noted. Conflicting evidence may be briefly pointed up. "Hard" facts must be included. Both must be *relevant* in order to be listed in the facts entry. It is impossible to tell what is relevant until the entire case is read, as the ultimate determination of the rights and liabilities of the parties may turn on something buried deep in the opinion.

Generally, the facts entry should not be longer than three to five *short* sentences.

It is often helpful to identify the role played by a party in a given context. For example, in a construction contract case the identification of a party as the "contractor" or "builder" alleviates the need to tell that that party was the one who was supposed to have built the house.

It is always helpful, and a good general practice, to identify the "plaintiff" and the "defendant." This may seem elementary and uncomplicated, but, especially in view of the creative editing practiced by some casebook editors, it is sometimes a difficult or even impossible task. Bear in mind that the *party presently* seeking something from this court may not be the plaintiff, and that sometimes only the cross-claim of a defendant is treated in the excerpt. Confusing or misaligning the parties can ruin your analysis and understanding of the case.

ISSUE: A statement of the general legal question answered by or illustrated in the case. For clarity, the issue is best put in the form of a question capable of a "yes" or "no" answer. In reality, the issue is simply the Rule of Law put in the form of a question (e.g., "May an offer be accepted by performance?").

The major problem presented in discerning what is *the* issue in the case is that an opinion usually purports to raise and answer several questions. However, except for rare cases, only one such question is really the issue in the case. Collateral issues not necessary to the resolution of the matter in controversy are handled by the court by language known as *"obiter dictum"* or merely *"dictum."* While dicta may be included later in the brief, they have no place under the issue heading.

To find the issue, ask *who wants what* and then go on to ask *why did that party succeed or fail in getting it.* Once this is determined, the "why" should be turned into a question.

The complexity of the issues in the cases will vary, but in all cases a single-sentence question should sum up the issue. *In a few cases,* there will be two, or even more rarely, three issues of equal importance to the resolution of the case. Each should be expressed in a single-sentence question.

Since many issues are resolved by a court in coming to a final disposition of a case, the casebook editor will reproduce the portion of the opinion containing the issue or issues most relevant to the area of law under scrutiny. A noted law professor gave this advice: "Close the book; look at the title on the cover." Chances are, if it is Property, you need not concern yourself with whether, for example, the federal government's treatment of the plaintiff's land really raises a federal question sufficient to support jurisdiction on this ground in federal court.

The same rule applies to chapter headings designating sub-areas within the subjects. They tip you off as to what the text is designed to teach. The cases are arranged in a casebook to show a progression or development of the law, so that the preceding cases may also help.

It is also most important to remember to *read the notes and questions* at the end of a case to determine what the editors wanted you to have gleaned from it.

HOLDING AND DECISION: This section should succinctly explain the rationale of the court in arriving at its decision. In capsulizing the "reasoning" of the court, it should always include an application of the general rule or rules of law to the specific facts of the case. Hidden justifications come to light in this entry: the reasons for the state of the law, the public policies, the biases and prejudices, those considerations that influence the justices' thinking and, ultimately, the outcome of the case. At the end, there should be a short indication of the disposition or procedural resolution of the case (e.g., "Decision of the trial court for Mr. Smith (P) reversed").

The foregoing format is designed to help you "digest" the reams of case material with which you will be faced in your law school career. Once mastered by practice, it will place at your fingertips the information the authors of your casebooks have sought to impart to you in case-by-case illustration and analysis.

B. Be as Economical as Possible in Briefing Cases

Once armed with a format that encourages succinctness, it is as important to be economical with regard to the time spent on the actual reading of the case as it is to be economical in the writing of the brief itself. This does not mean "skimming" a case. Rather, it means reading the case with an "eye" trained to recognize into which "section" of your brief a particular passage or line fits and having a system for quickly and precisely marking the case so that the passages fitting any one particular part of

the brief can be easily identified and brought together in a concise and accurate manner when the brief is actually written.

It is of no use to simply repeat everything in the opinion of the court; record only enough information to trigger your recollection of what the court said. Nevertheless, an accurate statement of the "law of the case," i.e., the legal principle applied to the facts, is absolutely essential to class preparation and to learning the law under the case method.

To that end, it is important to develop a "shorthand" that you can use to make marginal notations. These notations will tell you at a glance in which section of the brief you will be placing that particular passage or portion of the opinion.

Some students prefer to underline all the salient portions of the opinion (with a pencil or colored underliner marker), making marginal notations as they go along. Others prefer the color-coded method of underlining, utilizing different colors of markers to underline the salient portions of the case, each separate color being used to represent a different section of the brief. For example, blue underlining could be used for passages relating to the rule of law, yellow for those relating to the issue, and green for those relating to the holding and decision, etc. While it has its advocates, the color-coded method can be confusing and time-consuming (all that time spent on changing colored markers). Furthermore, it can interfere with the continuity and concentration many students deem essential to the reading of a case for maximum comprehension. In the end, however, it is a matter of personal preference and style. Just remember, whatever method you use, underlining must be used sparingly or its value is lost.

If you take the marginal notation route, an efficient and easy method is to go along underlining the key portions of the case and placing in the margin alongside them the following "markers" to indicate where a particular passage or line "belongs" in the brief you will write:

N   (NATURE OF CASE)
RL   (RULE OF LAW)
I   (ISSUE)
HL   (HOLDING AND DECISION, relates to
        the RULE OF LAW behind the decision)
HR   (HOLDING AND DECISION, gives the
        RATIONALE or reasoning behind the
        decision)
HA   (HOLDING AND DECISION, applies the
        general principle(s) of law to the facts of
        the case to arrive at the decision)

Remember that a particular passage may well contain information necessary to more than one part of your brief, in which case you simply note that in the margin. If you are using the color-coded underlining method instead of marginal notation, simply make asterisks or checks in the margin next to the passage in question in the colors that indicate the additional sections of the brief where it might be utilized.

The economy of utilizing "shorthand" in marking cases for briefing can be maintained in the actual brief writing process itself by utilizing "law student shorthand" within the brief. There are many commonly used words and phrases for which abbreviations can be substituted in your briefs (and in your class notes also). You can develop abbreviations that are personal to you and which will save you a lot of time. A reference list of briefing abbreviations can be found on page x of this book.

C. Use Both the Briefing Process and the Brief as a Learning Tool

Now that you have a format and the tools for briefing cases efficiently, the most important thing is to make the time spent in briefing profitable to you and to make the most advantageous use of the briefs you create. Of course, the briefs are invaluable for classroom reference when you are called upon to explain or analyze a particular

case. However, they are also useful in reviewing for exams. A quick glance at the fact summary should bring the case to mind, and a rereading of the rule of law should enable you to go over the underlying legal concept in your mind, how it was applied in that particular case, and how it might apply in other factual settings.

As to the value to be derived from engaging in the briefing process itself, there is an immediate benefit that arises from being forced to sift through the essential facts and reasoning from the court's opinion and to succinctly express them in your own words in your brief. The process ensures that you understand the case and the point that it illustrates, and that means you will be ready to absorb further analysis and information brought forth in class. It also ensures you will have something to say when called upon in class. The briefing process helps develop a mental agility for getting to the *gist* of a case and for identifying, expounding on, and applying the legal concepts and issues found there. The briefing process is the mental process on which you must rely in taking law school examinations; it is also the mental process upon which a lawyer relies in serving his clients and in making his living.

Abbreviations for Briefs

acceptance	acp	offer	O
affirmed	aff	offeree	OE
answer	ans	offeror	OR
assumption of risk	a/r	ordinance	ord
attorney	atty	pain and suffering	p/s
beyond a reasonable doubt	b/r/d	parol evidence	p/e
bona fide purchaser	BFP	plaintiff	P
breach of contract	br/k	prima facie	p/f
cause of action	c/a	probable cause	p/c
common law	c/l	proximate cause	px/c
Constitution	Con	real property	r/p
constitutional	con	reasonable doubt	r/d
contract	K	reasonable man	r/m
contributory negligence	c/n	rebuttable presumption	rb/p
cross	x	remanded	rem
cross-complaint	x/c	res ipsa loquitur	RIL
cross-examination	x/ex	respondeat superior	r/s
cruel and unusual punishment	c/u/p	Restatement	RS
defendant	D	reversed	rev
dismissed	dis	Rule Against Perpetuities	RAP
double jeopardy	d/j	search and seizure	s/s
due process	d/p	search warrant	s/w
equal protection	e/p	self-defense	s/d
equity	eq	specific performance	s/p
evidence	ev	statute	S
exclude	exc	statute of frauds	S/F
exclusionary rule	exc/r	statute of limitations	S/L
felony	f/n	summary judgment	s/j
freedom of speech	f/s	tenancy at will	t/w
good faith	g/f	tenancy in common	t/c
habeas corpus	h/c	tenant	t
hearsay	hr	third party	TP
husband	H	third party beneficiary	TPB
injunction	inj	transferred intent	TI
in loco parentis	ILP	unconscionable	uncon
inter vivos	I/v	unconstitutional	unconst
joint tenancy	j/t	undue influence	u/e
judgment	judgt	Uniform Commercial Code	UCC
jurisdiction	jur	unilateral	uni
last clear chance	LCC	vendee	VE
long-arm statute	LAS	vendor	VR
majority view	maj	versus	v
meeting of minds	MOM	void for vagueness	VFV
minority view	min	weight of authority	w/a
Miranda rule	Mir/r	weight of the evidence	w/e
Miranda warnings	Mir/w	wife	W
negligence	neg	with	w/
notice	ntc	within	w/i
nuisance	nus	without	w/o
obligation	ob	without prejudice	w/o/p
obscene	obs	wrongful death	wr/d

Table of Cases

CHAPTER 1

Acting Through Others: The Law of Agency

Quick Reference Rules of Law

Jenson Farms Co. v. Cargill, Inc.

Creditors (P) v. Debtor's financier (D)

Minn. Sup. Ct., 309 N.W.2d 285 (1981).

NATURE OF CASE: Appeal from jury verdict in favor of plaintiffs in contract default action.

FACT SUMMARY: Cargill, Inc. (Cargill) (D) contended that it was not the principal for Warren Grain & Seed Co. (Warren) by virtue of its course of conduct, and, therefore, could not be held jointly liable with Warren for Warren's contract defaults with Warren's creditors.

🏛 RULE OF LAW
An agency is created through a course of conduct where the facts, taken as a whole, show that one party (first party) has manifested consent that another party (second party) be its agent; the second party acts on behalf of the first party; and the first party exercises control over the second party.

FACTS: Warren Grain & Seed Co. (Warren) operated a grain elevator and purchased grain from local farmers. Warren applied for financing from Cargill, Inc. (Cargill) (D), and the two parties entered into a security agreement whereby Cargill (D) would loan money for working capital to Warren. Under this contract, Warren would receive funds and pay its expenses by issuing drafts drawn on Cargill (D) through various banks. The drafts were imprinted with both Warren's and Cargill's (D) names. Proceeds from Warren's sales would be deposited with Cargill (D) and credited to its account. In return for this financing, Warren appointed Cargill (D) as its grain agent for transaction with the Commodity Credit Corporation. Cargill (D) was also given a right of first refusal to purchase market grain sold by Warren to the terminal market. Over a period of 13 years, new financing contracts were negotiated between these two parties. Per the contracts Warren would provide Cargill (D) with annual financial statements and either Cargill (D) would keep the books for Warren or an independent firm would conduct an audit. Cargill (D) was given the right of access to Warren's books for inspection. In addition, Warren was not to make capital improvements or repairs in excess of $5,000 without Cargill's (D) prior consent. Further, Warren was not to become liable as guarantor on another's indebtedness, or encumber its assets except with Cargill's (D) permission, and consent by Cargill (D) was required before Warren would be allowed to declare a dividend or sell and purchase stock. Cargill (D) also entered into other agreements with Warren under which Warren agreed to act as Cargill's (D) agent for certain purposes. During this period, Cargill (D) offered suggestions to Warren for how Warren could improve its operations, but Warren did not act on these.

Warren was at that time shipping Cargill 90 percent of its cash grain. With time, it became clear to Cargill (D) that Warren was losing money. As Warren's indebtedness continued to be in excess of its credit line, Cargill (D) began to contact Warren daily regarding its financial affairs. Cargill headquarters informed Warren's regional office that, since Cargill (D) money was being used, Warren should realize that Cargill (D) had the right to make some critical decisions regarding the use of the funds. Cargill (D) headquarters also told Warren that a regional manager would be working with Warren on a day-to-day basis as well as in monthly planning meetings. At some point, Cargill's (D) regional office began to keep a daily debit position on Warren. A bank account was opened in Warren's name on which Warren could draw checks funded by drafts drawn on Cargill (D) by the local bank. Eventually, Warren defaulted on its contracts, owing $3.6 million to Cargill (D) and $2 million to other creditors (P), who brought suit for damages against both Warren and Cargill (D). A jury returned a verdict in favor of the plaintiffs, finding Cargill (D) jointly liable with Warren for Warren's debts on an agency theory. The state's highest court granted review.

ISSUE: Is an agency created through a course of conduct where the facts, taken as a whole, show that one party (first party) has manifested consent that another party (second party) be its agent; the second party acts on behalf of the first party; and the first party exercises control over the second party?

HOLDING AND DECISION: [Judge not stated in casebook excerpt.] Yes. An agency is created through a course of conduct where the facts, taken as a whole, show that one party (first party) has manifested consent that another party (second party) be its agent; the second party acts on behalf of the first party; and the first party exercises control over the second party. Agency results from the manifestation of consent by one person to another that the other will act on his behalf and subject to his control, and consent by the other so to act. For there to be an agency there must be an agreement, but not necessarily a contract between the parties. The existence of the agency may be proved by circumstantial evidence that shows a course of dealing between the two parties. Here, all three elements of agency were present. The facts showed that by directing Warren to implement its recommendations, Cargill (D) manifested its consent that Warren would be its agent. Warren acted on Cargill's (D) behalf in procuring

Continued on next page.

grain for Cargill (D) as the part of its normal operations, which were totally financed by Cargill (D). Cargill (D) exercised more than nominal control over Warren and was an active participant in Warren's operations rather than simply a financier. Taken as a whole, Cargill's (D) course of dealing with Warren was a paternalistic relationship in which Cargill (D) made the key economic decisions and kept Warren in existence. Although considerable interest was paid by Warren on the loan, the reason for Cargill's (D) financing of Warren was not to make money as a lender but, rather, to establish a source of market grain for its business. When viewing all these factors together, there was sufficient evidence from which the jury could find that Cargill (D) was Warren's principal. Affirmed.

▶ ANALYSIS

The Restatement (Third) Agency § 1.01 defines agency as the "fiduciary relationship that arises when one person (a 'principal') manifests assent to another person (an 'agent') that the agent shall act on the principal's behalf and subject to the principal's control, and the agent manifests assent or otherwise consent so to act."

Quicknotes

AGENCY A fiduciary relationship whereby authority is granted to an agent to act on behalf of the principal in order to effectuate the principal's objective.

AGENT An individual who has the authority to act on behalf of another.

APPARENT CONSENT The manifestation by actions, or by the failure to act, of an agreement of the minds, or of the acquiescence by one party to the will of another.

GUARANTOR A party who agrees to be liable for the debt or default of another.

PRINCIPAL A person or entity who authorizes another (the agent) to act on its behalf and subject to its authority to the extent that the principal may be held liable for the actions of the agent.

White v. Thomas

Principal (D) v. Third party contracting with agent (P)

Ark. Ct. App., 1991 LEXIS 109 (1991).

NATURE OF CASE: Appeal from order of specific performance and release of mortgage lien on property.

FACT SUMMARY: White (D) contended that his agent, Simpson, did not have apparent authority to enter into a contract for the sale of land to Thomas (P), and that, therefore, an order of specific performance of the contract was erroneous.

> ## RULE OF LAW
> In the absence of a principal and any indicia that an agent has authority to engage in a specific action on the principal's behalf, the agent does not have apparent authority to engage in such action merely because the agent asserts she has such authority.

FACTS: White (D) authorized Simpson, his agent, to attend a land auction and bid, in his behalf, up to $250,000.00 on an entire 220-acre farm, except for the three acres on which a house sat. He signed a blank check for her to use in depositing the required 10 percent of the bid. Simpson was given no other instructions, and White (D) left on a trip before the sale was held. Thomas (P) was the successful bidder on the three-acre tract on which the residence was located. Thomas (P) also unsuccessfully bid on acreage adjoining the homesite. The 217-acre balance of the land, including that additional acreage in which Thomas (P) had shown an interest, was struck off and sold to Simpson for $327,500.00. When Simpson realized that her bid had exceeded the amount authorized by White (D), she approached Thomas (P) about purchasing from her some of the lands surrounding their house. She signed the agreement with the auctioneer to purchase the 217-acre tract. She then entered into an offer and acceptance with Thomas (P) in which she agreed to sell to Thomas (P) approximately 45 acres of the land that she had just purchased for White (D). At the time, Simpson indicated to Thomas (P) that she had a power of attorney to convey the land, but Thomas (P) did not ask to see it. In fact, no such power of attorney existed. The contract was signed by Thomas (P) and by Simpson, "POA, Power of Attorney" for White (D). When White (D) returned from his trip and learned of what had happened, he informed Thomas (P) that he repudiated Simpson's action in signing the offer and acceptance. White's (D) purchase of the 217-acre tract was consummated in part with the proceeds of a bank-issued purchase-money loan, secured by a lien on the real estate. Thomas (P) then brought suit for specific performance of the contract and release of the land embraced in the contract from the mortgage. The trial court, finding Simpson

had acted with apparent authority on behalf of White (D), based on her assertion that she had a power of attorney, ruled in favor of Thomas (P). The appellate court granted review.

ISSUE: In the absence of a principal and any indicia that an agent has authority to engage in a specific action on the principal's behalf, does the agent have apparent authority to engage in such action merely because the agent asserts she has such authority?

HOLDING AND DECISION: (Cracraft, C.J.) No. In the absence of a principal and any indicia that an agent has authority to engage in a specific action on the principal's behalf, the agent does not have apparent authority to engage in such action merely because the agent asserts she has such authority. Here, it was undisputed that Simpson was not expressly authorized to sell White's (D) property; she was expressly authorized only to purchase a 217-acre tract of land for her principal if she could do so for no more than $250,000. Nor did she have the implied authority to contract to sell to Thomas (P) a portion of the property that she had purchased, as that act was not necessary to accomplish her assigned task of purchasing the entire tract. Therefore, for White (D) to be liable for Simpson's actions in entering into the offer and acceptance with Thomas (P), her actions must have fallen within the scope of her apparent authority. Here, Thomas (P) knew that Simpson's actions at the auction were purportedly being taken on behalf of White (D). Although Simpson's possession of a blank check signed by White (D) may have indicated some limited authority on her part to make a purchase for him, there was no evidence that White (D) knowingly permitted her to enter into a contract to sell or that he ever held her out as having such authority. Nor are purchasing and selling so closely related that a third person could reasonably believe that authority to do the one carries with it authority to do the other. In fact, Thomas (P) was sufficiently concerned about Simpson's authority to contract to sell White's (D) property that Thomas (P) specifically asked her whether she was so authorized. Thomas (P) made no attempt to contact White (D) concerning Simpson's authority and did not even demand to see the alleged written power of attorney under which Simpson claimed to be acting. Instead, Thomas (P) chose to rely solely upon an admitted agent's own declarations as to her authority. While the declarations of an alleged agent may be used to corroborate other evidence of the scope of agency, neither agency nor the extent of the agent's

Continued on next page.

authority can be shown solely by his own declarations or actions in the absence of the party to be affected. For these reasons, the trial court's decision was clearly erroneous. Reversed and dismissed.

▶ **ANALYSIS**

In this case, the court also ruled that there could be no basis for finding White (D) estopped to deny Simpson's authority, either, given that there was no evidence that he knew or should have known of her action or declarations. This case illustrates the point that an agent's apparent authority is authority that a reasonable third party would infer from the actions or statements of the principal (not those of the agent). Thus, apparent authority is in the nature of an equitable remedy designed to prevent fraud or unfairness to third parties who reasonably rely on the principal's actions or statements in dealing with the agent.

Quicknotes

AGENT An individual who has the authority to act on behalf of another.

APPARENT AUTHORITY The authority granted to an agent to act on behalf of the principal in order to effectuate the principal's objective, which may not be expressly granted, but which is inferred from the conduct of the principal and the agent.

EQUITABLE REMEDY A remedy that is based upon principles of fairness as opposed to rules of law; a remedy involving specific performance rather than money damages.

POWER OF ATTORNEY A written instrument that allows a person to appoint an agent and confer authority to perform certain specified acts on his behalf.

PRINCIPAL A person or entity who authorizes another (the agent) to act on its behalf and subject to its authority to the extent that the principal may be held liable for the actions of the agent.

SPECIFIC PERFORMANCE An equitable remedy whereby the court requires the parties to perform their obligations pursuant to a contract.

Gallant Ins. Co. v. Isaac

Insurer (P) v. Insured (D)

Ind. Ct. App., 732 N.E.2d 1262 (2000).

NATURE OF CASE: Appeal from summary judgment for defendant in declaratory judgment action.

FACT SUMMARY: Gallant Ins. Co. (Gallant) (P), an insurer, contended that its agent, Thompson-Harris, did not have inherent authority to bind Gallant (P) on an insurance policy issued to Isaac (D).

RULE OF LAW
An agent has inherent authority to bind its principal where the agent acts within the usual and ordinary scope of its authority, a third party can reasonably believe that the agent has authority to conduct the act in question, and the third party is not on notice that the agent is not so authorized.

FACTS: Gallant Ins. Co. (Gallant) (P) was an insurer, and Thompson-Harris was its agent. Thompson-Harris's authority included the power to bind Gallant (P) on new insurance policies, as well as interim policy endorsement such as adding a new driver, or changing and adding a vehicle insured under a policy. Although no written agreement described the relation between Gallant (P) and Thompson-Harris, Gallant (P) became bound to provide insurance coverage at the time and date on which Thompson-Harris faxed or called the required information to Gallant's (P) producing agent, and premiums were paid to Thompson-Harris. Isaac (D) had a Gallant insurance policy on her car. On the last day of the insurance policy, Isaac (D) traded her car in for a newer car. To obtain the newly purchased car, the financing bank required Isaac (D) to obtain full coverage on it. That same day, a Friday, Isaac (D) contacted Thompson-Harris to notify it that she was purchasing the new car, and to discuss enhancing the existing insurance policy to meet bank requirements. Isaac (D) told a Thompson-Harris employee that she must obtain "full insurance coverage" as a condition to receiving a loan. She also told the employee at Thompson-Harris that her current coverage expired on the next day (an inaccurate statement). In response, the Thompson-Harris employee informed Isaac (D) that because their agency was about to close for the weekend, she would immediately "bind" coverage on the new car. This statement was contrary to instructions from Gallant (P) and to the policy itself. It was decided that Isaac (D) would come in to Thompson-Harris on the following Monday to complete the paperwork and pay the down payment on the premium. Thompson-Harris faxed the paperwork for the new coverage on Saturday. On Sunday, Isaac (D) was in an accident while driving her new car. On Monday, as planned, Isaac (D) paid the premium. Thompson-Harris,

on behalf of Gallant (P), completed a form that notified the state police that Isaac (D) had insurance coverage at the time of the accident. A few weeks later, Gallant (P) renewed Isaac's (D) insurance policy, with an effective period starting on the Tuesday after the accident. Gallant (P) then brought a declaratory judgment action seeking a judgment that Gallant (P) was not liable for any losses incurred because the policy was not in force since the policy renewal premium was not paid as dictated in the policy and since Thompson-Harris had no authority to renew the insurance policy or orally contract in a manner contrary to what the policy stated without the approval of Gallant's (P) producing agent. The trial court granted summary judgment to Isaac (D), and the intermediate court of appeals granted review.

ISSUE: Does an agent have inherent authority to bind its principal where the agent acts within the usual and ordinary scope of its authority, a third party can reasonably believe that the agent has authority to conduct the act in question, and the third party is not on notice that the agent is not so authorized?

HOLDING AND DECISION: (Riley, J.) Yes. An agent has inherent authority to bind its principal where the agent acts within the usual and ordinary scope of its authority, a third party can reasonably believe that the agent has authority to conduct the act in question, and the third party is not on notice that the agent is not so authorized. Inherent agency power indicates the power of an agent that is derived not from authority, apparent or estoppel, but from the agency relation itself. This inherent authority theory exists for the protection of persons harmed by or dealing with a principal's servant or agent. Here, Thompson-Harris's renewal of Isaac's (D) insurance policy constituted an act that usually accompanies or is incidental to insurance transactions that it is authorized to conduct. Examining Gallant (P) and Thompson-Harris's agency relation reveals that, as an agent, Thompson-Harris was authorized to bind Gallant (P) on new insurance policies, as well as interim policy endorsements. In general, the power to bind its principal came into being once Thompson-Harris faxed the necessary paperwork to Gallant's (P) producing agent and payment was made. Thompson-Harris also had a common practice of telling its insured that they were "bound" despite not receiving payment until later, violating instructions by Gallant (P) and provisions found in the policy. This common practice of binding coverage verbally, in violation of Gallant's (P) orders, was

Continued on next page.

similar to Thompson-Harris's authorized conduct, given expressly by Gallant (P), to bind coverage by fax or phone. Therefore, Thompson-Harris acted within the usual and ordinary scope of its authority. The next issue as to whether inherent authority exists is whether a third party could have reasonably believed that the agent had authority to conduct the act in question, based on the agent's direct and indirect manifestations. Here, Isaac (D) could have reasonably believed that Thompson-Harris had authority to orally bind coverage. Isaac's (D) past dealings were all through Thompson-Harris, whether involving payment of premiums, changing or including a driver, or requesting a new estimate. Direct communication between Gallant (P) and Isaac (D) never occurred. Thus, it was reasonable for Isaac (D) to take at face value Thompson-Harris's communication that coverage was bound, and that she could come in at the end of the weekend to pay for the policy renewal. The reasonableness of Isaac's belief was bolstered by the fact that Thompson-Harris took care of all the paperwork necessary. Isaac (D) had no reason to second guess a direct communication by Thompson-Harris stating coverage was bound, particularly since that was a common practice of Thompson-Harris. Nothing in the record showed that Isaac (D) had notice that Thompson-Harris was not authorized to verbally bind coverage in the absence of payment. Here, too, Gallant (P) left Thompson-Harris unsupervised to establish common practice in violation of Gallant's (P) granted authority. For these reasons, Isaac's (D) insurance policy was in full force and effect on the day Isaac (D) was in the accident because Thompson-Harris had the inherent authority to bind coverage by Gallant (P) verbally. Affirmed.

▶ ANALYSIS

Under the traditional approach, the doctrine of inherent power gives a general agent the power to bind a principal, whether disclosed or undisclosed, to an unauthorized contract as long as a general agent would ordinarily have the power to enter such a contract and the third party is not on notice that the agent is not so authorized. This theory has been criticized as an unwarranted shift in the traditional balance of monitoring costs between principals and third parties.

Quicknotes

AGENT An individual who has the authority to act on behalf of another.

DECLARATORY JUDGMENT A judgment of the court establishing the rights of the parties.

PRINCIPAL A person or entity who authorizes another (the agent) to act on its behalf and subject to its authority to the extent that the principal may be held liable for the actions of the agent.

SUMMARY JUDGMENT Judgment rendered by a court in response to a motion made by one of the parties, claiming that the lack of a question of material fact in respect to an issue warrants disposition of the issue without consideration by the jury.

Humble Oil & Refining Co. v. Martin

Filling station owner (D) v. Injured bystander (P)

Tex. Sup. Ct., 148 Tex. 175, 222 S.W.2d 995 (1949).

NATURE OF CASE: Appeal from judgment awarding damages for personal injury.

FACT SUMMARY: Martin (P), injured when a car rolled out of a service station owned by Humble Oil & Refining Co. (Humble) (D), sought to hold Humble (D) liable for the station operator's negligence.

🏛 RULE OF LAW
A party may be liable for a contractor's torts if he exercises substantial control over the contractor's operations.

FACTS: Martin (P) and his two children (P) were injured when they were struck by a vehicle that rolled out of a service station owned by Humble Oil and Refining Co. (Humble) (D) and operated by Schneider. Martin (P) sued both Love (D), the owner of the vehicle that struck him, and Humble (D). The evidence showed that Humble (D) exercised substantial control over the details of the station's operation. The trial court rendered judgment against both Love (D) and Humble (D), and the appellate court affirmed. Humble (D) appealed, contending that it was not responsible for the torts of its independent contractors.

ISSUE: May a party be liable for a contractor's torts if he exercises substantial control over the contractor's operations?

HOLDING AND DECISION: (Garwood, J.) Yes. A party may be liable for a contractor's torts if he exercises substantial control over the contractor's operations. A party is not normally liable for the torts of his contractors. However, when that party so substantially controls the manner of the contractor's operations, the contractor relationship breaks down and a master-servant relationship is formed. Here, Schneider was obligated to perform any duty Humble (D) might impose on him. Humble (D) paid some of Schneider's operating expenses, and also controlled the station's hours. The evidence showed that Humble (D) mandated much of the day-to-day operations of the station, certainly enough to justify the trial court's finding of a master-servant relationship rather than a contractor relationship. Affirmed.

▶ ANALYSIS

According to the Restatement (Second) of Agency, a master-servant relationship is one in which the servant has agreed to work and also to be subject to the master's control. An independent contractor, on the other hand, agrees to work, but is not under the principal's control insofar as the manner in which the job is accomplished.

In general, liability will not be imputed to the principal for the tortious conduct of an independent contractor. Under the theory of "apparent agency," the mere appearance of a master-servant-type relationship may subject the principal to liability.

◼▬◼

Quicknotes

APPARENT AUTHORITY The authority granted to an agent to act on behalf of the principal in order to effectuate the principal's objective, which may not be expressly granted, but which is inferred from the conduct of the principal and the agent.

INDEPENDENT CONTRACTOR A party undertaking a particular assignment for another who retains control over the manner in which it is executed.

NEGLIGENCE Conduct falling below the standard of care that a reasonable person would demonstrate under similar conditions.

TORT A legal wrong resulting in a breach of duty by the wrongdoer, causing damages as a result of the breach.

◼▬◼

Hoover v. Sun Oil Co.

Injured motorist (P) v. Filling station owner (D)

Del. Sup. Ct., 212 A.2d 214 (1965).

NATURE OF CASE: Summary judgment for the defense in action seeking damages for personal injury.

FACT SUMMARY: Hoover (P) sought to hold franchisor Sun Oil Co. (D) responsible after he was injured in a fire at a service station franchise operated by Barone (D).

🏛 RULE OF LAW
A franchisee is considered an independent contractor of the franchisor if the franchisee retains control of inventory and operations.

FACTS: Barone (D) operated as a franchisee of Sun Oil Co. (Sun) (D). The agreement called for a certain level of compliance by Barone (D) with Sun (D) standards, but Barone (D) was left in control of day-to-day operations of the station, and made all inventory decisions. He carried primarily Sun (D) products, but was allowed to carry products by other companies as well. Hoover (P) suffered burns when a fire started while his vehicle was being filled by an employee at the station. He sued Sun (D) and Barone (D). Sun (D) moved for summary judgment, contending that it could not be liable under any form of vicarious liability. The trial court granted the motion, and Hoover (P) appealed.

ISSUE: Will a franchisee be considered an independent contractor of the franchisor if the franchisee retains control of inventory and operations?

HOLDING AND DECISION: (Christie, J.) Yes. A franchisee is considered an independent contractor of the franchisor if the franchisee retains control of inventory and operations. The test in such a situation is whether the franchisor retains the right to control the details of the day-to-day operations of the franchisee. A franchisor's control or influence over the results alone is insufficient to establish a principal-agent relationship. Here, while Sun (D) obviously had some control over the operation of Barone's (D) business, Barone (D) retained full control over his operations, including what inventory to stock. This clearly falls on the contractor side of the issue. Motion granted.

▶ ANALYSIS

It is difficult in cases dealing with the issue here to find one single determinant of whether one will be considered an agent or a contractor. Different courts focus on different factors. A franchise agreement that would lead to a result of no vicarious liability in one jurisdiction could well lead to the opposite conclusion in another jurisdiction.

▬▬▬

Quicknotes

AGENT An individual who has the authority to act on behalf of another.

FRANCHISEE A party, whom a supplier of goods or services agrees to permit to sell the good or service, or to otherwise conduct business on behalf of the franchise.

FRANCHISOR A supplier of goods or services, who agrees to permit a re-seller to sell the good or service, or to otherwise conduct business on behalf of the franchise.

INDEPENDENT CONTRACTOR A party undertaking a particular assignment for another who retains control over the manner in which it is executed.

PRINCIPAL A person or entity who authorizes another (the agent) to act on its behalf and subject to its authority to the extent that the principal may be held liable for the actions of the agent.

VICARIOUS LIABILITY The imputed liability of one party for the unlawful acts of another.

▬▬▬

Tarnowski v. Resop

Buyer (P) v. Agent (D)

Minn. Sup. Ct., 51 N.W.2d 801 (1952).

NATURE OF CASE: Appeal from jury verdict granting a principal recovery of various damages resulting from the principal's agent's fraudulent actions.

FACT SUMMARY: Tarnowski (P) contended that Resop (D), while acting as agent for him, was liable to Tarnowski (P) for a secret commission he collected for consummating a sale and for various damages Tarnowski (P) incurred in rescinding the sale and pursuing the action, given that the representations about the business made by Resop (D) were fraudulent.

RULE OF LAW
(1) An agent is liable to a principal for the agent's profits made during the course of the agency.
(2) An agent is liable to a principal for the damages caused by the agent's breach of his duty of loyalty.

FACTS: Tarnowski (P) hired Resop (D) as his agent to investigate and negotiate for the purchase of a coin-operated machine route. Relying on the advice of Resop (D) and the investigation he had made, Tarnowski (P) bought such a business from Loechler and Mayer. Tarnowski (P) contended that Resop (D) represented that he had done a thorough investigation of the route. As a matter of fact, Resop (D) had made only a superficial investigation and had adopted false representations of Loechler and Mayer as to the health of the business and had passed them on to Tarnowski (P) as his own. Tarnowski (P) also contended that Resop (D) collected a secret commission from Loechler and Mayer for consummating the sale. Tarnowski (P) then sued Resop (D for the amount of the secret commission and for the various damages Tarnowski (P) incurred in rescinding the sale and pursuing the action. These damages included: (1) losses suffered in the operation of the business prior to rescission; (2) loss of time devoted to operation; (3) expenses in connection with rescission of the sale and investigation therewith; (4) nontaxable expenses in connection with the prosecution of the suit against the sellers; and (5) attorneys' fees in connection with the suit. The jury returned a verdict for Tarnowski (P), and Resop (D) appealed. The state's highest court granted review.

ISSUE:
(1) Is an agent liable to a principal for the agent's profits made during the course of the agency?
(2) Is an agent liable to a principal for the damages caused by the agent's breach of his duty of loyalty?

HOLDING AND DECISION: (Knutson, J.)
(1) Yes. An agent is liable to a principal for the agent's profits made during the course of the agency. It is not material that no actual injury to the principal resulted, or that the principal made a profit on the transaction. It is also irrelevant that the principal, upon discovering a fraud, has rescinded the contract and recovered that with which he parted. The principal has an absolute right to recovery of the agent's profits made during the agency. Therefore, Tarnowski (P) has the absolute right to recover the money that Resop (D) received as a secret commission. Affirmed as to this issue.
(2) Yes. An agent is liable to a principal for the damages caused by the agent's breach of his duty of loyalty. The general rule is stated in Restatement, Agency, § 407(1), as follows: "If an agent has received a benefit as a result of violating his duty of loyalty, the principal is entitled to recover from him what he has so received, its value, or its proceeds, and also the amount of damage thereby caused." Regardless of whether the principal recovers his property, the agent is still liable for all losses to the principal resulting from the agent's breach of his duty. If the agent's wrongdoing requires the principal to sue to recover, the principal is also entitled to attorneys' fees from the agent, since the attorneys' fees are directly attributable to the agent's breach. Affirmed as to this issue.

ANALYSIS

Usually, an agent's primary duty is to make profits for the principal. His duty to account includes accounting for any unexpected and incidental accretions whether or not received in violation of duty. Thus, an agent who, without the principal's knowledge, receives something in connection with a transaction conducted for the principal, has a duty to pay this to the principal.

Quicknotes

AGENT An individual who has the authority to act on behalf of another.

PRINCIPAL A person or entity who authorizes another (the agent) to act on its behalf and subject to its authority to the extent that the principal may be held liable for the actions of the agent.

Continued on next page.

RESCIND To cancel an agreement restoring the parties to their original positions prior to the formation of the contract.

RESCISSION The canceling of an agreement and the return of the parties to their positions prior to the formation of the contract.

RESTATEMENT, AGENCY § 407(2) If an agent has violated a duty of loyalty to the principal, a third party action does not prevent the principal from recovering profits from the agent.

RESTATEMENT, TORTS § 910 A person injured by another's tort is entitled to recover all damages caused by the tort.

In re Gleeson

[Parties not identified]

Ill. App. Ct., 124 N.E.2d 624 (1954).

NATURE OF CASE: Appeal from acceptance by court of trustee report.

FACT SUMMARY: Trust beneficiaries of a trust holding real property claimed that Colbrook (D), the trustee, had to account for profits he personally made as a co-tenant of the trust property.

🏛 RULE OF LAW
A trustee of real property who is also a tenant of the trust property must account to the trust for profits made as tenant.

FACTS: Gleeson, in her will, appointed Colbrook (D) as trustee of her property, which included 160 acres of farm land, in trust for her three children. Colbrook (D) was also a co-tenant of the real property. Fifteen days after Gleeson died, Colbrook (D) and his co-tenant held over as tenants under the lease they had and farmed the land for another year. After he was confirmed as trustee, Colbrook (D) filed his first semi-annual report. After it was revised, the trial court accepted it, even though it did not contain an accounting for all monies received by Colbrook (D) personally as a profit by virtue of his being a co-tenant of the trust property. Gleeson's children, the beneficiaries, objected because the report had not included such an accounting, since Colbrook's (D) election was to act as trustee and, therefore, he could not deal with himself. The state appellate court granted review.

ISSUE: Must a trustee of real property who is also a tenant of the trust property account to the trust for profits made as tenant?

HOLDING AND DECISION: (Carroll, J.) Yes. A trustee of real property who is also a tenant of the trust property must account to the trust for profits made as tenant. A general principle of equity is that a trustee cannot deal in his individual capacity with the trust property. Colbrook (D) argues that the particular circumstances of this case warrant an exception to the general rule, since the death of Gleeson occurred only 15 days prior to the farm year; satisfactory farm tenants are not always available, especially on short notice; Colbrook (D) had sown crop on the land the year before; and that the co-tenants' holding over was in the best interest of the trust, which suffered no loss from the transaction. Colbrook's (D) argument for an exception to the general rule is rejected. There was no showing that Colbrook (D) tried to obtain a satisfactory tenant to replace the co-tenants, and the trust would not necessarily have suffered a loss if someone other than the co-tenants harvested the crop sown by the co-tenants since

an appropriate adjustment could easily have been made between the trust and the co-tenants to account for this crop. Further, the fact Colbrook (D) acted in good faith and honesty is unavailing, because he should have either chosen to continue as a tenant or to act as trustee. His election was to act as trustee and as such he could not deal with himself. Therefore, the trial court erred. Reversed.

▶ ANALYSIS

The private trust is a legal device that allows a trustee to hold legal title to trust property, which the trustee is under a fiduciary duty to manage for the benefit of the trust beneficiary. The trust resembles the agency relationship insofar as the trustee has obvious power to affect the interests of the beneficiary. The trust differs from agency insofar as the trustee is subject to the terms of the trust.

Quicknotes

CO-TENANT A tenant possessing property with one or more persons jointly or whose interest is derived from a common grantor.

TRUSTEE A person who is entrusted to keep or administer property for the benefit of another.

Joint Ownership of a Business: The Law of Partnerships and Limited Liability Companies

Quick Reference Rules of Law

Vohland v. Sweet

Partner (D) v. Partner (P)

Ind. Ct. App., 433 N.E.2d 860 (1982).

NATURE OF CASE: Appeal of order awarding damages pursuant to dissolution of partnership.

FACT SUMMARY: Sweet (P) contributed labor and expertise into a nursery business, from which he took 20 percent of the profits.

RULE OF LAW

For purposes of creating a partnership, one partner's contribution may consist of labor and expertise.

FACTS: Sweet (P) began working as a youngster for Charles Vohland in a nursery. When Paul Vohland (Vohland) (D), Charles's son, took over the business, inventory was nearly depleted. Sweet (P) and Vohland (D) agreed that Sweet (P) would manage the nursery grounds and that Vohland (D) would contribute capital and handle the finances. They worked out a plan to increase inventory. Sweet (P) was to receive 20 percent of the net profits after expenses. No partnership tax returns were filed, and each man filed individual tax returns showing they were self-employed. Vohland's (D) return showed the nursery as his business, and payments to Sweet (P) as "commissions." Sweet (P) reported he was a salesman for the nursery. The cost of planting and maintaining the nursery stock was assigned to expenses before Sweet received his 20 percent. The acquisition and enlargement of the existing inventory of nursery stock was paid for with earnings and, therefore, was financed partly with Sweet's money. After more than 10 years, Sweet (P) brought an action seeking dissolution of the partnership and a portion of the assets. At trial, Sweet (P) testified that Vohland (D) promised to "take care of" Sweet (P), and Vohland (D) acknowledged that Sweet (P) refused to permit his 20 percent to be charged with the cost of a truck unless his name was on the title. Sweet (P) testified that he intended to enter into a partnership. Vohland (D) asserted that no partnership was intended and that Sweet (P) was merely an employee, working on a commission. The trial court held that a partnership did exist, ordered its dissolution, and awarded Sweet (P) $58,733. Vohland (D) appealed and the state's intermediate appellate court granted review.

ISSUE: For purposes of creating a partnership, may one partner's contribution consist of labor and expertise?

HOLDING AND DECISION: (Neal, J.) Yes. For purposes of creating a partnership, one partner's contribution may consist of labor and expertise. A partnership may be defined as two or more persons carrying on as co-owners of a business for profit. No one element or test exists for identifying a partnership, but, generally speaking, a partnership relation involves mutual contribution and mutual share of the profits. The trial court here found an agreement to share the profits 80–20. While Sweet's (P) 20 percent was called a "commission," it was structured more as profit sharing than compensation. Sweet (P) did not contribute capital; however, there is no rule requiring capital contribution as a condition for partnership. If a contribution of labor and expertise is integral to the business operations, such contribution will suffice for purposes of creating a partnership. Here, the trial court found that Sweet (P) did contribute by means other than capital, and this was not beyond its discretion. Affirmed.

ANALYSIS

Usually partners in a partnership intend to create such a relationship. However, such an intention is not necessary. It is the intention to do the acts creating a partnership, not the intention to create a partnership itself, which controls.

■▭■

Quicknotes

PARTNERSHIP A voluntary agreement entered into by two or more parties to engage in business and to share any attendant profits and losses.

■▭■

National Biscuit Co. v. Stroud

Food distributor (P) v. Grocery partner (D)

N.C. Sup. Ct., 249 N.C. 467, 106 S.E.2d 692 (1959).

NATURE OF CASE: Suit to recover for goods sold.

FACT SUMMARY: Stroud (D) advised National Biscuit Co. (National) (P) he would not be responsible for any bread National (P) sold to his partner. Nevertheless, National (P) continued to make deliveries.

🏛 RULE OF LAW
The acts of a partner, if performed on behalf of the partnership and within the scope of its business, are binding upon all co-partners.

FACTS: Stroud (D) and Freeman entered into a general partnership to sell groceries under the name of Stroud's Food Center. Both partners apparently had an equal right to manage the business. The partnership periodically ordered bread from National Biscuit Co. (National) (P). Eventually, however, Stroud (D) notified National (P) that he would not be responsible for any additional bread the company (D) sold to Stroud's Food Center. Nevertheless, National (P) sent, at Freeman's request, additional bread of a total value of $171.04. On the day of the last delivery, Stroud (D) and Freeman dissolved their partnership. Most of the firm's assets were assigned to Stroud (D), who agreed to liquidate the assets of the partnership and to discharge its liabilities. National (P) eventually sued Stroud (D) to recover the value of the bread which had been delivered but never paid for. Stroud (D) denied liability for the price of the bread, contending that his notice to the company (P) that he would not be responsible for further deliveries had relieved him of any obligation to pay for the bread. The trial court rendered judgment in favor of National (P), and Stroud (D) appealed.

ISSUE: May a partner escape liability for debts incurred by a co-partner merely by advising the creditor, in advance, that he will not be responsible for those debts?

HOLDING AND DECISION: (Parker, J.) No. The acts of a partner, if performed on behalf of the partnership and within the scope of its business, are binding upon all co-partners. According to the appropriate provisions of the Uniform Partnership Act, all partners are jointly and severally liable for all obligations incurred on behalf of the partnership. If a majority of the partners disapprove of a transaction before it is entered into, then they may escape liability for whatever obligations that transaction ultimately incurs. But Freeman and Stroud (D) were equal partners, with neither possessing the power to exercise a majority veto over the acts of the other. Freeman's acts were entered into on behalf of the partnership, were within the scope of its ordinary business, and probably conferred a benefit upon both Freeman and Stroud (D) as partners. Under these circumstances, it is proper to hold Stroud (D) liable for the price of the bread delivered by National (P) even after Stroud's (D) notice that he would not be held responsible for additional shipments. Affirmed.

▶ ANALYSIS

The rule adopted by the Uniform Partnership Act is consistent with traditional principles of agency law. In the absence of a contrary provision in the parties' partnership agreement, each partner acts as the agent of the partnership and of each other partner. Of course, only acts that are performed on behalf of the partnership and are consistent with its purposes are binding on other partners. However, even an act that was outside the scope of a partner's duties may bind his co-partners if they ratify it.

▬ ▬

Quicknotes

AGENT An individual who has the authority to act on behalf of another.

NORTH CAROLINA UNIFORM PARTNERSHIP ACT All partners are jointly and severally liable for the acts and obligations of the partnership.

PRINCIPAL A person or entity who authorizes another (the agent) to act on its behalf and subject to its authority to the extent that the principal may be held liable for the actions of the agent.

▬ ▬

Adams v. Jarvis

Partner (P) v. Partner (D)

Wis. Sup. Ct., 127 N.W.2d 400 (1964).

NATURE OF CASE: Suit seeking a declaratory judgment.

FACT SUMMARY: Adams (P), Jarvis (D), and a third doctor (D) entered into a partnership for the practice of medicine. Adams (P) later withdrew and claimed a right to share in the partnership's existing accounts receivable.

🏛 RULE OF LAW
A partnership agreement which provides for the continuation of the firm's business despite the withdrawal of one partner and which specifies the formula according to which partnership assets are to be distributed to the retiring partner is valid and enforceable.

FACTS: Adams (P), Jarvis (D), and a third doctor (D) entered into a medical partnership. They executed a partnership agreement that provided, among other things, that the firm would continue to operate as a partnership even if one of the doctors withdrew. The agreement also provided that a withdrawing partner was entitled to share in the profits earned for any partial year that he remained a member of the partnership but that all accounts receivable were to remain the property of the continuing partners. On June 1, 1961, Adams (P) withdrew from the partnership. Adams (P) later sued for a declaration that he was entitled to share in the assets of the partnership, including its accounts receivable. The trial court concluded Adams's (P) withdrawal had worked dissolution of the partnership, the provisions of the partnership agreement were not controlling since a statutory dissolution had been ordered, and Adams (P) was entitled to recover a third of the value of the partnership's assets, including the accounts receivable. From this judgment, the surviving partners (D) appealed, contending that the trial court should have given effect to the provisions of the partnership agreement.

ISSUE: Should a court enforce the provisions of a duly executed partnership agreement?

HOLDING AND DECISION: (Beilfuss, J.) Yes. A partnership agreement which provides for the continuation of the firm's business despite the withdrawal of one partner and which specifies the formula according to which partnership assets are to be distributed to the retiring partner is valid and enforceable. In this case, the parties unambiguously agreed that their partnership would not terminate when one of the doctors withdrew from the firm. There are obvious reasons why they would have made provision for the continuance of the partnership, and where an express

agreement has been reached, and to that effect, there is no reason why statutory rules relating to withdrawal should operate to effect dissolution. The doctors also agreed that a withdrawing partner would have no right to share in the firm's accounts receivable, and this provision is also enforceable, despite Adams's (P) contention that it is contrary to public policy. It is altogether reasonable that the remaining partners should be able to reserve exclusive control over the accounts of an ongoing firm's active customers. Of course, some of the accounts receivable were ultimately collected during the year of Adams's (P) withdrawal and thus constitute profits in which he is entitled to share. Since the court below failed to give effect to the provisions of the parties' partnership agreement, it is necessary that its judgment be reversed, with directions to conduct supplementary proceedings at which Adams's (P) proper distributive share of the partnership assets may be ascertained. Reversed with directions.

▶ ANALYSIS

In most jurisdictions, matters pertaining to the distribution of partnership assets and continuation of the firm following one partner's withdrawal are regulated by statute. However, partners usually prefer to reach agreement among themselves concerning these matters since a statute designed to apply to an infinite variety of situations will rarely achieve a problem-free result when applied to a particular firm. If such an agreement is struck at the beginning stages of the partnership, both withdrawing and continuing partners are likely to be dealt with fairly, because no individual is apt to know at the outset whether he is destined to be a surviving partner or a withdrawing one.

Quicknotes

DECLARATORY JUDGMENT A judgment of the courts establishing the rights of the parties.

DISSOLUTION Annulment or termination of a formal or legal bond, tie or contract.

Page v. Page

Partner (P) v. Partner (D)

Cal. Sup. Ct., 359 P.2d 41 (1961).

NATURE OF CASE: Action for a declaratory judgment.

FACT SUMMARY: Page (P) sought a declaratory judgment that the partnership he had with Page (D) was a partnership at will that he could dissolve.

🏛 **RULE OF LAW**
A partnership may be dissolved by the express will of any partner when no definite term or particular undertaking is specified.

FACTS: Page (P) and Page (D) were partners in a linen supply business they had entered into in 1949, pursuant to an oral agreement. Each had contributed about $43,000 to purchase linen, equipment, and land. It was not until 1958 that business began to show a profit. Page (P) was the sole owner of the corporation, which was the partnership's major creditor, holding a $47,000 demand note, and in 1959, he sought a declaratory judgment that it was a partnership at will that he could terminate. The trial court found the partnership to be for a term, namely such reasonable time as was necessary to repay from profits the original outlays of Page (P) and Page (D) for equipment, etc.

ISSUE: Can a partnership be dissolved by the express will of any partner when no definite term or particular undertaking is specified?

HOLDING AND DECISION: (Traynor, J.) Yes. When no definite term or particular undertaking is specified, a partnership may be dissolved by the express will of any partner. Partners may impliedly agree to continue in business until certain debts are paid, until one or more partners recoup their investments, etc., but there is no evidence in this case to support any implied agreement of that nature. All partnerships are ordinarily entered into with the hope they will be profitable, but that alone does not make them all partnerships for a term and obligate the partners to continue in the partnerships until all of the losses over a period of many years have been recovered or original investments recouped. In holding that this is a partnership terminable at will, it is noted that the power to dissolve it must be exercised in good faith and not to "freeze out" a copartner. Reversed.

▶ *ANALYSIS*

An important aspect of this leading case is the introduction of the concept that a partner holds his dissolution power as a fiduciary. That means he owes his partners fraternal duties of good faith and fair dealing in exercising his dissolution rights.

▬▬■

Quicknotes

DECLARATORY JUDGMENT A judgment of the courts establishing the rights of the parties.

DISSOLUTION Annulment or termination of a formal or legal bond, tie or contract.

FIDUCIARY DUTY A legal obligation to act for the benefit of another, including subordinating one's personal interests to that of the other person.

PARTNERSHIP AT WILL A voluntary agreement entered into by two or more parties to engage in business and to share any attendant profits and losses, which lasts for an unspecified time period and may be terminated by either of the parties at any time and for any reason.

▬▬■

Meinhard v. Salmon

Joint venturer (P) v. Joint venturer (D)

N.Y. Ct. App., 164 N.E. 545 (1928).

NATURE OF CASE: Award of an interest in a lease.

FACT SUMMARY: Meinhard (P) and Salmon (D) were coadventurers in a lease on a hotel, but prior to the expiration of that lease, Salmon (D) alone, without Meinhard's (P) knowledge, agreed to lease the same and adjacent property.

🏛 RULE OF LAW
Joint adventurers owe to one another, while their enterprise continues, the duty of finest loyalty, a standard of behavior most sensitive.

FACTS: Salmon (D) leased from Gerry a New York hotel on Fifth Avenue for a period of 20 years. Later, Salmon (D) entered into a joint adventure with Meinhard (P) who contributed money while Salmon (D) was to manage the enterprise. Near the end of the lease, Gerry, who owned adjacent property as well as the hotel, desired to raze those buildings and construct one large building. Gerry, unable to find a new lessee to carry out his intentions, approached Salmon (D) with the idea when there was less than four months to run on his and Meinhard's (P) lease. The result was a 20-year lease to Midpoint Realty Company, wholly owned and controlled by Salmon (D). Meinhard (P) was never informed of the planned project or of the negotiations for a new lease. After he learned of it, he made demand on Salmon (D) that the lease be held in trust as an asset of the venture, which was refused. This suit followed with an award to Meinhard (P) of a 25 percent interest in the lease, one-half of his value in the hotel lease proportionate to the new lease. On appeal it was increased to 50 percent. Salmon (D) appealed arguing that he breached no duty to Meinhard (P).

ISSUE: Do joint adventurers owe to one another, while their enterprise continues, the duty of finest loyalty, a standard of behavior most sensitive?

HOLDING AND DECISION: (Cardozo, C.J.) Yes. Joint adventurers owe to one another, while their enterprise continues, the duty of finest loyalty, a standard of behavior most sensitive. Many forms of conduct permissible in a workday world, for those acting at arm's length, are forbidden to those bound by fiduciary ties. Here, Salmon (D) excluded his coadventurer from any chance to compete and from any chance to enjoy the opportunity for benefit that had come to him alone by virtue of his agency. It was likely that Salmon (D) thought that with the approaching end of the lease he owed no duty to Meinhard (P), but here the subject matter of the new lease was an extension and enlargement of the subject matter of the old one. As for Meinhard's (P) remedy, he should have been awarded one share less than half of the shares in Midpoint Realty Company. As modified, affirmed.

DISSENT: (Andrews, J.) This was not a general partnership. Rather, Meinhard (P) and Salmon (D) entered into a venture for a limited purpose. The interest terminated when the joint adventure expired. There was no intent to renew the joint adventure after its expiration.

▶ ANALYSIS

One of the most important aspects of the partnership relation is the broad fiduciary duty between partners. "The unique feature is their symmetry; each partner is, roughly speaking, both a principal and an agent, both a trustee and a beneficiary, for he has the property, authority, and confidence of his co-partners, as they do of him. He shares their profits and losses, and is bound by their actions. Without this protection of fiduciary duties, each is at the other's mercy." J. Crane.

■■■■

Quicknotes

AGENT An individual who has the authority to act on behalf of another.

FIDUCIARY DUTY A legal obligation to act for the benefit of another, including subordinating one's personal interests to that of the other person.

GENERAL PARTNERSHIP A voluntary agreement entered into by two or more parties to engage in business whereby each of the parties is to share in any profits and losses therefrom equally and each is to participate equally in the management of the enterprise.

■■■■

Pappas v. Tzolis

Former LLC member (P) v. LLC owner (D)

N.Y. Ct. App., 20 N.Y.3d 231 (2012).

NATURE OF CASE: Appeal from reversal of dismissal of various claims, including breach of fiduciary duty, unjust enrichment, conversion, and fraud and misrepresentation arising from the sale of LLC membership interests.

FACT SUMMARY: Tzolis (D), who had formed a limited liability company (LLC) with Pappas (P) and Ifantopoulos (P), and who had purchased his former co-members' interests in the LLC, contended their claims for breach of fiduciary duty, unjust enrichment, conversion, and fraud and misrepresentation arising from the sale of their interests were barred by their certification in closing documents, that Tzolis (D) had "no fiduciary duty" to them, and they were "not relying on any representation" by him.

🏛 RULE OF LAW
(1) Where there is a buyout of LLC membership interests, claims of breach of fiduciary duty, fraud and misrepresentation, and unjust enrichment brought by the sellers are barred where the LLC's operating agreement provided that members could engage in business ventures and investments of any nature whatsoever, whether or not in competition with the LLC, without obligation of any kind to the LLC or to the other members, and where the sellers certified at closing that the buyer had "no fiduciary duty" to them and they were "not relying on any representation" by the buyer.
(2) Where there is a buyout of LLC membership interests, the seller's claim of conversion based on the sale of those interests must be dismissed where the buyer purchased those interests.

FACTS: Pappas (P), Ifantopoulos (P), and Tzolis (D) formed an LLC for the purpose of entering into a long-term lease on a building. The operating agreement provided that any of the three members of the LLC could "engage in business ventures and investments of any nature whatsoever, whether or not in competition with the LLC, without obligation of any kind to the LLC or to the other Members." Numerous business disputes among the parties ensued, and Pappas (P) and Ifantopoulos (P) concluded Tzolis (D) was not trustworthy. Then, in January 2007, Tzolis (D) purchased the other members' interests for an aggregate of around $1.5 million. Before the purchase, Tzolis (D) represented to Pappas (P) and Ifantopoulos (P) he was aware of no reasonable prospects of selling the lease for an amount in excess of $2,500,000 (which was 20 times what they had paid for this a year earlier). At closing,

the parties executed a certificate (the "Certificate") in which Pappas (P) and Ifantopoulos (P) represented, that as sellers, they had "performed their own due diligence in connection with [the] assignments . . . engaged [their] own legal counsel, and [were] not relying on any representation by Steve Tzolis[,] or any of his agents or representatives, except as set forth in the assignments & other documents delivered to the undersigned Sellers today," and that "Steve Tzolis has no fiduciary duty to the undersigned Sellers in connection with [the] assignments." Tzolis (D) made reciprocal representations as the buyer. A few months later in August 2007, Tzolis (D), as the sole owner of the LLC, leased the building to a subsidiary of Extell Development Company (Extell) for $17.5 million. In 2009, Pappas (P) and Ifantopoulos (P) came to believe Tzolis (D) had surreptitiously negotiated the sale with the development company before he bought their interests in the LLC. They brought suit alleging numerous claims arising from the sale of their interests to Tzolis (D). The trial court dismissed all the claims, basing its decision on the operating agreement and Certificate. The state's intermediate appellate court reversed as to claims for fiduciary duty, unjust enrichment, conversion, and fraud and misrepresentation. That court permitted appeal, and the question of whether the appellate court had correctly ruled was certified to the state's highest appellate court, which granted review.

ISSUE:
(1) Where there is a buyout of LLC membership interests, are claims of breach of fiduciary duty, fraud and misrepresentation, and unjust enrichment brought by the sellers barred where the LLC's operating agreement provided that members could engage in business ventures and investments of any nature whatsoever, whether or not in competition with the LLC, without obligation of any kind to the LLC or to the other members, and where the sellers certified at closing that the buyer had "no fiduciary duty" to them and they were "not relying on any representation" by the buyer?
(2) Where there is a buyout of LLC membership interests, must the seller's claim of conversion based on the sale of those interests be dismissed where the buyer purchased those interests?

HOLDING AND DECISION: [Judge not listed in casebook extract.]
(1) Yes. Where there is a buyout of LLC membership interests, claims of breach of fiduciary duty, fraud and misrepresentation, and unjust enrichment brought by the

Continued on next page.

sellers are barred where the LLC's operating agreement provided that members could engage in business ventures and investments of any nature whatsoever, whether or not in competition with the LLC, without obligation of any kind to the LLC or to the other members, and where the sellers certified at closing that the buyer had "no fiduciary duty" to them and they were "not relying on any representation" by the buyer. As to the breach of fiduciary claim, where a principal and fiduciary are sophisticated entities and their relationship is not one of trust, the principal cannot reasonably rely on the fiduciary without making additional inquiry. Here, Pappas (P) and Ifantopoulos (P) were sophisticated businessmen represented by counsel, and their own allegations make it clear that at the time of the buyout, the relationship between the parties was not one of trust, so that reliance on Tzolis's (D) representations as a fiduciary would not have been reasonable. Therefore, the release contained in the Certificate was valid, and the cause of action alleging breach of fiduciary duty is barred. The cause of action alleging fraud and misrepresentation must be dismissed for similar reasons. Pappas (P) and Ifantopoulos (P) base this claim on the fact that Tzolis (D) represented to them that he was aware of no reasonable prospects of selling the lease for an amount in excess of $2,500,000. However, in the Certificate, they clearly announced and stipulated they were not relying on any representations as to the very matter as to which they now claim they were defrauded. Moreover, they do not allege the release was itself induced by any fraudulent action separate from the alleged fraud consisting of Tzolis's (D) failure to disclose his negotiations to sell the lease. Accordingly, this claim is barred by the release. Finally, as to the unjust enrichment claim, the equitable doctrine of unjust enrichment may be triggered in the absence of an agreement between the parties as to the subject of the claim. Here, however, the sale of interests in the LLC was controlled by contracts, including the operating agreement, and the Certificate, so that the unjust enrichment claim must fail as a matter of law. Reversed as to these claims.

(2) Yes. Where there is a buyout of LLC membership interests, the seller's claim of conversion based on the sale of those interests must be dismissed where the buyer purchased those interests. Two key elements of conversion are (1) the plaintiff's possessory right or interest in the property and (2) the defendant's dominion over the property or interference with it, in derogation of plaintiff's rights. Here, since Tzolis (D) had purchased Pappas's (P) and Ifantopoulos's (P) interests in the LLC, there could be no interference with their property rights. Therefore, the conversion claim must be dismissed.

▶ *ANALYSIS*

Practically speaking, it was clear to the court that Pappas (P) and Ifantopoulos (P) were in a position to make a reasoned judgment about whether to agree to the sale of their interests to Tzolis (D). The need to use care to reach an independent assessment of the value of the lease should have been obvious to them, given that Tzolis (D) offered to buy their interests for 20 times what they had paid for them just a year earlier. However, it is unclear why they did not conduct such due diligence, and the decision sends a strong reminder to parties to buyouts that it is likely in their best interests to conduct a reasonable level of due diligence notwithstanding its added cost.

Quicknotes

BREACH OF FIDUCIARY DUTY The failure of a fiduciary to observe the standard of care exercised by professionals of similar education and experience.

CONVERSION The act of depriving an owner of his property without permission or justification.

FRAUD A false representation of facts with the intent that another will rely on the misrepresentation to his detriment.

MISREPRESENTATION A statement or conduct by one party to another that constitutes a false representation of fact.

UNJUST ENRICHMENT Principle one should not be unjustly enriched at the expense of another.

The Corporate Form

Quick Reference Rules of Law

Automatic Self-Cleansing Filter Syndicate Co., Ltd. v. Cunninghame

Company (P) v. Unidentified party (D)

Eng. C.A., 2 Ch. 34 (1906).

NATURE OF CASE: Appeal in action for order directing a board of directors to proceed with a sale of assets on specific terms.

FACT SUMMARY: A 55 percent-majority group of the shareholders (the "majority group") (P) of Automatic Self-Cleansing Filter Syndicate Co., Ltd. (the "company") contended that the company's board of directors could not override the majority group's (P) vote, made at an ordinary shareholders meeting, to sell the company's assets, notwithstanding that the company's charter required a 75 percent vote to limit the board's decision-making power.

🏛 RULE OF LAW
Where a company's charter requires a 75 percent vote of the shareholders, made as an "extraordinary resolution," to override a board of directors' decision, a mere majority resolution made at an ordinary shareholders meeting may not override the board's decision that is contrary to the majority's wishes.

FACTS: A 55 percent-majority group of the shareholders (the "majority group") (P) of Automatic Self-Cleansing Filter Syndicate Co., Ltd. (the "company") wanted to sell the company's assets. At a meeting of the company, a resolution was passed by this majority group (P)—55 percent to 45 percent—in favor of the sale. The board of directors, believing in good faith the sale was not in the company's best interests, refused to carry out the resolution. The company's charter provided that "the management of the business and the control of the company shall be vested in the directors, subject nevertheless . . . to such regulations . . . as may from time to time be made by extraordinary resolution" (i.e., a vote of 75 percent of the shareholders). The majority group (P) brought an action to order the board to proceed with the sale on specific terms, but the trial court rejected the action. The appellate court granted review.

ISSUE: Where a company's charter requires a 75 percent vote of the shareholders, made as an "extraordinary resolution," to override a board of directors' decision, may a mere majority resolution made at an ordinary shareholders meeting override the board's decision that is contrary to the majority's wishes?

HOLDING AND DECISION: (Collins, M.R.) No. Where a company's charter requires a 75 percent vote of the shareholders, made as an "extraordinary resolution," to override a board of directors' decision, a mere majority resolution made at an ordinary shareholders meeting may not override the board's decision that is contrary to the majority's wishes. The governing statute gives precedence to the directors' decision in this situation, and gives to the directors the absolute power to do all things other than those expressly reserved to the shareholders. The directors' power is subject to extraordinary resolutions (in this case, by a 75 percent vote), so that if the shareholders desire to alter the directors' powers, they must do so not by a resolution made by a majority vote at an ordinary meeting, but by an extraordinary resolution. Thus, as here, a mere majority vote made at a regular meeting may not alter the mandate originally given to the directors in the charter. The argument that the directors are mere agents of the majority of shareholders is inapposite. It is by the consensus of all the shareholders that the directors become agents and hold their rights as agents. Therefore, since minority shareholders must also be considered the "principal," it is not fair to say that a majority at a meeting is the principal so as to alter the mandate of the agent. There is a mechanism provided in the charter to override the minority, but that mechanism—a special resolution made by a 75 percent vote—must be adhered to. There would be no point to requiring a "special resolution" for removal of directors in the company's charter if the company could be sold by majority vote at a general shareholders' meeting over the objection of the board. Affirmed.

CONCURRENCE: (Lord Cozens-Hardy, J.) The charter is a contract between all shareholders of the company, who have stipulated that the company's affairs will be managed by the board of directors, subject to the board's removal by a 75 percent vote (special resolution). Once appointed, the directors are not mere agents; they are more like managing partners appointed by the mutual agreement of all the shareholders.

▶ ANALYSIS

This decision reflected English law early in the 20th century. Similarly, in the United States, corporate law makes the board the ultimate locus of managerial powers. Thus, board members are not required by duty to follow the wishes of a majority shareholder. However, if the board thwarts the will of the majority, dissatisfied shareholders can pass a resolution to remove the directors at a special shareholders' meeting, or, in some jurisdictions, by consent solicitation.

■■■

Continued on next page.

Quicknotes

AGENT An individual who has the authority to act on behalf of another.

MINORITY SHAREHOLDER A stockholder in a corporation controlling such a small portion of those shares which are outstanding that its votes have no influence in the management of the corporation.

PRINCIPAL A person or entity who authorizes another (the agent) to act on its behalf and subject to its authority to the extent that the principal may be held liable for the actions of the agent.

SHAREHOLDER An individual who owns shares of stock in a corporation.

Jennings v. Pittsburgh Mercantile Co.

Real estate broker (P) v. Company (D)

Pa. Sup. Ct., 202 A.2d 51 (1964).

NATURE OF CASE: Appeal from denial of motion for judgment n.o.v. following jury verdict for plaintiff in assumpsit action.

FACT SUMMARY: Pittsburgh Mercantile Co. (Mercantile) (D) contended that Egmore, Mercantile's (D) vice-president and treasurer-comptroller, did not have apparent authority to accept an offer for a sale and leaseback, and that, therefore, Jennings (P), a real estate broker, was not entitled to commissions for a sale and leaseback transaction that Egmore seemed to accept, but that Mercantile's (D) board of directors did not.

🏛 RULE OF LAW
A corporation's executive officer does not have apparent authority to accept an offer for a transaction that, for the corporation, is extraordinary.

FACTS: Pittsburgh Mercantile Co. (Mercantile) (D), desiring to raise cash, sought to enter into a sale and leaseback of all its real property (an extraordinary transaction for the company). Egmore, Mercantile's (D) vice-president and treasurer-comptroller, met with Jennings (P), a real estate broker, and, after giving Jennings (P) some Mercantile (D) financials, requested that Jennings (P) solicit offers for a sale and leaseback. At this meeting, Egmore made the following representations: (1) the executive committee, of which Egmore was a member, controlled Mercantile (D); (2) the executive committee would be responsible for determining whether the company would accept any of the offers produced by Jennings (P); and (3) subsequent board of directors' approval of the acceptance would be automatic. In fact, however, Egmore did not have actual authority to accept such an offer. Egmore promised the payment of a commission if Jennings (P) succeeded in bringing in an offer on terms acceptable to the executive committee. Jennings (P) presented several offers to Egmore, one of which came close to Egmore's original terms. Jennings (P) was initially informed that the executive committee had "agreed to the deal." However, within a week Egmore informed Jennings (P) that the offer had been rejected. Mercantile (D) refused to pay Jennings' (P) bill for commission of $32,000 and Jennings (P) instituted an action in assumpsit for the brokerage commission. The jury returned a verdict for Jennings (P), and Mercantile (D) moved for a judgment n.o.v., which was rejected. The state's highest court granted review.

ISSUE: Does a corporation's executive officer have apparent authority to accept an offer for a transaction that, for the corporation, is extraordinary?

HOLDING AND DECISION: (Cohen, J.) No. A corporation's executive officer does not have apparent authority to accept an offer for a transaction that, for the corporation, is extraordinary. Apparent authority is defined as that authority which, although not actually granted, the principal (1) knowingly permits the agent to exercise or (2) holds him out as possessing. Egmore's representations cannot give rise to the apparent authority asserted because an agent cannot, simply by his own words, invest himself with apparent authority. Such authority emanates from the actions of the principal and not the agent. Also rejected are Jennings (P) arguments that apparent authority arose by virtue of (1) certain prior dealings of Egmore and (2) the corporate offices held by Egmore. As to the first argument, for a reasonable inference of the existence of apparent authority to be drawn from prior dealings, these dealings must have (1) a measure of similarity to the act for which the principal is sought to be bound, and, granting this similarity, (2) a degree of repetitiveness. Although the required degree of repetitiveness might have been present here, the prior acts relied upon consisted solely of Egmore's provision of financial information to Jennings (P) and other brokers with regard to the sale and leaseback, and Egmore's solicitation of offers through them. The dissimilarities between these acts and the act of accepting the offer in issue are self-evident, and apparent authority to do the latter act cannot be inferred from the doing of the former. As to the second argument, the offices held by Egmore do not by themselves indicate that a corporation has endowed them with apparent authority to act on behalf of the corporation regarding an extraordinary action. To hold otherwise would improperly extend the usual scope of authority which attaches to the holding of various corporate offices, and would greatly undercut the proper role of the board of directors in corporate decision-making by thrusting upon them determinations on critical matters which they have never had the opportunity to consider. Finally, the extraordinary nature of this transaction placed Jennings (P) on notice to inquire as to Egmore's actual authority, particularly since he was an experienced real estate broker. Had he done so, he would have discovered that the board never considered any of the proposals and did not delegate actual authority to accept offers. Reversed.

▌ ANALYSIS

Generally, corporate officers, unlike directors, are unquestionable agents of the corporation and are therefore

Continued on next page.

subject to the fiduciary duty of agents. Moreover, the board of directors generally may delegate its powers to the officers as it sees fit. It seems, therefore, that if this case had involved an ordinary company transaction, rather than an extraordinary one, Egmore should have been deemed to have had apparent authority to enter into it. Thus, it seems this case places the burden on third parties of determining whether a corporate transaction is ordinary or extraordinary.

■═■

Quicknotes

ACTION IN ASSUMPSIT Action to recover damages for breach of an oral or written promise to perform or pay pursuant to a contract.

AGENT An individual who has the authority to act on behalf of another.

APPARENT AUTHORITY The authority granted to an agent to act on behalf of the principal in order to effectuate the principal's objective, which may not be expressly granted, but which is inferred from the conduct of the principal and the agent.

FIDUCIARY DUTY A legal obligation to act for the benefit of another, including subordinating one's personal interests to that of the other person.

JUDGMENT N.O.V. A judgment entered by the trial judge reversing a jury verdict if the jury's determination has no basis in law or fact.

PRINCIPAL A person or entity who authorizes another (the agent) to act on its behalf and subject to its authority to the extent that the principal may be held liable for the actions of the agent.

■═■

CHAPTER 4

The Protection of Creditors

Quick Reference Rules of Law

Costello v. Fazio

Trustee in bankruptcy (D) v. Creditor (P)

256 F.2d 903 (9th Cir. 1958).

NATURE OF CASE: Appeal from denial of motion for an order subordinating creditors' claims to the claims of general unsecured creditors.

FACT SUMMARY: The trustee (D) in bankruptcy for the bankruptcy estate of Leonard Plumbing and Heating Supply, Inc. (the "company"), contended that claims against the estate of the company's creditors, Ambrose (P) and Fazio (P), who were also its controlling shareholders, should be subordinated to those of general unsecured creditors because Ambrose (P) and Fazio (P) had converted the bulk of their capital contributions into loans and left the company grossly undercapitalized, to the detriment of the company and its creditors.

RULE OF LAW

Where, in connection with the incorporation of a partnership, and for their own personal and private benefit, partners who are to become officers, directors, and controlling stockholders of the corporation, convert the bulk of their capital contributions into loans, taking promissory notes, thereby leaving the partnership and succeeding corporation grossly undercapitalized, to the detriment of the corporation and its creditors, their claims against the estate of the subsequently bankrupted corporation should be subordinated to the claims of the general unsecured creditors.

FACTS: Fazio (P), Ambrose (P), and Leonard formed a partnership, known as Leonard Plumbing and Heating Supply Co. The capital contributions of the three partners totaled $51,620.78, distributed as follows: Fazio, $43,169.61; Ambrose, $6,451.17; and Leonard, $2,000. The three later decided to incorporate that partnership, and formed Leonard Plumbing and Heating Supply, Inc. (the "company"). In contemplation of the incorporation, Fazio (P) and Ambrose (P) withdrew all but $2,000 apiece of their capital contributions to the business. This was accomplished by the issuance to them of partnership promissory demand notes in the sum of $41,169.61 and $4,451.17, respectively. The capital contribution to the partnership business then stood at $6,000—$2,000 for each partner. The closing balance sheet of the partnership showed current assets to be $160,791.87, and current liabilities at $162,162.22. There were also fixed assets in the sum of $6,482.90, and other assets in the sum of $887.45. The partnership had cash on hand in the sum of $66.66, and an overdraft at the bank in the amount of $3,422.78. During the year of incorporation, the company experienced a net loss of $22,521.34. The corporation assumed all liabilities of the partnership, including the notes to Fazio (P) and Ambrose (P). After continuing to sustain losses, the company filed a voluntary petition in bankruptcy. At this time, the corporation was not indebted to any creditors whose obligations were incurred by the preexisting partnership, saving the promissory notes issued to Fazio (P) and Ambrose (P), who each filed claims against the company's bankruptcy estate on their notes. The bankruptcy trustee moved to have their claims subordinated to those of general unsecured creditors on the grounds that the amounts in question represented a portion of the capital investment in the partnership and that the transfer of this sum from the partnership capital to debt effectuated a scheme to place copartners in the same class as unsecured creditors. A hearing was held before the referee in bankruptcy, at which experts for the trustee testified that the company was undercapitalized at the time of incorporation and that the incorporation resulted in a transfer of capital to debt for the protection of Fazio (P) and Ambrose (P). Notwithstanding this testimony, the referee ruled that the amount paid-in stated capital of the corporation at the time of its incorporation was adequate for the continued operation of the business. He found that while Fazio (P) and Ambrose (P) controlled and dominated the corporation and its affairs they did not mismanage the business. He further found that they did not practice any fraud or deception, and did not act for their own personal or private benefit and to the detriment of the corporation or its stockholders and creditors. The referee also found that the transaction was not a part of any scheme or plan to place the claimants in the same class as unsecured creditors of the partnership. On the basis of these findings, the referee concluded that, in procuring the promissory notes, the Fazio (P) and Ambrose (P) acted in all respects in good faith and took no unfair advantage of the corporation, or of its stockholders or creditors. The district court affirmed, and the court of appeals granted review.

ISSUE: Where, in connection with the incorporation of a partnership, and for their own personal and private benefit, partners who are to become officers, directors, and controlling stockholders of the corporation, convert the bulk of their capital contributions into loans, taking promissory notes, thereby leaving the partnership and succeeding corporation grossly undercapitalized, to the detriment of the corporation and its creditors, should their claims against the estate of the subsequently bankrupted corporation be subordinated to the claims of the general unsecured creditors?

Continued on next page.

HOLDING AND DECISION: (Hamley, J.) Yes.

Where, in connection with the incorporation of a partnership, and for their own personal and private benefit, partners who are to become officers, directors, and controlling stockholders of the corporation, convert the bulk of their capital contributions into loans, taking promissory notes, thereby leaving the partnership and succeeding corporation grossly undercapitalized, to the detriment of the corporation and its creditors, their claims against the estate of the subsequently bankrupted corporation should be subordinated to the claims of the general unsecured creditors. The referee's findings here were clearly erroneous, and, therefore, his conclusions merit reversal. First, the corporation was grossly undercapitalized. Despite the company's precarious financial condition, Fazio (P) and Ambrose (P) withdrew $45,620.78 of the partnership capital—more than 88 percent of the total capital. The $6,000 capital left in the business was only 1/65 of the last annual net sales. The conclusion that the company was undercapitalized is confirmed by the expert testimony. Second, it was abundantly clear that the depletion of the capital account in favor of a debt account was for the purpose of equalizing the capital investments of the partners and to reduce tax liability when there were profits to distribute. It is therefore certain, contrary to the referee's findings, that, in withdrawing this capital, Fazio (P) and Ambrose (P) did act for their own personal benefit. It is equally certain, from the undisputed facts, that in so doing they acted to the detriment of the corporation and its creditors. Claims of controlling shareholders will be deferred or subordinated to outside creditors where a corporation in bankruptcy has not been adequately or honestly capitalized, or has been managed to the prejudice of creditors, or where to do otherwise would be unfair to creditors. Because the company was purposely undercapitalized for the personal benefit of its shareholder-creditors (Fazio (P) and Ambrose (P)), and because it would be inequitable to permit those shareholder-creditors to share in the assets of the bankrupt company, in the same parity with general unsecured creditors, since they would receive a portion of the capital invested which should have been used to satisfy the claims of creditors before any capital investment could be returned to the owners and stockholders of the company, the capital-to-debt transaction must be condemned. This is also true because the shareholder-creditors, as company fiduciaries, stood on both sides of the transaction, and, under all the circumstances the transaction did not carry the earmarks of an arm's length bargain. The shareholder-creditors took advantage of their fiduciary position; their inequitable conduct consisted not in acting to the detriment of creditors then known, but in acting to the detriment of present or future creditors. Reversed and remanded.

▶ ANALYSIS

Equitable subordination is a means of protecting unaffiliated creditors by giving them rights to corporate assets superior to those of other creditors who happen to also be significant shareholders of the firm. The critical question is what set of circumstances will permit a court to impose this subordination on a shareholder-creditor. The first requirement, as was the case here, is that the creditor be an equity holder and typically an officer or director of the company. In addition, this insider-creditor must have, in some fashion, behaved inequitably toward the corporation and its outside creditors.

Quicknotes

CREDITOR A person or party to whom a debt or obligation is owed.

SHAREHOLDER An individual who owns shares of stock in a corporation.

UNDERCAPITALIZATION Refers to a business that does not have sufficient funds to operate.

UNSECURED CREDITOR A creditor whose loan is not backed by specified collateral or a security agreement.

Sea-Land Services, Inc. v. The Pepper Source

Shipping company (P) v. Corporation/sole shareholder (D)

941 F.2d 519 (7th Cir. 1991).

NATURE OF CASE: Appeal from a grant of summary judgment for the plaintiff in an action for money owed.

FACT SUMMARY: When Sea-Land Services, Inc. (Sea-Land) (P) could not collect a shipping bill because The Pepper Source (PS) (D) had been dissolved, Sea-Land (P) sought to pierce the corporate veil to hold PS's (D) sole shareholder personally liable.

RULE OF LAW
The corporate veil will be pierced where there is a unity of interest and ownership between the corporation and an individual and where adherence to the fiction of a separate corporate existence would sanction a fraud or promote injustice.

FACTS: After Sea-Land Services, Inc. (Sea-Land) (P), an ocean carrier, shipped peppers for The Pepper Source (PS) (D), it could not collect on the substantial freight bill because PS (D) had been dissolved. Moreover, PS (D) apparently had no assets. Unable to recover on a default judgment against PS (D), Sea-Land (P) filed another lawsuit, seeking to pierce the corporate veil and hold Marchese (D), sole shareholder of PS (D) and other corporations, personally liable. PS (D) then took the necessary steps to be reinstated as a corporation in Illinois. Sea-Land (P) moved for summary judgment, which the court granted. Marchese (D) and PS (D) appealed.

ISSUE: Will the corporate veil be pierced where there is a unity of interest and ownership between a corporation and an individual and where adherence to the fiction of a separate corporate existence would sanction a fraud or promote injustice?

HOLDING AND DECISION: (Bauer, C.J.) Yes. The corporate veil will be pierced where there is a unity of interest and ownership between a corporation and an individual and where adherence to the fiction of a separate corporate existence would sanction a fraud or promote injustice. There can be no doubt that the unity of interest and ownership part of the test is met here. Corporate records and formalities have not been maintained, funds and assets have been commingled with abandon, PS (D) was undercapitalized, and corporate assets have been moved and tapped and borrowed without regard to their source. The second part of the test is more problematic, however. An unsatisfied judgment, by itself, is not enough to show that injustice would be promoted. Promoting injustice means something less than an affirmative showing of fraud. If, as Sea-Land (P) maintains, an unsatisfied

judgment is enough, then every plaintiff who brings a piercing the corporate veil would pass that test, since an unsatisfied judgment looms in every such case, and the test would collapse into a one-step "unity of interest and ownership" test. Case law requires a wrong beyond the inability to collect on a judgment. Here, although Sea-Land (P) has alleged an intentional asset-and-liability-shifting scheme, it has not adduced evidence of such wrongdoing. On remand, Sea-Land (P) is required to show the kind of injustice necessary to evoke the court's power to prevent injustice. Reversed and remanded.

ANALYSIS

On remand, judgment for Sea-Land (P) required Marchese (D) to pay the shipping debt plus post-judgment interest. On appeal, the judgment was affirmed, *Sea-Land Services, Inc. v. The Pepper Source,* 993 F.2d 1309 (7th Cir. 1993). The court in that case observed that Marchese (D) had received countless benefits at the expense of Sea-Land (P) and others, including loans and salaries paid in such a way as to insure that his corporations had insufficient funds with which to pay their debts.

Quicknotes

CORPORATE VEIL Refers to the shielding from personal liability of a corporation's officers, directors or shareholders for unlawful conduct engaged in by the corporation.

PERSONAL LIABILITY An obligation pursuant to which the personal assets of an individual may be required for payment.

UNDERCAPITALIZATION Refers to a business that does not have sufficient funds to operate.

Kinney Shoe Corp. v. Polan

Corporation (P) v. Sole shareholder (D)

939 F.2d 209 (4th Cir. 1991).

NATURE OF CASE: Appeal from a judgment for the defendant in an action to recover rent due on a building sublease.

FACT SUMMARY: After a corporation owned by Polan (D) defaulted on a building sublease with Kinney Shoe Corp. (Kinney) (P), Kinney (P) sought to hold Polan (D) personally liable, since his corporation was inadequately capitalized and Polan (D) had not observed any corporate formalities.

🏛 RULE OF LAW
In a breach of contract, the corporate veil will be pierced where a unity of interest and ownership blends the two personalities of the corporation and the individual shareholder, and where treating the acts as those of the corporation alone would produce an inequitable result.

FACTS: Polan (D) formed Industrial Realty Company (Industrial) and Polan Industries, Inc, to re-establish an industrial manufacturing business. Although certificates of incorporation were issued, no organizational meetings were held, and no officers were elected. Polan (D) negotiated with Kinney Shoe Corp. (Kinney) (P) for Industrial to sublease a building in which Kinney (P) held a leasehold interest. Industrial then subleased part of the building to Polan Industries. Other than the sublease, Industrial had no assets. Polan (D) made the first rental payment out of his personal funds but made no further payments. Kinney (P) sought to hold Polan (D) personally liable on the sublease debt. The district court ruled in Polan's (D) favor. Kinney (P) appealed.

ISSUE: In a breach of contract, will the corporate veil be pierced where a unity of interest and ownership blends the two personalities of the corporation and the individual shareholder, and where treating the acts as those of the corporation alone would produce an inequitable result?

HOLDING AND DECISION: (Chapman, J.) Yes. In a breach of contract, the corporate veil will be pierced where a unity of interest and ownership blends the two personalities of the corporation and the individual shareholder, and where treating the acts as those of the corporation alone would produce an inequitable result. In this case, it is undisputed that Industrial had no paid-in capital and that Polan (D) did not observe any corporate formalities. A third prong of the test may apply where a complaining party may be deemed to have assumed the risk of the gross undercapitalization where it would be reasonable for such party to protect itself by making a credit investigation. The district court erred in applying this prong to the instant case. Because Polan (D) failed to follow the simple formalities of maintaining a corporation, he cannot now extricate himself by asserting that Kinney (P) should have known better. Reversed and remanded.

▌ ANALYSIS

Some jurisdictions have held that inadequate capitalization is not of itself a badge of fraud. The general rule is that an individual may incorporate his business for the sole purpose of escaping individual liability for the corporate debts. Here, however, Polan (D) had attempted to protect his assets by placing them in Polan Industries, then interposing Industrial, a shell corporation, between Polan Industries and Kinney (P) to prevent Kinney (P) from going against the corporation with assets.

■■■

Quicknotes

BREACH OF CONTRACT Unlawful failure by a party to perform its obligations pursuant to contract.

CORPORATE VEIL Refers to the shielding from personal liability of a corporation's officers, directors or shareholders for unlawful conduct engaged in by the corporation.

■■■

Walkovszky v. Carlton

Injured pedestrian (P) v. Cab company owner (D)

N.Y. Ct. App., 223 N.E.2d 6 (1966).

NATURE OF CASE: Appeal from reversal of grant of a motion to dismiss for failure to state a cause of action to recover damages for personal injury.

FACT SUMMARY: Walkovszky (P), run down by a taxicab owned by Seon Cab Corporation (D), sued Carlton (D), a stockholder of ten corporations, including Seon (D), each of which had only two cabs registered in its name.

RULE OF LAW
Whenever anyone uses control of the corporation to further his own rather than the corporation's business, he will be liable for the corporation's acts. Upon the principle of respondeat superior, the liability extends to negligent acts as well as commercial dealings. However, where a corporation is a fragment of a larger corporate combine that actually conducts the business, a court will not "pierce the corporate veil" to hold individual shareholders liable.

FACTS: Walkovszky (P) was run down by a taxicab owned by Seon Cab Corporation (Seon) (D). In his complaint, Walkovszky (P) alleged that Seon (D) was one of ten cab companies of which Carlton (D) was a shareholder and that each corporation had but two cabs registered in its name. The complaint, by this, implied that each cab corporation carried only the minimum automobile liability insurance required by law ($10,000). It was further alleged that these corporations were operated as a single entity with regard to financing, supplies, repairs, employees, and garaging. Each corporation and its shareholders were named as defendants because the multiple corporate structures, Walkovszky (P) claimed, constituted an unlawful attempt to "defraud members of the general public."

ISSUE: Did Walkovszky's (P) complaint state a sufficient cause of action so as to recover against each cab corporation, Carlton (D) as shareholder, and each corporation's shareholders?

HOLDING AND DECISION: (Fuld, J.) No. While the law permits the incorporation of a business for the purpose of minimizing personal liability, this privilege should not be abused. Courts will disregard the corporate form ("pierce the corporate veil") to prevent fraud or to achieve equity. General rules of agency—respondeat superior—will apply to hold an individual liable for a corporation's negligent acts. The court here had earlier invoked the doctrine in a case where the owner of several cab companies (and whose name was prominently displayed on the cabs) actually serviced, inspected, repaired, and dispatched them. However, in such instances, it must be shown that the stockholder was conducting the business in his individual capacity. In this respect, Walkovszky's (P) complaint is deficient. The corporate form may not be disregarded simply because the assets of the corporation, together with liability insurance, are insufficient to assure recovery. If the insurance coverage is inadequate, the remedy lies with the legislature and not the courts. It is not fraudulent for the owner of a single cab corporation to take out no more than minimum insurance. Fraud goes to whether Carlton (D) and his associates (D) were "shuttling their funds in and out of the corporations without regard to formality and to suit their own convenience." Order reversed.

DISSENT: (Keating, J.) The corporations formed by Carlton (D) were intentionally undercapitalized for the purpose of avoiding liability likely to arise from the operation of a large taxi fleet, and all income was continually drained out of the corporations for the same purpose. Given these circumstances, the shareholders (D) should all be held individually liable to Walkovszky (P) for the injuries he suffered. Contrary to Carlton's (D) assertion, merely because the minimum amount of insurance required by the statute was obtained does not mean that the corporate veil may not be pierced. In requiring the minimum liability insurance of $10,000, the legislature did not intend to shield those individuals who organized corporations with the specific intent of avoiding responsibility to the public. Thus, the court should have held that a participating shareholder of a corporation vested with a public interest, organized with capital insufficient to meet liabilities, which are certain to arise in the ordinary course of the corporation's business, may be held personally responsible for such liabilities. Under such a holding, the only types of corporate enterprises that will be discouraged will be those designed solely to abuse the corporate privilege at the expense of the public interest—as is the case here.

ANALYSIS

Courts, in justifying disregard of the corporate entity so as to pierce the corporate veil, advance an estoppel argument. If the entity is not respected by the shareholders, they cannot complain if the court, likewise, disregards the corporate arrangement—this is to prevent abuse of the form. Since the corporate veil may be dismissed even in instances where there has been no reliance on a

Continued on next page.

company's seeming healthiness, as in tort claims, whether or not creditors have been misled is not of primary importance. Rather, a court will look at the degree to which the corporate shell has been perfected and the corporation's use as a mere business conduit of its shareholders.

■■■■

Quicknotes

CORPORATE VEIL Refers to the shielding from personal liability of a corporation's officers, directors or shareholders for unlawful conduct engaged in by the corporation.

ESTOPPEL An equitable doctrine precluding a party from asserting a right to the detriment of another whom justifiably relied on the conduct.

NEGLIGENCE Conduct falling below the standard of care that a reasonable person would demonstrate under similar conditions.

RESPONDEAT SUPERIOR The rule the principal is responsible for tortious acts committed by its agents in the scope of their agency or authority.

■■■■

CHAPTER 5

Debt, Equity, and Economic Value

Quick Reference Rules of Law

PAGE

1. *In Re Emerging Communications Inc., Shareholder Litigation.* (1) For purposes of determining a company's fair value, premiums will not be added to the company's cost of capital where there is neither theoretical nor evidentiary support for such premiums. (2) For purposes of determining a company's fair value, a publicly traded company's market price will not be given significant weight as corroborative of the company's fair value where the record does not support a finding that the company's stock was traded in an efficient market. 36

In re Emerging Communications, Inc. Shareholders Litigation

[Parties not identified]

Del. Ch. Ct., 2004 Del. Ch. LEXIS 70 (2004).

NATURE OF CASE: Court's determination of fair value in consolidated statutory appraisal and class actions for breach of fiduciary duty.

FACT SUMMARY: Minority shareholders of Emerging Communications, Inc. (ECM) contended that the board of directors and a majority shareholder of ECM undervalued the company when its majority owner, Prosser, took it private, and that, therefore, they were paid an unfair price as a result of unfair dealing. The court evaluated the opinions of both sides' experts as to the company's cost of capital, as well as the company's market price, in determining the fair value of the company's shares.

RULE OF LAW

(1) For purposes of determining a company's fair value, premiums will not be added to the company's cost of capital where there is neither theoretical nor evidentiary support for such premiums.

(2) For purposes of determining a company's fair value, a publicly traded company's market price will not be given significant weight as corroborative of the company's fair value where the record does not support a finding that the company's stock was traded in an efficient market.

FACTS: [In a two-step going-private transaction, the publicly owned shares of Emerging Communications, Inc. (ECM) were acquired by Innovative Communications Corp., LLC (Innovative), ECM's majority shareholder, for $10.25 per share. At the time, 52 percent of the outstanding shares of ECM, and 100 percent of the outstanding shares of Innovative, were owned by Innovative Communication Company, LLC (ICC). ICC, in turn, was wholly owned by ECM's Chairman and CEO, Prosser. Thus, Prosser had voting control of both of the parties to the privatization transaction. The shareholders approved the transaction, and the merger was consummated. Minority shareholders brought actions for statutory appraisal, as well as class actions for breach of fiduciary duties. These actions were consolidated by the Chancery Court.] One of the issues before the court was, for statutory appraisal purposes, the fair value of ECM on the merger date, and, in light of that value whether the transaction price of $10.25 was a "fair price" within the meaning of fiduciary duty case law. Both sides presented experts on this issue. As part of the fair value determination, the experts opined as to ECM's cost of equity. The plaintiffs' expert, Zmijewski, determined a

cost of equity of between 10.3 percent and 10.4 percent. The defendants' expert, Bayston, initially determined a cost of equity of 9.9 percent, but then added several premiums to this figure, amounting to 4.1 percent, to raise the cost of equity to 14 percent. More specifically, Bayston added a "small stock premium" of 1.7 percent and a "company-specific premium" of 2.4 percent, the latter consisting of a 1 to 1.5 percent "super-small stock premium" and a .9 to 1.4 percent "hurricane risk premium." Those "premiums" accounted for most of the difference between the two experts' cost of equity inputs. Accordingly, the issue for the court was whether either of these premiums was appropriate in these circumstances. The court also addressed whether ECM's market price of $7.00 was corroborative of ECM's fair value.

ISSUE:

(1) For purposes of determining a company's fair value, will premiums be added to the company's cost of capital where there is neither theoretical nor evidentiary support for such premiums?

(2) For purposes of determining a company's fair value, will a publicly traded company's market price be given significant weight as corroborative of the company's fair value where the record does not support a finding that the company's stock was traded in an efficient market?

HOLDING AND DECISION: [Judge not stated in casebook excerpt.]

(1) No. For purposes of determining a company's fair value, premiums will not be added to the company's cost of capital where there is neither theoretical nor evidentiary support for such premiums. The party seeking to add a premium (here, the defendants) has the burden to establish that the premium is appropriate. As to the "small firm/small stock premium," there is finance literature supporting the position that stocks of smaller companies are riskier than securities of large ones and, therefore, command a higher expected rate of return in the market. The use of such premiums has been upheld by case law, and the use of this premium here is appropriate theoretically, and is supported by the evidence presented by Bayston. Far more controversial, and less grounded in finance theory and legal precedent, is the additional 2.4 percent premium added by Bayston to account for what he determined was the incremental risk of ECM being both a "supersmall" firm and also subject to unusually hazardous weather risk, specifically, hurricanes. As to the "supersmall"

Continued on next page.

firm premium, other than baldly asserting that the premium reflects the reality of investment returns in micro-cap companies such as ECM, the defendants offer no analysis, discussion of specific data, reference to any finance text, or other rationale for their "supersmall" firm premium. Defendants' support for an incremental premium falls woefully short of the showing that is required. The defendants offer nothing to persuade the court that ECM's risk profile fits what they contend is the "reality" of investment returns for micro-cap companies. ECM may be small, but it is also a utility that was unusually protected from the hazards of the marketplace. ECM was well established, it had no competition, it was able to borrow at below-market rates, and it was cushioned by regulators from extraordinary hazards. Implicit in this position is the assumption that these advantages, however extraordinary, were not enough to offset the added risk created by ECM's "supersmall" size. It is the defendant's burden to support that assumption, and they have not done that. Therefore, this premium will not be added to the cost of equity. As to the weather-related premium, the defendants similarly have failed to provide either theoretical or empirical support for the premium. The defendants argued that the premium was appropriate based on unreimbursed hurricane-related damages of around $80 million, and that ECM would not be able to obtain hurricane insurance going forward. First, there was evidence that in fact the amount of unreimbursed hurricane damages was around $55 million. Second, defendants' claim that management knew as of the merger date its hurricane insurance would not continue, relied entirely on Prosser's trial testimony, which was not corroborated by any contemporaneous document and was inconsistent with ECM's SEC filings and loan documents, none of which indicated any impending loss of hurricane loss coverage. Third, even assuming the risk of future storm losses should be accounted for in some way, the defendants did not support their argument that the appropriate way to do that is by increasing the cost of equity. They cited no finance literature supporting that approach, nor did they support their argument empirically, such as (for example) by comparing ECM's company-specific weather-related risk (net of mitigation factors) to the "average" or "mean" weather-related risk for all companies, or even for all "small" companies. This absence of theoretical and evidentiary support fails to persuade the court that the risk of unrecoverable hurricane damage loss is so embedded in ECM's business as to require a structural increase in ECM's cost of equity. A better approach would have been to spread the risk of hurricane loss over ECM's cash flows over a number of years. For these reasons, the defendants' hurricane-related premium is rejected, and will not be added to ECM's cost of equity. Based on the court's findings, the appropriate discount rate for a discounted cash flow (DCF)

analysis is 8.69 percent, and, applying that discount rate, the fair value of ECM as of the merger date is determined to be $38.05 per share. [The court's determination that ECM's fair value on the merger date was $38.05 led it to rule that the $10.25 transaction price was not a "fair price."]

(2) No. For purposes of determining a company's fair value, a publicly traded company's market price will not be given significant weight as corroborative of the company's fair value where the record does not support a finding that the company's stock was traded in an efficient market. Case law recognizes that while market price should be considered in an appraisal, it is not always indicative of fair value. Here, the evidence does not support the defendants' expert Malkiel's assertion that ECM's common stock was traded in an efficient market. First, it was precisely because ECM's stock market price did not reflect ECM's underlying values that Prosser decided to acquire the ECM minority interest. Prosser himself told his fellow ECM directors that the ECM stock price had failed to reach the desired appreciation as a result of the small public float and the fact that the stock was not being followed by Wall Street analysts. Moreover, because Prosser always owned the majority interest, the market price of ECM stock always reflected a minority discount. Further, while the stock was trading freely, (i.e., before Prosser announced the privatization), the market never had the benefit of any disclosed earnings or projections of future results. For these reasons, the defendants' argument, that the market price of ECM stock corroborates the $10.25 price as the fair or intrinsic value of ECM on the date of the merge, is rejected. In this case, ECM's unaffected stock market price merits little or no weight.

▶ ANALYSIS

Typical in litigation of this kind, the overriding question—what the company was intrinsically worth on the merger date—involves a proverbial "battle of the experts." In this case, the plaintiffs' expert valued ECM at over $41 per share, whereas the defendants' expert valued ECM at $10.38 per share. These widely differing valuations of the same company result from quite different financial assumptions that each sponsoring side exhorts the court to accept. As this case illustrates, to evaluate the parties' competing approaches requires the court to resolve a multitude of valuation issues, some of which are factual and others of which are conceptual. Ultimately, the court makes an independent determination of value based on the evidence presented by both sides.

Continued on next page.

Quicknotes

BREACH OF FIDUCIARY DUTY The failure of a fiduciary to observe the standard of care exercised by professionals of similar education and experience.

BURDEN OF PROOF The duty of a party to introduce evidence to support a fact that is in dispute in an action.

EXCULPATORY CLAUSE A clause in a contract relieving one party from liability for certain unlawful conduct.

FIDUCIARY DUTY A legal obligation to act for the benefit of another, including subordinating one's personal interests to that of the other person.

Normal Governance: The Voting System

Quick Reference Rules of Law

Rosenfeld v. Fairchild Engine & Airplane Corp.

Shareholder (P) v. Corporation (D)

N.Y. Ct. App., 128 N.E.2d 291 (1955).

NATURE OF CASE: Appeal from dismissal of a shareholder's derivative suit.

FACT SUMMARY: Rosenfeld (P) brought a derivative suit to have the $261,522 that had been paid to both sides of a proxy contest returned to the corporation (D).

🏛 RULE OF LAW
Directors may make reasonable and proper expenditures from the corporate treasury to persuade stockholders of the correctness of the directors' policy positions and to solicit shareholder support for policies that the directors believe, in good faith, are in the corporation's best interests.

FACTS: $261,522 was paid out of Fairchild Engine & Airplane Corp.'s (D) corporate treasury to reimburse both sides in a proxy contest. Of the $261,522 at issue, $106,000 of corporate funds was spent by the old board of directors in defense of their positions in the proxy contest. The new board paid $28,000 to the old board for the remaining expenses incurred after the proxy contest was over. The new board found this to be fair and reasonable. The new board was paid expenses in the proxy contest. This was ratified by stockholders. Stockholder Rosenfeld (P) admitted the sums were reasonable. Rosenfeld (P), however, argued that they were not legal charges that could be reimbursed and sued to compel the return of the $261,522. The appellate division affirmed the judgment of an official referee, who had dismissed Rosenfeld's (P) complaint, having concluded that this was a contest over corporate policy. Rosenfeld (P) appealed.

ISSUE: May directors make reasonable and proper expenditures from the corporate treasury to persuade stockholders of the correctness of the directors' policy positions and to solicit shareholder support for policies that the directors believe, in good faith, are in the corporation's best interests?

HOLDING AND DECISION: (Froeseel, J.) Yes. Directors may make reasonable and proper expenditures from the corporate treasury to persuade stockholders of the correctness of the directors' policy positions and to solicit shareholder support for policies that the directors believe, in good faith, are in the corporation's best interests. If not, incumbent directors would be unable to defend their positions and corporate policies. As such, the old board was reimbursed for reasonable and proper expenditures in defending their positions. Stockholders also have the right to reimburse successful contestants for their reasonable

expenses. As such, the new board was also reimbursed for its expenditures by the stockholders. Judgment of the appellate division affirmed, without costs.

▶ ANALYSIS

This case represents the popularity of proxy contests in the 1950s. One of the advantages of proxy contests is that they are considered to be cheaper than tender offers where a bidder offers to buy voting shares at a particular price. Another advantage is that insurgent groups may be reimbursed for their expenses, as in this case. Lastly, proxy contests are often considered successful in contests alleging incompetence.

Quicknotes

PROXY A person authorized to act for another.

SHAREHOLDER'S DERIVATIVE ACTION Action asserted by a shareholder in rder to enforce a cause of action on behalf of the corporation.

Speiser v. Baker

50 percent common stock owner (P) v. 50 percent common stock owner (D)

Del. Ch. Ct., 525 A.2d 1001 (1987).

NATURE OF CASE: Motion by plaintiff seeking judgment on the pleadings and dismissal of defendant's affirmative claim for declaratory relief, asserted as cross-claims and counterclaims, in action seeking an order requiring the convening of an annual meeting of shareholders.

FACT SUMMARY: Speiser (P), a 50 percent owner of the common shares of Health Med Corporation's (Health Med's) and one of its two directors, contended that the corporation was required to hold an annual stockholders meeting to elect directors; Baker (D), the other 50 percent owner of Health Med's common shares and its other director, counterclaimed that Health Med could not vote its 42 percent stock interest in Health Chem (Chem), a publicly traded company, at such a stockholders meeting because to do so would contravene a statutory prohibition on the voting of shares "belonging to" a corporation—despite the fact that Chem (through a subsidiary) did not hold, even indirectly, a majority of the stock "entitled to vote" in Health Med's election of directors.

> ## 🏛 RULE OF LAW
> (1) Where a corporation has failed to hold an annual stockholders meeting for the election of directors, in contravention of statutory law, such a meeting must be held even if it means that one of two directors will be removed.
> (2) Where a statute prohibits the voting by a corporation of stock "belonging to the corporation," stock held by a corporate subsidiary may "belong to" the issuer and thus be prohibited from voting, even if the issuer does not hold a majority of shares entitled to vote at the election of directors of the subsidiary.

FACTS: Speiser (P) and Baker (D) were each 50 percent owners of Health Med Corporation's (Health Med's) common stock and were its two directors. Health Med held the stock of Health Chem (Chem), a publicly traded company. Chem's stock was held as follows: the public (40%), Speiser (P) (10%), Baker (D) (8%) and Health Med (42%). However, Chem itself indirectly, along with Baker (D) and Speiser (P), through a wholly owned subsidiary, owned 95 percent of Health Med's equity. However, Chem's 95 percent equity ownership in Health Med did not represent 95 percent of the Health Med's voting power, since what Chem owned was an issue of convertible preferred stock which, while bearing an unqualified right to be converted immediately into common stock of Health Med represent-

ing 95 percent of Health Med's voting power, while it was unconverted, carried the right to only approximately 9 percent of Health Med's vote. In its unconverted state the preferred stock commanded the same dividend rights as it would if converted to common stock. Speiser (P) and Baker (D) owned the balance of Health Med's voting power. This circular voting structure enabled Speiser (P) and Baker (D) to retain control of all the companies, while owning only 35 percent of Chem's equity. Conversion of the preferred stock would destroy this control mechanism, since it would increase the public shareholders' voting power from 40 percent to 65.6 percent. Speiser (P), who was president of all three corporations—Health Med, Chem, and the wholly owned subsidiary—was able to control Health Med's vote. Speiser (P) and Baker (D) had a falling out and Health Med did not have an annual stockholders' meeting for several years. Speiser (P) brought a statutory action for an order requiring the convening of an annual meeting of Health Med shareholders. Baker (D) argued that Speiser (P) was seeking a Health Med stockholders meeting for the purpose of removing Baker (D) as one of Health Med's two directors. The case raised two independent legal issues: whether Baker (D) raised an affirmative defense to Speiser's (P) prima facie case for requiring an annual stockholders meeting, and whether the circular ownership of stock among the companies was illegal so that Health Med was precluded from exercising its rights as a Chem shareholder.

ISSUE:
(1) Where a corporation has failed to hold an annual stockholders meeting for the election of directors, in contravention of statutory law, must such a meeting be held even if it means that one of two directors will be removed?
(2) Where a statute prohibits the voting by a corporation of stock "belonging to the corporation," may stock held by a corporate subsidiary "belong to" the issuer and thus be prohibited from voting, even if the issuer does not hold a majority of shares entitled to vote at the election of directors of the subsidiary?

HOLDING AND DECISION: (Allen, J.)
(1) Yes. Where a corporation has failed to hold an annual stockholders meeting for the election of directors, in contravention of statutory law, such a meeting must be held even if it means that one of two directors will be removed. Baker's (D) affirmative defenses allege no wrong to Health Med or its shareholders that will occur by reason of the holding of Health Med's annual

Continued on next page.

meeting. The essence of his defense is that he will likely be voted out of office as a Health Med director and the company will fall under Speiser's (P) complete domination. As a legal matter, there would be nothing wrong with that result. Motion on the pleadings granted as to this issue.

(2) Yes. Where a statute prohibits the voting by a corporation of stock "belonging to the corporation," stock held by a corporate subsidiary may "belong to" the issuer and thus be prohibited from voting, even if the issuer does not hold a majority of shares entitled to vote at the election of directors of the subsidiary. Baker's (D) counterclaim seeks a declaratory judgment that Health Med may not vote its 42 percent stock interest in Chem. This counterclaim is based on a statute that says: "Shares of its own capital stock belonging to the corporation or to another corporation, if a majority of the shares entitled to vote in the election of directors of such other corporation is held directly or indirectly, by the corporation, shall neither be entitled to vote nor counted for quorum purposes." A literal reading of this language does not prohibit the voting of Health Med's stock in Chem since Chem (through its subsidiary) does not hold, even indirectly, a majority of the stock "entitled to vote" in Health Med's election of directors. That conclusion, however, does not end the inquiry, because other portions of the statutory language may be read to extend the statute's prohibition to the voting of Health Med's Chem holdings. Specifically, the phrase "belonging to the corporation," when interpreted in light of the statute's history and underlying policy, can reach the particular set of facts presented by this case. Basically, the statute and its common law origins are intended to address the dangers posed by mechanisms that permit directors, by virtue of their office, to control votes belonging to shares of company stock owned by the corporation, its nominee, or its agent, and thereby deprive the true owners of the corporation of a say in who will run the corporation. The legislative history does not indicate an intent to create a statutory presumption that in no event would stock owned by another corporation that does not satisfy the "majority of shares entitled to vote" test be deemed to be stock "belonging to the corporation." Therefore, the statute is applicable here, where the capital of one corporation (Chem) has been invested in another corporation (Health Med) and that investment, in turn, is used solely to control votes of the first corporation. The only effect of this structure is to muffle the voice of the public shareholders of Chem in the governance of Chem. The motion to dismiss the counterclaim is denied.

ANALYSIS

The circular control structure involved in this case was not materially different from the various schemes repeatedly struck down for more than 150 years by American courts. See, e.g., *Italo Petroleum Corp. v. Producers Oil Corporation*, 174 A. 276 (Del. Ch. 1934).

Quicknotes

COMMON STOCK A class of stock representing the corporation's ownership, the holders of which are entitled to dividends only after the holders of preferred stock are paid.

CONVERTIBLE STOCK Stock that may be converted into common stock or some other type of security pursuant to its terms.

COUNTERCLAIM An independent cause of action brought by a defendant to a lawsuit in order to oppose or deduct from the plaintiff's claim.

CROSS-CLAIM A claim asserted by a plaintiff or defendant to an action against a co-plaintiff or co-defendant, and not against an opposing party, arising out of the same transaction or occurrence as the subject matter of the action.

DECLARATORY JUDGMENT A judgment of the court establishing the rights of the parties.

JUDGMENT ON THE PLEADINGS Motion for judgment after the pleadings are closed.

PREFERRED STOCK Shares of stock entitled to payment of dividends and other distributions before the holders of common stock.

PRIMA FACIE CASE An action where the plaintiff introduces sufficient evidence to submit the issue to the judge or jury for determination.

Schreiber v. Carney

Shareholder (P) v. Corporation (D)

Del. Ch. Ct., 447 A.2d 17 (1982).

NATURE OF CASE: Action seeking to void a loan transaction.

FACT SUMMARY: Jet Capital (D), a shareholder of Texas International Airlines (Texas International) (D), agreed to withdraw opposition to a merger if it received a loan from Texas International (D).

RULE OF LAW

Corporate vote-buying is permissible if it does not work to the prejudice of other shareholders.

FACTS: Texas International Airlines (Texas International) (D) and Texas Air (D) entered merger discussions. Jet Capital, Inc. (D) was a 35 percent shareholder in Texas International (D) and had effective veto power over any merger. The merger would have been financially adverse to Jet Capital (D) unless it exercised certain warrants it had in Texas International (D). Not having sufficient capital to exercise the warrants, Jet Capital (D) made it known that it would not support the merger unless it received a loan. A committee of noninterested directors and an independent counsel formulated a loan plan, which the shareholders of Texas International (D) overwhelmingly approved. Schreiber (P), a dissenting shareholder of Texas International (D), sued to enjoin the transaction as vote-buying, void under public policy.

ISSUE: Is corporate vote-buying permissible if it does not work to the prejudice of other shareholders?

HOLDING AND DECISION: (Hartnett, V. Chan.) Yes. Corporate vote-buying is permissible if it does not work to the prejudice of other shareholders. Vote-buying appears to be uniformly rejected in published opinions. However, a common thread in all these opinions is that the challenged plan worked to the detriment of the nonparticipating shareholders. A per se prohibition has never been established. It should also be noted that most of these decisions come from a time when buying and selling voting rights was strictly prohibited. Today, the law is much more lenient towards these types of transactions; witness the legalization of voting trusts. In light of this, this court holds that vote-buying is not void, but rather voidable only. In this instance, shareholder approval precludes voiding the transaction.

ANALYSIS

The old view was that vote-buying violated public policy as a breach of the duty shareholders owed to each other. This principle maintained that each shareholder voting his own interests was essential to preserving the interest of the stockholders collectively. In today's corporate environment this concept has been largely abandoned.

■ ■ ■

Quicknotes

MERGER The acquisition of one company by another, after which the acquired company ceases to exist as an independent entity.

VOTING TRUST An agreement establishing a trust, whereby shareholders transfer their title to shares to a trustee who is authorized to exercise their voting powers.

■ ■ ■

Virginia Bankshares, Inc. v. Sandberg

Corporation (D) v. Minority shareholder (P)

501 U.S. 1083 (1990).

NATURE OF CASE: Appeal from a jury award of damages in a minority shareholder action.

FACT SUMMARY: After a freeze-out merger, in which the minority shareholders of First American Bank of Virginia (Bank) lost their interest, Sandberg (P) and other minority shareholders sued for damages, alleging violation of § 14(a) and Rule 14a-9 and a breach of the fiduciary duties.

RULE OF LAW

(1) An individual is permitted to prove a specific statement of reason knowingly false or materially misleading, even when the statement is couched in conclusory terms.

(2) Causation of damages compensable through a federal implied private right of action cannot be demonstrated by minority shareholders whose votes are not required to authorize the transaction giving rise to the claim.

FACTS: In a freeze-out merger, the First American Bank of Virginia (the "Bank") merged into Virginia Bankshares, Inc. (D) (VBI). First American Bankshares, Inc. (FABI) (D), the parent company of VBI (D), hired an investment banking firm to give its opinion on the appropriate price for shares of the minority holders who would lose their interest as a result of the merger. The investment banking firm concluded that $42 a share would be a fair price based on market quotations and unverified information from FABI (D). The merger proposal was approved at that price, according to the directors' proxy solicitation, because it was an opportunity for the minority shareholders to achieve a high value and a fair price for their minority stock. Sandberg (P), who had not voted for the merger, then filed suit against VBI (D) and FABI (D), alleging violation of § 14(a) and Rule 14a-9 and breach of fiduciary duties owed the minority shareholders under state law. The jury held for Sandberg (P), finding that she would have received $60 per share had her stock been properly valued. The court of appeals affirmed, and VBI (D) appealed.

ISSUE:

(1) Is an individual permitted to prove a specific statement of reason knowingly false or materially misleading, even when the statement is couched in conclusory terms?

(2) Can causation of damages compensable through a federal implied private right of action be demonstrated by minority shareholders whose votes are not required to authorize the transaction giving rise to the claim?

HOLDING AND DECISION: (Souter, J.)

(1) Yes. An individual is permitted to prove a specific statement of reason knowingly false or materially misleading, even when the statement is couched in conclusory terms. Here, there was evidence of a "going concern" value for the Bank in excess of $60 per share of common stock, a fact never disclosed. Thus the directors' statement was materially misleading on its face. The evidence invoked by VBI (D) fell short of compelling the jury to find that the facial materiality of the misleading statement was neutralized or that the risk of real deception was nullified by any true statements in the proxy solicitation.

(2) No. Causation of damages compensable through a federal implied private right of action cannot be demonstrated by minority shareholders whose votes are not required to authorize the transaction giving rise to the claim. Application of the "essential link" causation test to the facts of this case would extend the private right of action beyond the scope congressionally intended by the Securities Exchange Act of 1934. Causation would then turn on inferences about what the corporate directors would have thought and done without the minority shareholder approval unneeded to authorize action. Assuming that the material facts about the merger were not accurately disclosed, the minority votes were inadequate to ratify the merger under state law, and there was no loss of a state appraisal remedy to connect the proxy solicitation with harm to minority shareholders. The judgment of the court of appeal is reversed.

CONCURRENCE AND DISSENT: (Kennedy, J.) The severe limits the majority places upon possible proof of nonvoting causation in a § 14(a) private action are justified neither by the Court's precedents nor by any case in the court of appeals. In restricting a well-established implied right of action, the majority presumes that a majority shareholder will vote in favor of management's proposal even if proxy disclosure suggests that the transaction is unfair to minority shareholders or that the board of directors or majority shareholder have breached their fiduciary duties to the minority. However, in such a situation, where there has been full disclosure, a majority shareholder has the option of cancelling the meeting at which a vote would be taken on the majority shareholder's proposal. The result is that the transaction does not go forward and the minority is not injured. Further, the majority's attempt to distinguish between voting and nonvoting causation is

Continued on next page.

unclear. There is no authority for limiting § 14(a) only to those situations where the minority has enough strength to successfully oppose a proposal. Instead, that section is designed to protect all investors through adequate disclosure, especially those who do not have the strength to vote down a proposal, since the voting process involves more than just casting ballots. With appropriate disclosures, the "nonvoting" minority can bring court action, negotiate an increased price, or otherwise participate in a deliberative process. Such practicalities can result in causation sufficient to support recovery, and the facts of this case exemplify that point. The facts in this case showed that had there been full disclosure, the transaction may not have been pursued, especially had it been known that the price was unfair to the minority. The evidence clearly showed that there was a link between the nondisclosure and the completion of the merger. The case shows that nonvoting causation theories are quite plausible where the misstatement or omission is material and the damage sustained by minority shareholders is serious. Finally, there is no support for the proposition, implicit in the majority's ruling, that the state statute governing director conflicts of interest incorporates the same definition of materiality used in the federal proxy rules.

▶ ANALYSIS

While a materially misleading statement, may lose its deceptive edge simply by joinder with others that are true, not every mixture with the true will neutralize the deception. Sandberg (P) invoked language from the Court's opinion in *Mills v. Electric Auto-Lite Co.*, 396 U.S. 375 (1970), permitting the jury could find for the plaintiff without a showing of her own reliance on the alleged misstatements, so long as the misstatements were material and the proxy solicitation was an "essential link" in the merger process. Justice Souter, however, distinguished *Mills*, where a majority stockholder controlled just over half of the corporation's shares and a two-thirds vote was needed to approve the merger proposal, from the instant case.

■━■

Quicknotes

FIDUCIARY DUTY A legal obligation to act for the benefit of another, including subordinating one's personal interests to that of the other person.

MAJORITY STOCKHOLDER A stockholder of a corporation who holds in excess of fifty percent of the corporation's shares.

MATERIALITY Importance; the degree of relevance or necessity to the particular matter.

MINORITY SHAREHOLDER A stockholder in a corporation controlling such a small portion of outstanding shares that its votes have no influence in the management of the corporation.

RULE 14a-9 No proxy solicitation shall contain false and misleading statements or omissions regarding material facts.

■━■

Schnell v. Chris-Craft Industries, Inc.

Shareholder (P) v. Corporation (D)

Del Sup. Ct., 285 A.2d 437 (1971).

NATURE OF CASE: Appeal from the denial of a petition by dissident stockholders for injunctive relief.

FACT SUMMARY: The managing directors of Chris-Craft Industries, Inc. (D) amended the bylaws in accordance with the new Delaware Corporation Law, advancing the date of the annual stockholders' meeting.

🏛 RULE OF LAW
Inequitable action does not become permissible simply because it is legally permissible.

FACTS: A dissident group of shareholders of Chris-Craft Industries, Inc. (D) attempted to wage a proxy fight. To give the insurgents less time, the Board reset the date of the annual shareholders' meeting by over a month. Schnell (P) and other insurgents sought an injunction resetting the meeting date. The trial court denied the relief, and Schnell (P) appealed.

ISSUE: Does inequitable action become permissible simply because it is legally permissible?

HOLDING AND DECISION: (Herrmann, J.) No. Inequitable action does not become permissible simply because it is legally permissible. There is no indication of any prior warning of management's intent to amend the bylaws to change the annual stockholders' meeting date. Rather, it appears that management attempted to conceal its action as long as possible. Stockholders may not be charged with the duty of anticipating inequitable action by management and of seeking anticipatory injunctive relief to foreclose such action. Until management changed the date of the meeting, the stockholders had no need of judicial assistance. Reversed and remanded.

DISSENT: (Wolcott, C.J.) In view of the length of time leading up to the immediate events that caused the filing of this action, the lower court was correct that the application for injunctive relief came too late.

▶ ANALYSIS

The Delaware Supreme Court declared that when the bylaws of a corporation designate the date of the annual meeting of stockholders, it is to be expected that those who intend to contest the reelection of incumbent management will gear their campaign to the bylaw date. It is not to be expected that management will attempt to advance that date in order to obtain an inequitable advantage in the contest. The advancement by directors of the bylaw date of a stockholders' meeting for such purposes may not be permitted to stand.

▄■▄

Quicknotes

BYLAWS Rules promulgated by a corporation regulating its governance.

▄■▄

CHAPTER 7

Normal Governance: The Duty of Care

Quick Reference Rules of Law

Gagliardi v. TriFoods International, Inc.

Shareholder (P) v. Corporation (D)

Del. Ch. Ct., 683 A.2d 1049 (1996).

NATURE OF CASE: Motion to dismiss a shareholder action against corporate directors.

FACT SUMMARY: Shareholders (P) of TriFoods International, Inc. (TriFoods) brought a derivative action against TriFoods directors (D) for recovery of losses allegedly sustained by reason of mismanagement unaffected by directly conflicting interests; the directors (D) moved to dismiss.

🏛 RULE OF LAW

To sustain a derivative action for the recovery of corporate losses resulting from mismanagement unaffected by directly conflicting financial interests, a shareholder must plead that a director/officer did not act in good faith and/or failed to act as an ordinary prudent person would have acted under similar circumstances.

FACTS: Shareholders (P) of TriFoods International, Inc. (TriFoods) brought a derivative action against TriFoods directors (D) for recovery of losses allegedly sustained by reason of mismanagement unaffected by directly conflicting interests. The directors (D) moved to dismiss the action. The issue was thus what the shareholders (P) had to plead to sustain their action.

ISSUE: To sustain a derivative action for the recovery of corporate losses resulting from mismanagement unaffected by directly conflicting financial interests, must a shareholder plead that a director/officer did not act in good faith and/or failed to act as an ordinary prudent person would have acted under similar circumstances?

HOLDING AND DECISION: (Allen, Chan.) Yes. To sustain a derivative action for the recovery of corporate losses resulting from mismanagement unaffected by directly conflicting financial interests, a shareholder must plead that a director/officer did not act in good faith and/or failed to act as an ordinary prudent person would have acted under similar circumstances. First, absent a direct financial conflict, a director or officer is not liable for corporate losses suffered as a result of a decision that individual made or authorized in good faith. Also, the actions of officers and directors is protected by the business judgment rule, which provides that if a director is independent and disinterested, there can be no liability for corporate loss, unless the facts were such that no person could possibly authorize such a transaction if he or she were attempting in good faith to meet their fiduciary duty. These precepts make economic sense, since shareholders would not rationally want directors or officers to be risk

averse. In today's corporate environment, it would take only a very small probability of director/officer liability based on negligence, inattention, waste, or like theories to inhibit directors or officers from taking any risk if the directors/officers were liable for any corporate loss from a risky project. Accordingly, it is in the shareholders' economic interest to offer sufficient protection to directors and officers from liability for negligence, inattention, waste, etc., so as to enable directors or officers to be confident that if they act in good faith and meet minimal standards of attention, they will not face liability as a result of a business loss. That is why corporations are authorized to pay for director and officer liability insurance or to indemnify their directors/officers.

▶ ANALYSIS

In addition to requiring that a corporate director discharge the duties of that office in good faith and with a stated standard of care, usually phrased in terms of the care that an ordinarily prudent person would exercise under similar circumstances, numerous jurisdictions also require that a director perform these duties in a manner that she reasonably believes to be in the best interests of the corporation.

Quicknotes

BUSINESS JUDGMENT RULE Doctrine relieving corporate directors and/or officers from liability for decisions honestly and rationally made in the corporation's best interests.

FIDUCIARY DUTY A legal obligation to act for the benefit of another, including subordinating one's personal interests to that of the other person.

GOOD FAITH An honest intention to abstain from taking advantage of another.

INDEMNIFICATION The payment by a corporation of expenses incurred by its officers or directors as a result of litigation involving the corporation.

NEGLIGENCE Conduct falling below the standard of care that a reasonable person would demonstrate under similar conditions.

ORDINARY CARE The degree of care exercised by a reasonable person when conducting everyday activities or under similar circumstances; synonymous with due care.

Continued on next page.

SHAREHOLDER'S DERIVATIVE ACTION Action asserted by a shareholder in order to enforce a cause of action on behalf of the corporation.

Waltuch v. Conticommodity Services, Inc.

Employee (P) v. Employer (D)

88 F.3d 87 (2d Cir. 1996).

NATURE OF CASE: Appeal from suit for indemnification.

FACT SUMMARY: When Conticommodity Services, Inc. (Conti) (D) refused to indemnify Waltuch (P) for legal fees resulting from litigation that arose out of his former employment with Conti (D), Waltuch (P) brought suit for indemnification.

⚖ RULE OF LAW

(1) A provision of a corporation's articles of incorporation that provides for indemnification without including a good-faith limitation runs afoul of a statute that permits indemnification only if the prospective indemnitee acted in good faith, even if the statute also permits the corporation to grant rights in addition to indemnification rights.

(2) To the extent a director, officer, employee or agent of a corporation has been successful on the merits or otherwise in defense of any action, suit or proceeding, or in defense of any claim, issue or matter therein, he shall be indemnified against expenses (including attorney's fees) actually and reasonably incurred by him in connection therewith.

FACTS: As a former employee of Conticommodity Services, Inc. (Conti) (D), Waltuch (P) traded silver for the firm's clients, as well as for his personal account. When the silver market fell, clients brought suit against Waltuch (P) and Conti (D) alleging fraud, market manipulation and antitrust violations. All of the suits eventually settled and were dismissed with prejudice, pursuant to settlements in which Conti (D) paid over $35 million to the various suitors. Waltuch (P) himself was dismissed from the suits with no settlement contribution. His unreimbursed legal expenses in these actions totaled approximately $1.2 million. After the actions had been settled, Waltuch (P) sought indemnification from Conti (D), which refused, and Waltuch (P) brought suit for indemnification for his unreimbursed expenses. The ninth article of Conti's (D) articles of incorporation (Article Ninth) required Conti (D) to indemnify Waltuch (P). Conti (D) contended that Waltuch's (P) claim was barred by subsection (a) of § 145 of Delaware's General Corporation Law, which permits indemnification only if the corporate officer acted "in good faith," something that Waltuch (P) had not established. Waltuch (P) countered that § 145(f) permits a corporation to grant indemnification rights outside the limits of subsection (a), and that Conti (D) did so with Article Nine

(which had no stated good-faith limitation). The district court held that, notwithstanding § 145(f), Waltuch (P) could recover under Article Nine only if Waltuch (P) met the "good faith" requirement of § 145 (a). Waltuch (P) also claimed that § 145(c) required Conti (D) to indemnify him because he was "successful on the merits or otherwise" in the lawsuits. The court of appeals granted review.

ISSUE:

(1) Does a provision of a corporation's articles of incorporation that provides for indemnification without including a good-faith limitation run afoul of a statute that permits indemnification only if the prospective indemnitee acted in good faith, even if the statute also permits the corporation to grant rights in addition to indemnification rights?

(2) To the extent a director, officer, employee or agent of a corporation has been successful on the merits or otherwise in defense of any action, suit or proceeding, or in defense of any claim, issue or matter therein, shall he be indemnified against expenses (including attorney's fees) actually and reasonably incurred by him in connection therewith?

HOLDING AND DECISION: (Jacobs, J.)

(1) Yes. A provision of a corporation's articles of incorporation that provides for indemnification without including a good-faith limitation runs afoul of a statute that permits indemnification only if the prospective indemnitee acted in good faith, even if the statute also permits the corporation to grant rights in addition to indemnification rights. Section 145(a) limits a corporation's indemnification powers to situations where the officer or director to be indemnified acted in good faith. Critically, § 145(f) merely acknowledges that one seeking indemnification may be entitled to rights in addition to that of indemnification; it does not speak in terms of corporate power, and therefore cannot be read to free a corporation from the good faith limit explicitly imposed in § 145(a). To hold otherwise would require ignoring the explicit terms of § 145. Additionally, such an interpretation does not render § 145(f) meaningless, since a corporation may grant additional rights that are not inconsistent with § 145(a). For these reasons, Waltuch (P) is not entitled to indemnification under Article Nine, which exceeds the scope of § 145(a). Affirmed as to this issue.

(2) Yes. To the extent a director, officer, employee or agent of a corporation has been successful on the merits or otherwise in defense of any action, suit or proceeding,

Continued on next page.

or in defense of any claim, issue or matter therein, he shall be indemnified against expenses (including attorney's fees) actually and reasonably incurred by him in connection therewith. Conti (D) argued that the successful settlements could not be attributed to Waltuch (P), but were the result of Conti's (D) efforts. This application is overbroad. Escape from an adverse judgment or other detriment, for whatever reason, is determinative. "Success is vindication." To go behind the "successful" result is inappropriate. Once Waltuch (P) achieved his settlement gratis, he achieved success "on the merits or otherwise." Accordingly, Conti (D) must indemnify Waltuch (P) under § 145(c) for the $1.2 million in unreimbursed legal fees he spent defending the private lawsuits. Reversed.

▶ ANALYSIS

This is the first time the court considered the application of the section with respect to civil litigation. It extends the holding in *Merritt-Chapman & Scott Corp. v. Wolfson*, 321 A.2d 138 (1974), to the present case. There the corporation's agents were charged with criminal conduct and reached a "settlement" with the prosecutor's office. The court considered the defendants' guilty plea to achieve dismissals as "success" and "vindication," which is sufficient to invoke the protections of § 154(c).

▬■▬■▬

Quicknotes

INDEMNIFICATION The payment by a corporation of expenses incurred by its officers or directors as a result of litigation involving the corporation.

OVERBROAD Refers to a statute that proscribes lawful as well as unlawful conduct.

▬■▬■▬

Kamin v. American Express Co.

Shareholder (P) v. Corporation (D)

N.Y. Sup. Ct., 54 A.D.2d 654 (1976).

NATURE OF CASE: Derivative action for damages for waste of corporate assets.

FACT SUMMARY: Kamin (P) brought a shareholders' derivative suit claiming American Express Co. (D) had engaged in waste of corporate assets by declaring a certain dividend in kind.

▥ RULE OF LAW
Whether or not a dividend is to be declared or a distribution made is exclusively a matter of business judgment for the board of directors, and the courts will not, therefore, interfere as long as the decision is made in good faith.

FACTS: American Express Co. (D) had acquired for investment almost two million shares of common stock in Donaldson, Lufken and Jenrette (DLJ) at a cost of $29.9 million. Kamin (P), a minority stockholder in American Express (D), charged that the subsequent decision to declare a special dividend to all stockholders resulting in a distribution of the shares of DLJ in kind was a negligent violation of the directors' fiduciary duty. He argued that the market value of the DLJ shares was only $4 million and that American Express (D) should have sold the DLJ shares on the market so as to be able to offset the $25 million capital loss against taxable capital gains on other investments and thus obtain an $8 million tax saving that would be otherwise unavailable. In a shareholders' derivative action, Kamin (P) sought a declaration that the dividend in kind constituted a waste of corporate assets and sought damages therefor. American Express (D) moved to dismiss the complaint.

ISSUE: Should the courts interfere with a board of directors' good faith business judgment as to whether or not to declare a dividend or make a distribution?

HOLDING AND DECISION: (Greenfield, J.) No. Whether or not to declare a dividend or make a distribution is exclusively a matter of business judgment for the board of directors, and thus the courts will not interfere with their decision as long as it is made in good faith. It is not enough to charge, as Kamin (P) has in this case, that the directors made an imprudent decision or that some other course of action would have been more advantageous. Such a charge cannot give rise to a cause of action. Thus, the motion for summary judgment and dismissal of the complaint is granted.

▶ ANALYSIS

The "business judgment rule" illustrated in this expresses the traditional and still valid view, of a director's duty of care. This common-law standard is designed to allow the directors a wide berth in conducting the affairs of the corporation so that they can act effectively and efficiently in pursuing the corporation's best interests rather than being constantly influenced by the need to practice "defensive management" to prevent being held liable in this type of action.

▬▬

Quicknotes

BUSINESS CORPORATION LAW, § 720 Permits an action against directors for failure to perform duties in managing corporate assets.

BUSINESS JUDGMENT RULE Doctrine relieving corporate directors and/or officers from liability for decisions honestly and rationally made in the corporation's best interests.

COMMON STOCK A class of stock representing the corporation's ownership, the holders of which are entitled to dividends only after the holders of preferred stock are paid.

DUTY OF CARE Duty that an officer or director owes to the corporation, by virtue of his fiduciary relationship, to act for the benefit of the corporation.

FIDUCIARY DUTY A legal obligation to act for the benefit of another, including subordinating one's personal interests to that of the other person.

▬▬

Francis v. United Jersey Bank

[Parties not identified]

N.J. Sup. Ct., 432 A.2d 814 (1981).

NATURE OF CASE: Review of Appellate Division decision holding director of corporation liable for clients' losses.

FACT SUMMARY: Mrs. Pritchard (D) ignored her duties as a director, allowing her sons to withdraw over $12 million from client trust accounts.

🏛 **RULE OF LAW**
Liability of a corporation's directors to its clients requires a demonstration that: (1) a duty existed; (2) the directors breached that duty; and (3) the breach was a proximate cause of the client's losses.

FACTS: Mrs. Pritchard (D) inherited an interest in Pritchard & Baird, a reinsurance broker, from her husband. She and her two sons, Charles, Jr., and William, served as directors of the corporation. Her sons withdrew millions of dollars in the form of loans from client trust accounts, and the firm went bankrupt. Mrs. Pritchard (D) was completely ignorant as to the fundamentals of the reinsurance business and paid no attention to the affairs of the corporation, the business of which she was completely unfamiliar. After her husband died, she began to drink heavily, her health declined rapidly, and she died. The bankruptcy trustee brought suit, claiming that Mrs. Pritchard (D) had been negligent in the discharge of her duties as director. The trial court held her liable for the clients' losses, finding that although she was competent to act, despite her drinking and distraught psychological state of mind following her husband's death, she had made no effort to exercise her duties as a director.

ISSUE: Does individual liability of a corporation's directors to its clients require a duty, a breach, and proximate cause?

HOLDING AND DECISION: (Pollock, J.) Yes. Individual liability of a corporation's directors to its clients requires a demonstration that: (1) a duty existed; (2) the directors breached that duty; and (3) the breach was a proximate cause of the client's losses. This is a departure from the general rule that a director is immune from liability and is not an insurer of the corporation's success. The director of a corporation stands in a fiduciary relationship to both the corporation and its stockholders. Inherent in this role is a duty to acquire a basic understanding of the corporation's business and a continuing duty to keep informed of its activities. This entails an overall monitoring of the corporation's affairs, and a regular review of its financial statements. Such a review may present a duty of further inquiry. Here, Mrs. Pritchard (D) failed to exercise supervision over the corporation, including the examination of its financial statements, which would have revealed the misappropriation of funds by her sons. The cumulative effect of her negligence was a substantial factor contributing to the clients' losses. Affirmed.

▶ **ANALYSIS**

Directors do not ordinarily owe a duty of care to third parties unless the corporation is insolvent. Due to the nature of certain types of enterprises, the director stands in a fiduciary capacity to third parties. Because the reinsurance business relies on the entrustment of capital within the company, and on the transmission of funds to the appropriate parties, Mrs. Pritchard (D) owed a duty of care to third-party clients of Pritchard & Baird.

■■■

Quicknotes

FIDUCIARY DUTY A legal obligation to act for the benefit of another, including subordinating one's personal interests to that of the other person.

NEW JERSEY BUSINESS CORPORATION ACT § 14A Directors are obligated to discharge their duties in good faith and with skill of ordinary prudent person in similar position.

PROXIMATE CAUSE The natural sequence of events without which an injury would not have been sustained.

■■■

Graham v. Allis-Chalmers Manufacturing Co.

Shareholder (P) v. Corporation (D)

Del. Sup. Ct., 188 A.2d 125 (1963).

NATURE OF CASE: Appeal from judgment in derivative action that defendant-directors were not liable for failing to learn of unlawful employee conduct.

FACT SUMMARY: Shareholders of Allis Chalmers Manufacturing Co. (Allis-Chalmers) (D) contended in a derivative action that the corporation's directors were liable as a matter of law for failing to take action to learn of and prevent antitrust activity of non-director employees.

RULE OF LAW

A corporate director who has no knowledge of suspicion of wrongdoing by employees is not liable for such wrongdoing as a matter of law.

FACTS: Allis Chalmers Manufacturing Co. (Allis-Chalmers) (D), a very large corporation employing over 31,000 individuals, and several non-director employees were indicted for, and pleaded guilty to, violating federal antitrust laws. Shareholders (P) brought a derivative action for damages allegedly suffered by the corporation by reason of the indictments. No director had any actual knowledge of the antitrust activity, or had actual knowledge of any facts that would have put them on notice that antitrust activity was being carried on by some of their employees. Additionally, the operating policy of the company was to decentralize by the delegation of authority to the lowest possible management level capable of fulfilling the delegated responsibility. The shareholders (P) contended that the directors were liable as a matter of law because they failed to take action designed to learn of and prevent the illegal conduct, noting that over 20 years earlier the company had signed consent decrees that it would not engage in such antitrust activities. The few (3 of 14) directors who knew about the decrees satisfied themselves that the company was in compliance with them. The chancery court held that the directors were not liable. The state's highest court granted review.

ISSUE: Is a corporate director who has no knowledge of suspicion of wrongdoing by employees liable for such wrongdoing as a matter of law?

HOLDING AND DECISION: (Wolcott, J.) No. A corporate director who has no knowledge of suspicion of wrongdoing by employees is not liable for such wrongdoing as a matter of law. First, knowledge by three of the directors that over 20 years earlier the company had consented to the entry of decrees enjoining it from doing something they had satisfied themselves it had never done, did not put the board on notice of the possibility of future illegal antitrust activity. Therefore, the shareholders (P) must rely on the legal proposition that directors of a corporation, as a matter of law, are liable for losses suffered by the corporation as a consequence of their gross inattention to the common law duty of actively supervising and managing the corporation's affairs. This requires a degree of watchfulness by the board that is premised on employee dishonesty. To the contrary, a board may rely on the honesty and trustworthiness of its employees until something occurs to put the board on suspicion that something is wrong. "[A]bsent cause for suspicion there is no duty upon the directors to install and operate a corporate system of espionage to ferret out wrongdoing which they have no reason to suspect exists." Here, it was impossible for the board to know every employee, and thus it was appropriate that the board focused on broad policy decisions. As soon as it had knowledge of suspicions of wrongdoing, the board responded appropriately to put an end to any wrongdoing and prevent its recurrence. There is "no rule of law which requires a corporate director to assume, with no justification whatsoever, that all corporate employees are incipient law violators who, but for a tight checkrein, will give free vent to their unlawful propensities." Affirmed.

ANALYSIS

Corporate boards must tread carefully in discharging their duty to monitor corporate affairs, since monitoring too closely may lead to lawsuits for employment law violations or invasion of privacy. Such suits could have a negative impact for the company and shareholders.

Quicknotes

ANTITRUST LAW Body of federal law prohibiting business conduct that constitutes a restraint on trade.

CONSENT DECREE A decree issued by a court of equity ratifying an agreement between the parties to a lawsuit; an agreement by a defendant to cease illegal activity.

SHAREHOLDER'S DERIVATIVE ACTION Action asserted by a shareholder in order to enforce a cause of action on behalf of the corporation.

In the Matter of Michael Marchese

Securities and Exchange Commission (P) v. Outside director (D)

SEC Enforcement Action, Release Nos. 34-47732; AAER-1764; Administrative Proceeding File No. 3-11092 (April 24, 2003).

NATURE OF CASE: Securities and Exchange Commission (SEC) enforcement action.

FACT SUMMARY: The Securities and Exchange Commission (SEC) (P) contended that Marchese (D), an outside director of Chancellor who served on Chancellor's audit committee, violated, and caused Chancellor to violate, various provisions of the Exchange Act and Rules thereunder because he failed to adequately monitor the company's financial statements.

🏛 **RULE OF LAW**
An outside director of a corporation, who serves on its audit committee, violates and causes his corporation to violate, the Exchange Act and Rules thereunder by recklessly failing to inquire into the corporation's financials when he has knowledge of facts to put him on notice that such inquiry is warranted.

FACTS: Marchese (D) was an outside director of Chancellor who served on its audit committee and was an acquaintance of Adley, who was Chancellor's controlling shareholder, chairman and chief executive officer (CEO). As part of an acquisition of another company, a dispute arose between Chancellor's management and its auditors regarding the appropriate acquisition date for accounting purposes, and Chancellor dismissed the auditors. Adley directed that documents be backdated or fabricated to support a date earlier than accepted by the auditors, and new auditors were hired. Based on the falsified records, the new auditors approved the date desired by Adley and management. Marchese (D) approved the decision to dismiss the original auditors; he was aware of the disagreement between Chancellor's management and the auditors regarding the appropriate acquisition date for accounting purposes; he knew that the disagreement formed part of the reason for the auditors' dismissal; and he approved the engagement of the new auditors. Despite this knowledge, Marchese (D) made no inquiry into the reasons for the different views held by the different auditors, and he did not determine whether there was any factual support for the earlier acquisition date. Additionally, in connection with the acquisition, Adley caused Chancellor to record $3.3 million in fees to a private corporation he owned, purportedly for consulting services. However, in fact, no significant consulting services had been rendered to Chancellor by Adley's private company. Again, Adley directed the fabrication of documents to support the accounting for the fees, and directed that the fees be recorded as an asset on Chancellor's balance sheet,

rather than as an expense on its income statement. As with the acquisition date, such accounting was inconsistent with generally accepted accounting principles (GAAP), which provide that costs payable to an outside consultant in business combinations may be capitalized only if the consultant has no affiliation with the companies involved in the acquisition. The year before, in connection with the preparation of Chancellor's year-end results, Chancellor's auditors had required the company to write off $1.14 million in related party payments to Adley-controlled entities because there was no substantiation for the payments. Although Marchese (D) knew of these write-offs of payments to Adley's entities, he took no steps to determine whether the $3.3 million consulting fee to Adley's personal company was substantiated. He inquired neither of the auditor nor of Adley about related party transactions. As a result of the inappropriate accounting, both as to the acquisition date and the consulting fees, Marchese (D), along with others, signed a Form 10-KSB that was misleading and falsely represented that the value of Chancellor's assets was higher than it really were, and that Chancellor had net income, rather than a loss. Marchese (D) never reviewed Chancellor's accounting procedures or internal controls.

ISSUE: Does an outside director of a corporation who serves on its audit committee violate, and cause his corporation to violate, the Exchange Act and Rules thereunder by recklessly failing to inquire into the corporation's financials when he has knowledge of facts to put him on notice that such inquiry is warranted?

HOLDING AND DECISION: (Katz, Commn. Secy.) Yes. An outside director of a corporation who serves on its audit committee violates, and causes his corporation to violate, the Exchange Act and Rules thereunder by recklessly failing to inquire into the corporation's financials when he has knowledge of facts to put him on notice that such inquiry is warranted. First, Marchese (D) violated and caused Chancellor's violation of Section 10(b) of the Exchange Act and Rule 10b-5 thereunder when he signed Chancellor's Form 10-KSB. That is because despite his knowledge surrounding the dispute with the original auditors that led to the new auditors approving an earlier acquisition date, Marchese (D) recklessly failed to make any inquiry into the circumstances leading to the new audit firm's approval of the acquisition date, or whether it was correct, and, despite his knowledge of the previous year's write-offs based on related-party fees, he recklessly

Continued on next page.

failed to make any inquiry into the existence of documents substantiating the services for which the fees were purportedly due. Second, Marchese (D) caused Chancellor's violations of Sections 13(a), 13(b)(2)(A) and 13(b)(2)(B) of the Exchange Act and Rules 12b-20 and 13a-1 thereunder, since those provisions and rules require that annual reports be accurate; that every reporting company make and keep books, records and accounts that accurately and fairly reflect the issuer's transactions; and that a company devise and maintain a system of internal controls sufficient to provide reasonable assurances that transactions are recorded as necessary to permit the preparation of financial statements in conformity with GAAP. Here, Marchese (D) was reckless in not knowing that Chancellor's Form 10-KSB contained materially misleading statements, and signed that form without inquiring into the basis for the consultant fees payable to Adley's company or the basis for the new audit firm's approval of the earlier acquisition date. Accordingly, Marchese (D) must cease and desist from committing or causing similar violations of these rules and statutory provisions.

▶ *ANALYSIS*

As this SEC enforcement action demonstrates, in today's regulatory environment, directors need to be concerned with their duty to monitor and duty of care not only because of the potential of shareholder derivative actions brought under state law, but also because of the potential of SEC enforcement actions. These concerns have grown in the wake of corporate accounting scandals, and, in response to increasing regulatory demands and potentially massive regulatory fines, the designing of corporate compliance programs has developed into a new legal subspecialty.

■=■

Quicknotes

DUTY OF CARE Duty that an officer or director owes to the corporation, by virtue of his fiduciary relationship, to act for the benefit of the corporation.

RECKLESSNESS The conscious disregard of substantial and justifiable risk.

■=■

In re Caremark International Inc. Derivative Litigation

Healthcare company's board of directors (D) v. Shareholders (P)

Del. Ch. Ct., 698 A.2d 959 (1996).

NATURE OF CASE: Motion to approve a settlement of a consolidated derivative action.

FACT SUMMARY: Caremark International, Inc. (Caremark), a managed health-care provider, entered into contractual arrangements with physicians and hospitals, often for "consultation" or "research," without first clarifying the unsettled law surrounding prohibitions against referral fee payments.

> 🏛 **RULE OF LAW**
> A board of directors has an affirmative duty to attempt in good faith to assure that a corporate information and reporting system exists and is adequate.

FACTS: Caremark International, Inc. (Caremark) was involved in providing patient health care and managed health-care services. Much of Caremark's revenue came from third-party payments, insurers, and Medicare and Medicaid reimbursement programs. The Anti-Referral Payments Law (ARPL) applied to Caremark, prohibiting payments to induce the referral of Medicare or Medicaid patients. Caremark had a practice of entering into service contracts, including consultation and research, with physicians who at times prescribed Caremark products or services to Medicare recipients. Such contracts were not prohibited by the ARPL, but they raised the issue of unlawful kickbacks. Caremark's board of directors (D) attempted to monitor these contracts internally, seeking legal advice and devising guidelines for employees. However, the government began investigating Caremark. Caremark began making structural changes in response to the investigation, centralizing management. In spite of this, Caremark and two officers were indicted. Several shareholder derivative actions were subsequently filed, charging the board of directors (D) with failure to adequately monitor as part of its duty of care. Settlement negotiations began. Caremark agreed in the settlement to cease all payments to third parties that referred patients to Caremark and to establish an ethics committee, which it had, in effect, already done. Caremark also agreed to make reimbursement payments to private and public parties totaling $250 million. All other claims were waived in the proposed settlement. The proposed settlement was submitted to the court for approval.

ISSUE: Does a board of directors have an affirmative duty to attempt in good faith to assure that a corporate information and reporting system exists and is adequate?

HOLDING AND DECISION: (Allen, Chan.) Yes. A board of directors has an affirmative duty to attempt in

good faith to assure that a corporate information and reporting system exists and is adequate. Directors generally do not monitor day-to-day operations in a company. The United States Supreme Court has said where there is no basis for suspicion, directors cannot be liable. However, it would be extending this holding too far to say that directors have no obligation whatsoever to determine whether they are receiving accurate information. The duty of care implies that a board will make a good faith effort to ensure that a corporation's information and reporting system is adequate. In this case, acts that resulted in indictments do not, by themselves, prove that the Caremark board (D) was not adequately monitoring corporate behavior. On the contrary, the board (D) appears to have been making structural changes all along to gain greater centralized control of the company. And an ethics monitoring group was in place well before the settlement was reached. Given that the evidence on the record suggests that success in the derivative suit was unlikely, but that Caremark is giving up little in the way of concessions not already in place, the settlement is fair.

▶ **ANALYSIS**

A duty to monitor does not require a board to be aware of all the details of corporate activity. In fact, such oversight would be physically impossible in a large company. The duty does, however, require the board to be aware of major activities and related issues that could pose a threat to the company. The choice of what structure to use in informational gathering is still subject to the safe harbor of the business judgment rule; therefore, a claim that the duty to monitor has been breached is tremendously difficult to prove successfully.

■—■—■

Quicknotes

BUSINESS JUDGMENT RULE Doctrine relieving corporate directors and/or officers from liability for decisions honestly and rationally made in the corporation's best interests.

■—■—■

In re Citigroup Inc. Shareholder Derivative Litigation

Shareholders (P) v. Corporate directors and officers (D)

Del. Ch. Ct., 2009 WL 481906 (Feb. 24, 2009).

NATURE OF CASE: Shareholder derivative action.

FACT SUMMARY: Shareholders (P) of Citigroup brought suit against the company's directors (D) and officers (D) on a theory that they breached their fiduciary duties to the company by ignoring "red flags" indicating the demise of the subprime mortgage market.

▥ RULE OF LAW

Directors do not breach their fiduciary duties by failing adequately to oversee a company's exposure to problems in the subprime mortgage market and to ensure that financial and other disclosures were accurate.

FACTS: Citigroup shareholders (P) brought suit against certain current and former Citigroup officials (D), alleging, in essence, that the officials (D) breached their fiduciary duties by failing properly to monitor and manage the risks the company faced from problems in the subprime lending market, and by failing properly to disclose Citigroup's exposure to subprime assets. The shareholders (P) claimed that there were "red flags" that should have given the officials (D) notice of the problems that were brewing in the real estate and credit markets, and that the officials (D) ignored these warnings in the pursuit of short-term profits and at the expense of the company's long-term viability.

ISSUE: Do directors breach their fiduciary duties by failing adequately to oversee a company's exposure to problems in the subprime mortgage market and to ensure that financial and other disclosures were accurate?

HOLDING AND DECISION: (Chandler, Chan.) No. Directors do not breach their fiduciary duties by failing adequately to oversee a company's exposure to problems in the subprime mortgage market and to ensure that financial and other disclosures were accurate. The shareholders' (P) theory essentially amounts to a claim that the directors (D) should be personally liable to the company because they failed to fully recognize the risk posed by subprime securities. To allow shareholders (P) to succeed on a theory that a director (D) is liable for a failure to monitor business risk would invite courts to perform a hindsight evaluation of the reasonableness or prudence of directors' (D) business decisions. In sum, the shareholders (P) failed to state a claim sufficient to support a theory that the directors (D) did not fulfill their oversight obligations by failing to monitor the business risk of the company. Ultimately, the discretion granted directors and managers (D) allows them to maximize shareholder (P) value in the long term

by taking risks without the debilitating fear that they will be held personally liable if the company experiences losses. This doctrine also means, however, that when the company suffers losses, shareholders may not be able to hold the directors personally liable.

▶ ANALYSIS

Shareholder derivative actions rose sharply in the aftermath of the tanking of the subprime mortgage market. Derivative lawsuits are brought on behalf of the corporation itself, and typically include claims of breach of fiduciary duty, corporate waste, and unjust enrichment directed at the corporation's directors and officers. Derivative lawsuits ordinarily are premised on the directors' alleged failure to adequately consider and protect the company against risk, or to fully disclose a company's subprime exposure. But others include claims that the defendants profited personally and committed securities fraud by offloading their shares of company stock at artificially-inflated prices. Where fraud or bad faith is not alleged or cannot be proved, the shareholder's burden in derivative lawsuits is particularly heavy.

━━━

Quicknotes

BUSINESS PURPOSE RULE Doctrine relieving corporate directors and/or officers from liability for decisions honestly and rationally made in the corporation's best interests.

DERIVATIVE SUIT Action asserted by a shareholder in order to enforce a cause of action on behalf of the corporation.

FIDUCIARY DUTY A legal obligation to act for the benefit of another, including subordinating one's personal interests to that of the other person.

━━━

Miller v. AT&T

Shareholder (P) v. Corporation (D)

507 F.2d. 759 (3d Cir. 1974).

NATURE OF CASE: Action against corporate directors for breach of fiduciary duty and violation of the campaign contribution law.

FACT SUMMARY: Shareholders (P) of American Telephone & Telegraph Co. (D) brought suit when the corporate directors forgave a $1.5 million debt owed it by the Democratic National Convention.

🏛 RULE OF LAW
The business judgment rule will not insulate directors from liability where it is alleged that they have committed illegal or immoral acts.

FACTS: The Democratic National Convention owed American Telephone & Telegraph Co. (AT&T) (D) $1.5 million. The directors of AT&T (D) made no attempt to collect this debt for the Corporation (D). Several AT&T (D) shareholders, including Miller (P), brought a derivative suit against all but one director for breach of their fiduciary duty. The complaint also alleged that forgiveness of the debt was an illegal campaign contribution under 18 U.S.C. § 610. The directors (D) pleaded a valid business decision and the court dismissed the case on the basis of the business judgment rule.

ISSUE: Is the business judgment rule a defense to an action charging illegal or immoral conduct?

HOLDING AND DECISION: (Seitz, C.J.) No. The business judgment rule is based on a judicial recognition of the impossibility of intervening in corporate decision-making if the directors' judgment is uninfluenced by personal considerations and was made in good faith after the use of reasonable diligence in ascertaining the facts. However, the sound business judgment rule has no application to situations charging the directors with illegal or immoral acts. Business judgment has no place in the decision to commit such acts. Here, the directors (D) are charged with violations of the campaign contribution laws. A prima facie case has been stated by the complaint. Reversed and remanded.

▶ ANALYSIS

Even though the illegal acts benefit the corporation, the business judgment rule is no defense. In *Roth v. Robertson*, 64 Misc. 343 (1909), bribery to protect the corporation exposed the directors to liability. In *Abrams v. Allen*, 297 N.Y. 52 (1947), the complaint alleged that the directors had caused their plant to be moved to injure workers engaged in a labor dispute. The court found that the action was

immoral and against public policy. The business judgment rule was found to be no defense.

━━■

Quicknotes

BUSINESS JUDGMENT RULE Doctrine relieving corporate directors and/or officers from liability for decisions honestly and rationally made in the corporation's best interests.

FIDUCIARY DUTY A legal obligation to act for the benefit of another, including subordinating one's personal interests to that of the other person.

SHAREHOLDER'S DERIVATIVE ACTION Action asserted by a shareholder in order to enforce a cause of action on behalf of the corporation.

18 U.S.C. § 610 Prohibits certain corporate campaign spending.

━━■

Quick Reference Rules of Law

A.P. Smith Manufacturing Co. v. Barlow

Corporation (P) v. Shareholder (D)

N.J. Sup. Ct., 98 A.2d 581 (1953).

NATURE OF CASE: Appeal in action to determine validity of a corporate donation.

FACT SUMMARY: Barlow (D) and other shareholders of A.P. Smith Mfg. (P) challenged its authority to make a donation to Princeton University.

RULE OF LAW

State legislation adopted in the public interest can be constitutionally applied to preexisting corporations under the reserved power.

FACTS: A.P. Smith Mfg. (P) made a contribution to Princeton University. Shareholders (D) of A.P. Smith Mfg. (P) questioned the corporation's authority to make the contribution on two grounds: (1) its certificate of incorporation did not expressly authorize the donation and A.P. Smith Mfg. (P) possessed no implied power to make it; and (2) the New Jersey statutes that would have expressly authorized the contribution did not constitutionally apply to A.P. Smith Mfg. (P) because it was incorporated long before their enactment. The state's highest court reviewed the matter on appeal.

ISSUE: Can state legislation adopted in the public interest be constitutionally applied to preexisting corporations under the reserved power?

HOLDING AND DECISION: (Jacobs, J.) Yes. State legislation adopted in the public interest can be constitutionally applied to preexisting corporations under the reserved power. Fifty years before the incorporation of A.P. Smith Mfg. (P), the New Jersey legislature provided that every corporate charter thereafter granted would be subject to alteration and modification at the discretion of the legislature. A similar reserved power was incorporated into the state constitution. New Jersey courts have repeatedly recognized that, where justified by the advancement of the public interest, the reserved power may be invoked to sustain later charter alterations even though they affect contractual rights between the corporation and its stockholders. Therefore, a statute enacted in 1930 encouraging and expressly authorizing reasonable charitable contributions is applicable to A.P. Smith Mfg. (P) and must be upheld as a lawful exercise of A.P. Smith Mfg.'s (P) implied and incidental powers under common law principles. Affirmed.

ANALYSIS

The court was clearly swayed as much by philanthropic concerns and social policy as by statutory law. It dedicated a large portion of its opinion to discussing the economic and social importance of corporate contributions, particularly those made to universities. The opinion was quite prophetic as such donations have grown even more significantly in the forty-five years since the opinion was written.

Quicknotes

PUBLIC INTEREST Something in which the public has either a monetary or legal interest.

State ex rel. Hayes Oyster Co. v. Keypoint Oyster Co.

Corporation (P) v. Corporation (D)

Wash. Sup. Ct., 391 P.2d 979 (1964).

NATURE OF CASE: Appeal from judgment for defendant in breach of fiduciary duty and disgorgement action.

FACT SUMMARY: Coast Oyster Co. (Coast) claimed that Hayes (D), its chief executive officer (CEO), director, and shareholder, breached his fiduciary duty to Coast by failing to disclose a secret profit and personal advantage he would gain from the approval of Coast's sale of oyster beds to Keypoint Oyster Co. (Keypoint) (D). Coast sought disgorgement of such secret profit from Hayes or his company, Hayes Oyster Co.

🏛 RULE OF LAW
A corporation's director or officer breaches his fiduciary duty to the corporation by failing to disclose the potential profit or advantage that would accrue to him if a transaction involving the corporation were approved.

FACTS: Hayes (D) was Coast Oyster Co.'s (Coast's) chief executive officer (CEO), director, and 23 percent shareholder. Hayes (D) was permitted to be involved with his family corporation, Hayes Oyster Co. (Hayes Oyster), in which he held a 25 percent interest. Hayes (D) suggested that Coast sell some of its oyster beds to raise cash, and he brokered a deal between Coast and Engman, a Coast employee, whereby Hayes Oyster would help finance Engman's purchase of the oyster beds. Coast's board approved Hayes's (D) plan to sell the oyster beds to Keypoint Oyster Co. (Keypoint) (D), a corporation to be formed by Engman, for $250,000, payable $25,000 per year, with 5 percent interest. Shortly thereafter, Hayes (D) and Engman agreed that Keypoint's (D) shares would be owned half by Engman and half by Hayes Oyster. Subsequently, Coast shareholders approved the sale to Keypoint (D)—Hayes voting his Coast shares and others for which he held proxies (in total constituting a majority) in favor. At none of these times did any person connected with Coast (other than Hayes and Engman) know of Hayes's (D) or Hayes Oyster's interest in Keypoint (D). After the transaction was approved, Hayes (D) signed a detailed executory contract between Coast and Keypoint (D) setting forth the terms of the deal. A couple of years later, after Hayes (D) had left Coast, Coast's new management brought suit alleging that Hayes (D) had breached his fiduciary duties to Coast by acquiring a secret profit and personal advantage to himself in his acquisition of the Keypoint (D) stock. Coast's suit also sought disgorgement of that profit. The trial court found no breach of duties, and the state's highest court granted review.

ISSUE: Does a corporation's director or officer breach his fiduciary duty to the corporation by failing to disclose the potential profit or advantage that would accrue to him if a transaction involving the corporation were approved?

HOLDING AND DECISION: (Denney, J.) Yes. A corporation's director or officer breaches his fiduciary duty to the corporation by failing to disclose the potential profit or advantage that would accrue to him if a transaction involving the corporation were approved. Although not every transaction involving corporate property in which a director has an interest is voidable at the option of the corporation, since such a contract cannot be voided if the director or officer can show that the transaction was fair to the corporation, nondisclosure by an interested director or officer is per se unfair. At the time Hayes (D) voted his majority shares and proxies to approve the transaction, he knew that he had an interest in Keypoint (D) and that Coast and Keypoint (D) would enter into an executory contract as a result of the transaction going forward. It was at this point that Hayes (D) had a duty to disclose his interest in Keypoint (D) so that Coast shareholders and directors could make an informed determination as to the advisability of retaining Hayes (D) as CEO under the circumstances, and to determine whether or not it was wise to enter into the contract at all, in light of Hayes' (D) conduct, especially given that there was a possibility, or even a probability, that some controversy might arise between Coast and Keypoint (D) relative to the numerous provisions of the contract. Moreover, there was a clear conflict of interest in the acquisition by Hayes (D) or Hayes Oyster of a 50 percent interest in Keypoint (D). It is irrelevant that Coast may not have suffered any direct harm, or that Hayes (D) had no intent to defraud Coast. What matters is that Hayes (D) was not loyal to Coast. "Fidelity in the agent is what is aimed at, and as a means of securing it, the law will not permit the agent to place himself in a situation in which he may be tempted by his own private interest to disregard that of his principal." Accordingly, Coast may assert the principle that whatever a director or officer acquires in his corporate capacity, except in open dealings with the company, belongs not to the director or officer, but to the company. Even if Hayes (D) had been acting on behalf of Hayes Oyster when he entered his bargain with Engman, this did not vitiate Hayes's (D) duties to Coast. Equity requires that Hayes (D) and Hayes Oyster be held jointly liable. Therefore,

Continued on next page.

Keypoint (D) is ordered to cancel its shares held by Hayes Oyster and to issue the same number of such cancelled shares to Coast. Reversed with directions.

▶ ANALYSIS

The duty to disclose raises the issue of the scope of disclosure. For example, in Delaware, the legal standard for disclosure by a conflicted fiduciary is that a director or controlling shareholder must disclose *all* material information relevant to the transaction. Although the Delaware Supreme Court has encouraged the use of special committees of independent directors to simulate arm's-length negotiations, some Delaware cases indicate that a fiduciary is not required to state the best price that he would pay or accept.

Quicknotes

EQUITY Fairness; justice; the determination of a matter consistent with principles of fairness and not in strict compliance with rules of law.

EXECUTORY CONTRACT A contract in which performance of an obligation has yet to be rendered.

FIDUCIARY DUTY A legal obligation to act for the benefit of another, including subordinating one's personal interests to that of the other person.

PROXY A person authorized to act for another.

Cookies Food Products v. Lakes Warehouse

Shareholders (P) v. Majority shareholder (D)

Iowa Sup. Ct., 430 N.W.2d 447 (1988).

NATURE OF CASE: Appeal from a dismissal of a shareholders' derivative suit alleging breach of fiduciary duty.

FACT SUMMARY: After Herrig (D), a majority shareholder in Cookies Food Products (Cookies) (P) turned the company around by promoting and selling its products through his own distributing company, other Cookies (P) shareholders alleged that he had skimmed off profits through self-dealing transactions.

RULE OF LAW
Directors who engage in self-dealing must establish that they acted in good faith, honesty, and fairness.

FACTS: Because Cookies Food Products (Cookies) (P) was in dire straits, its board of directors approached Herrig (D), a shareholder and owner of Lakes Warehouse Distributing (D), about distributing Cookies' (P) product. Under their agreement, Lakes (D) assumed all costs of warehousing, marketing, sales, delivery, promotion, and advertising. Cookies' (P) sales soared. Herrig (D) subsequently gained control of Cookies (P) by buying a majority of its stock. He then replaced four of the five board members. The exclusive distributorship contract was extended, as it had been before Herrig (D) became majority shareholder, and the newly configured board later authorized increased compensation for Herrig (D) and Lakes (D). No dividends were paid to Cookies' (P) shareholders, however, due to the terms of Cookies' (P) Small Business Administration (SBA) loan. The minority shareholders (P) filed suit, alleging that Herrig (D) had violated his duty of loyalty to Cookies (P). The district court ruled in Herrig's (D) favor. Cookies (P) appealed.

ISSUE: Must directors who engage in self-dealing establish that they acted in good faith, honesty, and fairness?

HOLDING AND DECISION: (Neuman, J.) Yes. Directors who engage in self-dealing must establish that they acted in good faith, honesty, and fairness. This is in addition to the requirement that any such transactions must be fully disclosed and consented to by the board of directors or the shareholders, or at least be fair and reasonable to the corporation. Self-dealing transactions must have the earmarks of arms-length transactions before a court can find them to be fair or reasonable. But financial success is not the only measure of fairness or reasonableness. Although Cookies (P) profited under Herrig's (D) authority, the court must also look to the fairness of the bargain that he struck with Cookies (P). In this case, given

his hard work on Cookies' (P) behalf, Herrig's (D) services were neither unfairly priced nor inconsistent with Cookies' (P) corporate interest. Furthermore, Herrig (D) furnished sufficient pertinent information to Cookies' (P) board to enable it to make prudent decisions concerning the contracts. To tinker with such a successful venture and to punish Herrig (D) for this success would be inequitable. Affirmed.

DISSENT: (Schultz, J.) It was Herrig's (D) burden to demonstrate that all of his self-dealing transactions were fair to Cookies (P). While much credit is due to Herrig (D) for the success of the company, this does not mean that these transactions were fair to the company. Cookies (P) has put forth convincing testimony that Herrig (D) has been grossly overcompensated for his services based on their fair market value.

ANALYSIS

Corporate directors and officers may, under proper circumstances, transact business with the corporation, but it must be done in the strictest good faith and with full disclosure of the facts to, and with the consent of, all concerned. The burden is upon the corporate directors and officers to establish their good faith, honesty, and fairness. Such transactions are scanned by the courts with skepticism and the closest scrutiny, and may be nullified on slight grounds. These principles were embodied by the legislature in Iowa Code § 496A.34, applied by the court.

Quicknotes

FIDUCIARY DUTY A legal obligation to act for the benefit of another, including subordinating one's personal interests to that of the other person.

MINORITY SHAREHOLDER A stockholder in a corporation controlling such a small portion of outstanding shares that its votes have no influence in the management of the corporation.

SELF-DEALING Transaction in which a fiduciary uses property of another, held by virtue of the confidential relationship, for personal gain.

SHAREHOLDER'S DERIVATIVE ACTION Action asserted by a shareholder in order to enforce a cause of action on behalf of the corporation.

Cooke v. Oolie

Shareholders (P) v. Directors (D)

Del. Ch. Ct., 2000 Del. Ch. LEXIS 89 (May 24, 2000).

NATURE OF CASE: Motion for summary judgment to dismiss an action for breach of the fiduciary duty of loyalty.

FACT SUMMARY: Shareholders (P) of The Nostalgia Network, Inc. (TNN) contended that two TNN directors, Oolie (D) and Salkind (D), breached their duty of loyalty by electing to pursue a particular acquisition proposal that allegedly best protected their personal interests as TNN creditors, rather than pursue other proposals that allegedly offered superior value to TNN's shareholders. Oolie (D) and Salkind (D) maintained that because the board's disinterested directors also voted to approve the acquisition, their conduct was protected by the business judgment rule's safe harbor.

🏛 RULE OF LAW

An interested director's vote to pursue a transaction that would be beneficial to the director at the expense of the shareholders is protected by the business judgment rule where disinterested directors ratify the vote.

FACTS: Oolie (D) and Salkind (D) were directors, as well as creditors, of The Nostalgia Network, Inc. (TNN). They voted to pursue an acquisition proposal that allegedly best protected their personal interests as TNN creditors, instead of pursuing other proposals that allegedly offered superior value to TNN's shareholders. TNN's two disinterested directors also voted in favor of the acquisition. TNN shareholders (P) brought suit against Oolie (D) and Salkind (D) for breach of the fiduciary duty of loyalty.

ISSUE: Is an interested director's vote to pursue a transaction that would be beneficial to the director at the expense of the shareholders protected by the business judgment rule where disinterested directors ratify the vote?

HOLDING AND DECISION: (Chandler, Chan.) Yes. An interested director's vote to pursue a transaction that would be beneficial to the director at the expense of the shareholders is protected by the business judgment rule where disinterested directors ratify the vote. It is presumed that Oolie's (D) and Salkind's (D) vote was protected by the business judgment rule, and the shareholders (P) bear the burden of rebutting this presumption. Even if the facts support the shareholders' (P) claim that Oolie (D) and Salkind (D) failed to act with disinterest and independence, any taint of disloyalty is removed by the vote of the disinterested directors supporting the same deal. This is because the disinterested directors have no incentive to act disloyally and should be only concerned with advancing the corporation's best interests. "The Court will presume, therefore, that the vote of a disinterested director signals that the interested transaction furthers the best interests of the corporation despite the interest of one or more directors." Motion for summary judgment granted.

▶ ANALYSIS

In reaching its conclusion, the court relied on the policy rationale behind the safe harbor provisions of DGCL § 144. Under § 144(a)(1), the business judgment rule is applied to the actions of an interested director, who is not the majority shareholder, if the interested director fully discloses his interest and a majority of the disinterested directors ratify the interested transaction. Here, Oolie's (D) and Salkind's (D) actions did not fall explicitly within § 144, since the statute only applies to transactions between a corporation and its directors or another corporation in which the directors have a financial interest. Although a potential conflict existed between Oolie (D) and Salkind (D) as directors and Oolie (D) and Salkind (D) as creditors of TNN, they were neither on both sides of the potential transaction nor did they have a financial interest in the other company. Second, § 144 applies to a "contract or transaction," but, in this case, no transaction had occurred; the shareholders (P) merely challenged the directors' decision to pursue a transaction that ultimately never took place.

Quicknotes

BUSINESS JUDGMENT RULE Doctrine relieving corporate directors and/or officers from liability for decisions honestly and rationally made in the corporation's best interests.

DUTY OF LOYALTY A director's duty to refrain from self-dealing or to take a position that is adverse to the corporation's best interests.

INTERESTED DIRECTOR A director of a corporation who has a personal interest in the subject matter of a transaction between the corporation and another party.

MOTION FOR SUMMARY JUDGMENT Judgment rendered by a court in response to a motion by one of the parties, claiming that the lack of a question of material fact in respect to an issue warrants disposition of the issue without consideration by the jury.

Lewis v. Vogelstein

Shareholders (P) v. Directors (D)

Del. Ch. Ct., 699 A.2d 327 (1997).

NATURE OF CASE: [Nature of case not stated in casebook excerpt.]

FACT SUMMARY: [Fact summary not stated in casebook excerpt.]

🏛 RULE OF LAW
Unanimous shareholder approval is required to ratify a conflicted transaction that involves corporate waste.

FACTS: [Facts not stated in casebook excerpt.]

ISSUE: Is unanimous shareholder approval required to ratify a conflicted transaction that involves corporate waste?

HOLDING AND DECISION: (Allen, Chan.) Yes. Unanimous shareholder approval is required to ratify a conflicted transaction that involves corporate waste. Shareholder ratification of conflicted transactions differs from general agency ratification in three regards. First, decisions to affirm or ratify an act are subject to collective action disabilities, since there is not a single principal, but a principal that is a collective. One of these potential disabilities is that a portion of the ratifying class may have conflicting interests in the transaction. Another is that some dissenting members of the class may be able to show that the "will" of the principal is wrong or even corrupt and therefore should not to be binding on the class. Second, corporate "ratification" is ordinarily not directed to lack of legal authority of the agent but relates to the consistency of some authorized director action with the equitable duty of loyalty, so that ratification acts as an affirmation that the action taken is consistent with shareholder interests. Third, when a director-conflict transaction is the subject of ratification, the statutory law [DGCL § 144] may limit the effect of purported ratification. These differences may lead to the result that an attempted ratification is ineffectual (1) because a majority of those affirming the transaction had a conflicting interest with respect to it or (2) because the transaction that is ratified constituted a corporate waste. As to the second of these, it has long been held that shareholders may not ratify a waste except by a unanimous vote. The rationale for this rule is that a transaction that satisfies the high standard of waste constitutes a gift of corporate property and no one should be forced against their will to make a gift of their property. In all events, informed, uncoerced, disinterested shareholder ratification of a transaction in which corporate directors have a material conflict of interest has the effect of protecting the transaction from judicial review except on the basis of waste.

▶ ANALYSIS

Corporate waste entails an exchange of corporate assets for consideration so disproportionately small as to lie beyond the range at which any reasonable person might be willing to trade. Most often, the claim is associated with a transfer of corporate assets that serves no corporate purpose; or for which no consideration at all is received.

━■━

Quicknotes

DUTY OF LOYALTY A director's duty to refrain from self-dealing or to take a position that is adverse to the corporation's best interests.

RATIFICATION Affirmation of a prior action taken by either the individual himself or by an agent on behalf of the principal, which is then treated as if it had been initially authorized by the principal.

━■━

Sinclair Oil Corp. v. Levien

Corporation (D) v. Shareholder (P)

Del. Sup. Ct., 280 A.2d 717 (1971).

NATURE OF CASE: Appeal from an order requiring an accounting for damages.

FACT SUMMARY: Sinclair Oil Corp. (D) contended that, although it controlled its subsidiary Sinven and owed it a fiduciary duty, its business transactions with Sinven should be governed by the business judgment rule, and not by the intrinsic fairness test.

🏛 RULE OF LAW
The intrinsic fairness test should not be applied to business transactions where a fiduciary duty exists but is unaccompanied by self-dealing.

FACTS: Sinclair Oil Corp. (Sinclair) (D), the majority shareholder of Sinven, nominated all members of Sinven's board of directors and effectively controlled that company and its board of directors. A derivative action was brought by Levien (P), a minority shareholder of Sinven, who alleged that over the course of several years, Sinclair (D) had caused Sinven to pay out excessive dividends, denied Sinven industrial development opportunities and, through its wholly owned subsidiary Sinclair International Oil, breached a contract with Sinven. Levien (P) sought an accounting for damages sustained as a result of the above actions. Because the relationship between the companies gave rise to a fiduciary duty on the part of Sinclair (D), the Court of Chancery applied the intrinsic fairness test to the complained-of transactions and found for Levien (P) on all three claims. Sinclair (D) appealed, contending that the proper standard by which its conduct should have been measured was the business judgment rule.

ISSUE: Should the intrinsic fairness test be applied to business transactions where a fiduciary duty exists but is not accompanied by self-dealing?

HOLDING AND DECISION: (Wolcott, C.J.) No. The intrinsic fairness test should not be applied to business transactions where a fiduciary duty exists but is not accompanied by self-dealing, i.e., where the parent company receives some benefit to the detriment or exclusion of the minority shareholders of the subsidiary. Because Sinven's shareholders benefited from the payment of dividends and because Levien (P) could not show that Sinclair (D) took business opportunities away from Sinven that rightfully belonged to it, no self-dealing was demonstrated as to these claims. Accordingly, the business judgment rule applied to those transactions and Levien (P) did not demonstrate a violation of that rule. However, Sinclair (D) did engage in self-dealing when it forced Sinven to contract with Sinclair's (D) wholly owned subsidiary Sin-

clair International Oil and then failed to abide by the terms of that contract, thereby invoking the intrinsic fairness test. Because Sinclair (D) could not show that its actions under the contract were intrinsically fair to Sinven's minority shareholders, it was required to account for damages under that claim. Affirmed in part; reversed in part.

▸ ANALYSIS

The use of the intrinsic fairness test to shift the burden to the defendant to demonstrate the fairness of a particular transaction may not be as great a victory as it sounds for the plaintiff. Note that in order to invoke the test and to shift the burden in the first place, the plaintiff must, in addition to demonstrating the existence of a fiduciary duty, show self-dealing on the part of the defendant. Hasn't the plaintiff in such an instance already gone a long way toward rebutting the presumption of good faith afforded the defendant under the business judgment rule? Self-dealing will rarely, if ever, pass muster under the business judgment rule either.

■◼▬■

Quicknotes

BUSINESS JUDGMENT RULE Doctrine relieving corporate directors and/or officers from liability for decisions honestly and rationally made in the corporation's best interests.

FIDUCIARY DUTY A legal obligation to act for the benefit of another.

INTRINSIC FAIRNESS TEST A defense to a claim that a director engaged in an interested director transaction by showing the transaction's fairness to the corporation.

SELF-DEALING Transaction in which a fiduciary uses property of another, held by virtue of the confidential relationship, for personal gain.

SHAREHOLDER'S DERIVATIVE ACTION Action asserted by a shareholder in order to enforce a cause of action on behalf of the corporation.

■◼▬■

Weinberger v. UOP, Inc.

Minority shareholder (P) v. Corporation (D)

Del. Sup. Ct., 457 A.2d 701 (1983).

NATURE OF CASE: Appeal of class action to rescind a merger.

FACT SUMMARY: Claiming that a cash-out merger between UOP, Inc. (D) and Signal, Inc. (D) was unfair, Weinberger (P), a former minority shareholder of UOP (D), brought a class action to have the merger rescinded.

🏛 RULE OF LAW
When seeking to secure minority shareholder approval for a proposed cash-out merger, the corporations involved must comply with the fairness test, which has two basic interrelated aspects: (1) fair dealings—which imposes a duty on the corporations to completely disclose to the shareholders all information germane to the merger—and (2) fair price— which requires that the price being offered for the outstanding stock be equivalent to a price determined by an appraisal where "all relevant nonspeculative factors"—were considered.

FACTS: Signal, Inc. (D) owned 50.5 percent of UOP (D) stock. Seven of UOP's (D) thirteen directors, including the president, were also directors of or employees of Signal (D). Arledge and Chitiea, who were directors of UOP (D) and Signal (D), prepared a feasibility study for Signal (D). The study reported that it would be a good investment for Signal (D) to acquire the remaining 49.5 percent of UOP (D) shares through a cash-out merger at any price up to $24 per share. The study was given to all the Signal (D) directors, including those who also served as directors on UOP's (D) board. However, the evidence indicates that the study was never disclosed to UOP's (D) six non-Signal (D), i.e., outside, directors. Nor was it disclosed to the minority shareholders who owned the remaining 49.5 percent of UOP (D) stock. On February 28, Signal (D) offered UOP (D) a cash-out merger price of $21 per share. Four business days later, on March 6, the six non-Signal (D) UOP (D) directors (the seven common Signal-UOP (D) directors abstained from the voting) voted to approve the merger at $21 per share. The vote was largely due to the fact that at the time, UOP's (D) market price was only $14.50 per share, and also there was a "fairness opinion letter" from UOP's (D) investment banker stating that the $21 per share was a fair price. The merger was then approved by a majority (51.9%) of the minority, i.e., the remaining 49.5 percent, of UOP (D) shareholders. Weinberger (P), a former minority shareholder of UOP (D), then brought a class action to have the merger rescinded, claiming it was unfair to UOP's (D) former shareholders. The Court of Chancery

held for UOP (D) and Signal (D). Weinberger (P) appealed.

ISSUE: May a minority shareholder successfully challenge the approval of a cash-out merger that was approved by the majority of the minority shareholders?

HOLDING AND DECISION: (Moore, J.) Yes. A minority shareholder may successfully challenge the approval of a cash-out merger that was approved by the majority of the minority shareholders if he can demonstrate that the corporations involved failed to comply with the fairness test in securing the approval. The fairness test consists of two basic interrelated aspects. The first aspect is "fair dealings," which imposes a duty on the corporations involved to completely disclose to the minority shareholders all information germane to the merger. Here, Signal (D) failed to disclose to the non-Signal (D) UOP (D) directors and the minority shareholders of UOP (D) the Arledge-Chitiea feasibility study that reported it would be a "good investment" for Signal (D) to acquire the minority shares up to a price of $24 per share. In addition, UOP's (D) minority was given the impression that the "fairness opinion letter" from UOP's (D) investment banker had been drafted only after the banker had made a careful study, when, in fact, the investment banker had drafted the letter in three days with the price left blank. Consequently, Signal (D) did not meet the "fair dealings" aspect of the test. The second aspect of the fairness test is "fair price," which requires that the price being offered for the outstanding stock be equivalent to an appraisal where "all relevant nonspeculative factors" were considered. In this case, the Court of Chancery tested the fairness of Signal's (D) $21 per-share price against the Delaware weighted average method of valuation. This method shall no longer exclusively control the determination of "fair price." Rather, a new method that considers "all relevant nonspeculative factors" shall now be used for determining fair price. This new method is consistent with the method used in determining a shareholder's appraisal remedy. Here, the Court of Chancery did not consider the $24 per-share price determined by the Arledge-Chitiea study. Nor did the court consider Weinberger's (P) discounted cash flow analysis, which concluded that the UOP (D) stock was worth $26 per share on the date of merger. Therefore, since these factors were not considered, it cannot be said that the $21 per-share price paid by Signal (D) meets the new method of determining fair price. Finally, in view of the new, more liberal test for determining fair price,

Continued on next page.

together with the chancery court's broad remedial discretion, it is concluded that the business purpose requirement for mergers, as required by *Singer v. Magnavox Co.*, 380 A.2d 969 (1977), *Tanzer v. International General Industries, Inc.*, 379 A.2d 1121 (1977), and *Roland International Corp. v. Najjar*, 407 A.2d 1032 (1979), adds no further protection to minority shareholders. Accordingly, the business purpose requirement is no longer law. Reversed.

▶ ANALYSIS

This case demonstrates the use of a cash-out merger to eliminate or "freeze out" the minority interest. A footnote in the case suggests that Signal's (D) freeze-out of UOP's (D) minority interest would have met the court's fairness test if UOP (D) had appointed an independent negotiating committee of its non-Signal (D) directors to deal with Signal (D) at arm's length.

■■■

Quicknotes

CASH-OUT MERGER Occurs when a merging company prematurely redeems the securities of a holder as part of the merger.

CLASS ACTION A suit commenced by a representative on behalf of an ascertainable group that is too large to appear in court, who shares a commonality of interests and who will benefit from a successful result.

RESCISSION The canceling of an agreement and the return of the parties to their positions prior to the formation of the contract.

■■■

Donahue v. Rodd Electrotype Co.

Minority shareholder (P) v. Corporation (D)

Mass. Sup. Jud. Ct., 328 N.E.2d 505 (1975).

NATURE OF CASE: Action to rescind a corporate purchase of shares and recover the purchase price.

FACT SUMMARY: Donahue (P), a minority stockholder in a close corporation, sought to rescind a corporate purchase of shares of the controlling shareholder.

🏛 RULE OF LAW
A controlling stockholder (or group) in a close corporation who causes the corporation to purchase his stock breaches his fiduciary duty to the minority stockholders if he does not cause the corporation to offer each stockholder an equal opportunity to sell a ratable number of shares to the corporation at an identical price.

FACTS: As a controlling stockholder of Rodd Electrotype Co. (D), a close corporation, Harry Rodd (D) caused the corporation to reacquire 45 of his shares for $800 each ($36,000 total). He then divested the rest of his holding by making gifts and sales to his children. Donahue (P), a minority stockholder who had refused to ratify this action, offered to sell her shares on the same terms but was refused. A suit followed in which Donahue (P) sought to rescind the purchase of Harry Rodd's (D) stock and make him repay to Rodd Electrotype (D) the $36,000 purchase price with interest. Finding the purchase had been without prejudice to Donahue (P), the trial court dismissed the bill and the appellate court affirmed.

ISSUE: Does a controlling stockholder (or group) in a close corporation who causes the corporation to purchase his stock breach his fiduciary duty to the minority stockholders if he does not cause the corporation to offer each stockholder an equal opportunity to sell a ratable number of shares to the corporation at an identical price?

HOLDING AND DECISION: (Tauro, C.J.) Yes. A controlling stockholder (or group) in a close corporation who causes the corporation to purchase his stock breaches his fiduciary duty to the minority stockholders if he does not cause the corporation to offer each stockholder an equal opportunity to sell a ratable number of shares to the corporation at an identical price. A close corporation is typified by: (1) a small number of stockholders; (2) no ready market for the corporate stock; and (3) substantial majority stockholder participation in the management, direction and operations of the corporation. As thus defined, close corporations are different from other types of corporations in that they are very much like partnerships and require the utmost trust, confidence, and loyalty among the

members for success. In such corporations there is also an opportunity for the majority stockholders to oppress or disadvantage minority stockholders through "freezeouts." The minority shareholders in a close corporation who are being oppressed by the controlling shareholders are not readily able to sell their interests, since there is not a ready market for such interests, as there is with publicly traded companies. Therefore, the minority shareholders are at a disadvantage relative to the majority shareholders. However, given the partnership-like nature of a close corporation, minority shareholders are also able to take advantage of unsuspecting majority shareholders. For these reasons, a partnership-type fiduciary duty arises between all the stockholders in the close corporation. It is the basis for the rule herein announced, under which Donahue (P) must be given an equal opportunity to sell her shares. When a close corporation reacquires its own stock, the purchase is subject to the requirement that the stockholders, who, as directors or controlling stockholders, caused the corporation to enter into the stock purchase agreement, must have acted with the utmost good faith and loyalty to the other stockholders. To meet this test, if the stockholder whose shares were purchased was a member of the controlling group, the controlling stockholders must cause the corporation to offer each stockholder an equal opportunity to sell a ratable number of his shares to the corporation at an identical price. Purchase by the corporation confers substantial benefits on the members of the controlling group whose shares were purchased, since it turns corporate assets into their personal assets. These benefits are not available to the minority stockholders if the corporation does not also offer them an opportunity to sell their shares. The controlling group may not, consistent with its strict duty to the minority, utilize its control of the corporation to obtain special advantages and disproportionate benefit from its share ownership. These principles are applicable here. Since what the corporation purchased here was 100 percent of 45 of Rodd's (D) shares, Donahue (P) should be entitled to have 100 percent of 45 of her shares also purchased by the corporation. Reversed.

CONCURRENCE: (Wilkins, J.) I do not join in any implication that this rule applies to other activities of the corporation, like salaries and dividend policy, as they affect minority stockholders.

▶ ANALYSIS

A problem that exists with close corporations is that there is no ready market to which a minority stockholder can

Continued on next page.

turn when he wishes to liquidate his holdings. Knowing this fact, the controlling stockholder has a very powerful weapon that he would not have in a regular corporate setup. This is one of the reasons he is held to a higher degree of fiduciary duty in this case.

■■■

Quicknotes

FIDUCIARY DUTY A legal obligation to act for the benefit of another, including subordinating one's personal interests to that of the other person.

MINORITY STOCKHOLDER A stockholder in a corporation controlling such a small portion of those outstanding shares that its votes have no influence in the management of the corporation.

■■■

Smith v. Atlantic Properties, Inc.

Shareholder (P) v. Corporation (D)

Mass. App. Ct., 422 N.E.2d 798 (1981).

NATURE OF CASE: Action for a determination of dividends, removal of a director, and a reimbursement order for penalty taxes.

FACT SUMMARY: Wolfson (D), a minority stockholder acting pursuant to a provision in the articles of incorporation, was able to prevent the distribution of dividends, as a result of which the corporation, Atlantic Properties, Inc. (D), had to pay a penalty tax for accumulated earnings.

> 🏛 **RULE OF LAW**
> Where a closed corporation's articles of incorporation include a provision designed to protect minority stockholders, the minority stockholders have a fiduciary duty to use the provision reasonably.

FACTS: Wolfson (D) purchased land in Norwood. Wolfson (D) then offered a 25 percent interest each in the land to Smith (P), Zimble (P), and Burke (P). Smith (P) then organized defendant corporation, Atlantic (D) to operate the real estate. Each of the four subscribers received 25 shares. At Wolfson's (D) request, the article of incorporation included a provision that required an approval of 80 percent of the voting shares before any election, resolution, or action would be binding upon Atlantic Properties, Inc. (Atlantic) (D). After 10 years of operation, Atlantic (D) had accumulated $172,000 in earnings. Wolfson (D) wished to see the earnings devoted to repairs. Therefore he refused to vote for any dividends, and pursuant to the 80 percent provision Atlantic (D) was unable to declare any dividends. As a result, the Internal Revenue Service, pursuant to I.R.C. § 531 et seq., assessed and collected two penalty assessments for a total of approximately $45,000 for the unreasonable accumulation of earnings. Smith (P), Zimble (P), and Burke (P) then brought this action for determination of dividends, removal of Wolfson (D) from the Board of Directors, and a reimbursement of the penalty taxes from Wolfson (D). The trial court held for Smith (P) and Wolfson (D) appealed.

ISSUE: May a minority stockholder of a closed corporation use a provision in the articles of incorporation that is designed to protect minority stockholders in a manner that will unduly hamper the good-faith corporate interests of the majority stockholders?

HOLDING AND DECISION: (Cutter, J.) No. Where a closed corporation's articles of incorporation include a provision designed to protect minority stockholders, the minority stockholders have a fiduciary duty to use the provision reasonably so as not to unduly hamper the good-faith corporate interests of the majority stockholders. Here, 80 percent provision in Atlantic's (D) articles of incorporation, which was designed to protect minority stockholders, was unreasonably used by Wolfson (D). Wolfson (D) was warned of the penalty tax that could result from a failure to declare dividends. However, he refused to vote for any amount of dividends that would minimize the possibility of penalty tax. Consequently, the trial judge was correct in protecting the majority stockholders by ordering Wolfson (D) to reimburse Atlantic (D) for the penalty taxes. In addition, the trial judge's order to Atlantic's (D) directors to declare a dividend is to be modified and affirmed.

▌ *ANALYSIS*

As this case illustrates, sometimes the articles of incorporation provide minority shareholders with an opportunity to obtain ad hoc controlling interest. When this occurs, Heatherington, in the 1972 *Duke L.J.* at 944, states that the minority shareholder is bound by the same fiduciary standard imposed upon majority shareholders. In other words, both the majority shareholder and the ad hoc controlling minority shareholder should not exercise their corporate powers in a manner that is clearly adverse to the corporation's interest.

■=■

Quicknotes

DIVIDEND The payment of earnings to a corporation's shareholders in proportion to the amount of shares held.

FIDUCIARY DUTY A legal obligation to act for the benefit of another.

MINORITY SHAREHOLDER A stockholder in a corporation controlling such a small portion of outstanding shares that its votes have no influence in the management of the corporation.

■=■

CHAPTER 9

Executive Compensation

Quick Reference Rules of Law

In re The Goldman Sachs Group, Inc. Shareholder Litigation

Shareholders (P) v. Investment bank (D)

Del. Ch. Ct., 2011 WL 4826104 (Oct. 2011).

NATURE OF CASE: Motion to dismiss for failure to make a pre-suit demand upon the board and failure to state a claim.

FACT SUMMARY: Shareholders (P) of investment bank Goldman Sachs (Goldman) (D) claimed that Goldman's (D) compensation structure, which was based on a percentage of the firm's net revenue, motivated Goldman's employees to grow net revenue at any cost and without regard to risk. The shareholders (P) claimed that the firm's directors (D) breached their fiduciary duties by approving the compensation structure.

🏛 **RULE OF LAW**
Corporate directors may pursue corporate opportunities in any way that they see fit, if those opportunities are pursued in the exercise of their business judgment on behalf of the corporation, and their actions are within the boundaries of their duty to act as faithful fiduciaries to the corporation and its stockholders.

FACTS: Shareholders (P) of investment bank Goldman Sachs (Goldman) (D) claimed that Goldman's (D) compensation structure created a divergence of interest between Goldman's management (D) and its stockholders (P). Goldman's directors (D) based compensation for the firm's management on a percentage of net revenue, and the shareholders (P) claimed that Goldman's employees were therefore motivated to grow net revenue at any cost and without regard to risk. The shareholders (P) argued that Goldman's (D) employees would do this by engaging in highly risky trading practices and by over-leveraging the company's assets. If these practices turned a profit, Goldman's (D) employees would receive a windfall, but losses would fall on the stockholders (P). The shareholders (P) alleged that the directors (D) breached their fiduciary duties by approving the compensation structure, that the payments under this compensation structure constituted corporate waste, and that this compensation structure led to overly risky business decisions and unethical and illegal practices. The directors (D) moved for dismissal of this action on the grounds that the shareholders (P) failed to make a pre-suit demand on the board and to state a claim.

ISSUE: May corporate directors pursue corporate opportunities in any way that they see fit, if those opportunities are pursued in the exercise of their business judgment on behalf of the corporation, and their actions are within the boundaries of their duty to act as faithful fiduciaries to the corporation and its stockholders?

HOLDING AND DECISION: (Glasscock, V. Chan.) Yes. Corporate directors may pursue corporate opportunities in any way that they see fit, if those opportunities are pursued in the exercise of their business judgment on behalf of the corporation, and their actions are within the boundaries of their duty to act as faithful fiduciaries to the corporation and its stockholders. This broad freedom to pursue opportunity on behalf of the corporation is what allows corporations to produce wealth, and exercising that freedom is what directors and officers are elected by their shareholders to do. As long as such individuals act within the boundaries of their fiduciary duties, the business decisions of those chosen by the stockholders to fulfill that function should not be second-guessed. The actions taken by Goldman's directors (D) do not fall outside of the fiduciary boundaries existing under Delaware case law. Regarding the shareholders' (P) allegations that the directors (D) violated fiduciary duties in setting compensation levels and failing to oversee the risks that the compensation structure created are unsupported by the facts as pled. The facts pled in support of these allegations, if true, support only a conclusion that the directors (D) made poor business decisions. The shareholders (P) have failed to allege facts sufficient to demonstrate that the directors (D) were unable to properly exercise their business judgment. The shareholders (P) also failed to raise a reasonable doubt that the directors (D) were disinterested or independent, or that the compensation scheme was implemented in good faith and on an informed basis. Finally, the shareholders (P) failed to plead facts showing a substantial likelihood of liability on the directors' (D) part, because no reasonable inference could be made that the directors (D) consciously disregarded their duty to be informed about business risk, assuming that such a duty exists, which need not be decided. Shareholders' (P) claims dismissed.

▶ *ANALYSIS*

As this decision suggests, Delaware law gives corporate directors wide latitude to direct business strategy, and setting compensation structures is part of the business of running a company. But even if the law were not so permissive, the evaluation of pay for corporate officers by judges would still be controversial. Not only would it be difficult for a judge to evaluate executive pay, but many

Continued on next page.

would consider such evaluation inappropriate interference in commerce by the courts.

Quicknotes

BUSINESS JUDGMENT RULE Doctrine relieving corporate directors and/or officers from liability for decisions honestly and rationally made in the corporation's best interests.

FIDUCIARY DUTY A legal obligation to act for the benefit of another, including subordinating one's personal interests to that of the other person.

Calma v. Templeton

Shareholder (P) v. Director (D)

Del. Ch. Ct., C.A. 9579 (April 30, 2015).

NATURE OF CASE: Motion to dismiss for failure to state a claim in derivative action for, inter alia, breach of fiduciary duty.

FACT SUMMARY: Calma (P), a shareholder of Citrix Systems, Inc. (Citrix), brought a derivative action against Citrix's directors (D) asserting, inter alia, breach of fiduciary duty that arose from the grant of restricted stock units (RSUs) to non-employee directors pursuant to Citrix's shareholder-approved equity incentive plan, which covered multiple and varied classes of beneficiaries and contained a generic one million RSU limit, but did not specifically address non-employee director compensation. The directors (D) moved to dismiss the complaint for failure to state a claim, that arguing shareholder approval of the plan ratified it, so that any review of the RSU awards would have to be made under a waste standard, rather than an entire fairness standard, and that it was not reasonably conceivable that the RSU awards constituted waste.

🏛 RULE OF LAW
Where a majority of a corporation's disinterested stockholders in informed and uncoerced votes provides omnibus approval of a compensation plan that covers multiple and varied classes of beneficiaries, and that contains a single generic limit on the amount of compensation that may be awarded in a given year, such approval is not sufficient to establish a ratification defense for awards made under that plan to the company's non-employee directors where the shareholders were not asked to approve—and thus did not approve—any action bearing specifically on the magnitude of compensation for the non-employee directors.

FACTS: A majority of the disinterested shareholders of Citrix Systems, Inc. (Citrix), in informed and uncoerced votes, in 2005 approved the company's Equity Incentive Plan (the "Plan"). Under the Plan, the persons eligible to receive an equity award included Citrix's directors, officers, employees, consultants, and advisors. The Plan limited the total number of shares covered by an award that any beneficiary could receive under the Plan in a calendar year to 1 million shares. The Plan did not specify the compensation that the company's non-employee directors would receive annually, nor were there sub-limits varied by position with the company, such as a limit for non-employee directors and a different limit for officers. Thus, the compensation committee (or the board) effectively had the authority to decide how many awards it could grant to its

members and other directors, subject only to the amount of stock limitations. Pursuant to the Plan, non-employee directors were awarded restricted stock units (RSUs) in 2011, 2012, and 2013 (the "RSU Awards"). The majority of the directors' compensation consisted of these RSU Awards. Calma (P), a Citrix shareholder, brought a derivative suit in July 2014 against the Citrix directors (D), contending the RSU Awards were, when combined with the cash payments that Citrix's non-employee directors received, "excessive" in comparison with the compensation received by directors at certain of Citrix's "peers." Calma (P) asserted claims, inter alia, of breach of fiduciary duty. At the time Calma (P) brought suit, a grant of one million shares to a single person would have been worth over $55 million. Thus, Calma (P) asserted the directors (D) had to establish the entire fairness of the RSU Awards as conflicted compensation decisions because the Plan did not have any "meaningful limits" on the annual stock-based compensation Citrix directors could receive from the company. The directors (D) moved to dismiss for failure to state a claim upon which relief could be granted, contending Citrix stockholders ratified the Plan so any award of RSUs to the directors under the generic one million RSU limit in the Plan had to be reviewed under a waste standard, and they further contended it was not reasonably conceivable that the RSU Awards constituted waste. The Delaware Chancery Court considered the directors' (D) motion.

ISSUE: Where a majority of a corporation's disinterested stockholders in informed and uncoerced votes provides omnibus approval of a compensation plan that covers multiple and varied classes of beneficiaries, and that contains a single generic limit on the amount of compensation that may be awarded in a given year, is such approval sufficient to establish a ratification defense for awards made under that plan to the company's non-employee directors where the shareholders were not asked to approve—and thus did not approve—any action bearing specifically on the magnitude of compensation for the non-employee directors?

HOLDING AND DECISION: (Bouchard, J.) No. Where a majority of a corporation's disinterested stockholders in informed and uncoerced votes provides omnibus approval of a compensation plan that covers multiple and varied classes of beneficiaries, and that contains a single generic limit on the amount of compensation that may be awarded in a given year, such approval is not

Continued on next page.

sufficient to establish a ratification defense for awards made under that plan to the company's non-employee directors where the shareholders were not asked to approve—and thus did not approve—any action bearing specifically on the magnitude of compensation for the non-employee directors. When established, ratification works as an affirmative defense to the entire fairness standard. Ratification contemplates the ex post conferring upon or confirming of the legal authority of an agent in circumstances in which the agent had no authority or arguably had no authority. Case law precedent provides that ratification does not embrace a "blank check" or "carte blanche" theory. When uncoerced, fully informed, and disinterested stockholders approve a specific corporate action, the doctrine of ratification, in most situations, precludes claims for breach of fiduciary duty attacking that action. However, the mere approval by stockholders of a request by directors for the authority to take action within broad parameters does not insulate all future action by the directors within those parameters from attack. A corollary principal is that valid stockholder ratification leads to waste being the doctrinal standard of review for a breach of fiduciary duty claim. Approval by a mere majority of stockholders does not ratify waste because a waste of corporate assets is incapable of ratification without unanimous stockholder consent. Here, a majority of disinterested and informed shareholders approved the Plan, but they did not by so doing approve specific non-employee director compensation, because the Plan did not set forth the specific compensation to be granted to non-employee directors, nor did it set forth any director-specific "ceilings" on the compensation that could be granted to the company's directors. For these reasons, the directors' (D) motion to dismiss as to the breach of fiduciary claim is denied. [The court also denied the directors' (D) motion to dismiss as to an unjust enrichment claim, but granted the motion as to a claim for waste.]

▌ *ANALYSIS*

Important policy considerations support the ratification doctrine in the context of director compensation. Specifying the precise amount and form of director compensation in an equity compensation plan when it is submitted for stockholder approval helps to ensure integrity in the underlying principal-agent relationship between stockholders and directors by aligning the directors' interests with those of the shareholders by having a consistent, non-discretionary approach to their compensation. Likewise, obtaining stockholder approval of director compensation on an annual or regular basis facilitates the disclosure of inherently conflicted decisions and empowers stockholders with a meaningful role in the compensation of their fiduciaries.

Quicknotes

BREACH OF FIDUCIARY DUTY The failure of a fiduciary to observe the standard of care exercised by professionals of similar education and experience.

RATIFICATION Affirmation of a prior action taken by either the individual himself or by an agent on behalf of the principal, which is then treated as if it had been initially authorized by the principal.

WASTE The mistreatment of another's property by someone in lawful possession.

CHAPTER 10

Shareholder Lawsuits

Quick Reference Rules of Law

Fletcher v. A.J. Industries, Inc.

Shareholder (P) v. Directors/Corporations (D)

Cal. Ct. App., 266 Cal. App. 2d 313, 72 Cal. Rptr. 146 (1968).

NATURE OF CASE: Appeal from derivative action against directors.

FACT SUMMARY: Fletcher (P) requested attorney fees for successfully settling a derivative suit.

🏛 RULE OF LAW
Even though the corporation receives no money from a derivative suit, attorney fees are properly awarded if the corporation has substantially benefited from the action.

FACTS: Fletcher (P) brought a derivative suit alleging directorial mismanagement. The suit alleged that Ver Halen (D) totally dominated the corporation and that Malone's (D) salary as treasurer was excessive, etc. A settlement between Fletcher (P), A.J. Industries (D) (the "corporation" or "A.J.") and the various defendant directors was reached. Ver Halen's (D) authority was curtailed and his voting power was restricted. Malone (D) was made a director and ceased acting as treasurer. Various other board members were replaced. Monetary claims against officers/directors were referred to future arbitration. Attorney fees for Fletcher's (P) action were to be referred to the court for an award, in its discretion and A.J. (D) was free to dispute them since it was to pay any award rendered. The court, over A.J.'s (D) objection, awarded $64,000 in attorney fees and $2,100 in costs on the theory that the action had substantially benefited the corporation (D).

ISSUE: Even though the corporation receives no money from a derivative suit, are attorney fees properly awarded if the corporation has substantially benefited from the action?

HOLDING AND DECISION: (Rattigan, J.) Yes. Even though the corporation receives no money from a derivative suit, attorney fees are properly awarded if the corporation has substantially benefited from the action. Normally attorney fees are only awarded the prevailing party when authorized by statute or under an agreement between the parties. A judicial exception to this rule is the "common fund" rule. If a party brings an action to preserve, protect or create a common fund, he is entitled to attorney fees. This rule has been applied to derivative suits where the corporation obtains a monetary judgment. Here, any monetary judgment will be awarded in the future through arbitration. We find, however, that a second exception, an extension to the common fund doctrine, should be created. This is the "substantial benefit" rule. If the corporation receives a substantial benefit from the derivative action, even though nonmonetary, recovery of attorney fees should be allowed. Here, there was a restruc-

turing of corporate management, a restriction on the authority and voting rights of the majority shareholder, possible future monetary awards, and the saving of an excessive salary paid to the former treasurer. These were substantial corporate benefits. Affirmed.

DISSENT IN PART: (Christian, J.) The new rule announced herein is better left to the legislature whose statute specifically limits the right to attorney fees.

▶ ANALYSIS

In *Bosch v. Meeker Cooperative Light and Power Assn.*, 101 N.W. 2d 423 (1960), the court found that the prevention of ultra vires acts conferred a "substantial benefit" in that it was a deterrent to future irresponsible acts by the directors. Suits establishing violations of securities laws are generally deemed to be of a substantial benefit to the corporation. *Mills v. Electric Auto-Lite*, 396 U.S. 375 (1970). This decision was apparently bottomed in equity on the "common benefit" approach.

Quicknotes

DERIVATION SUIT Action asserted by a shareholder in order to enforce a cause of action on behalf of the corporation.

Levine v. Smith

Shareholder (P) v. Directors (D)

Del. Sup. Ct., 591 A.2d 194 (1991).

NATURE OF CASE: Appeal of dismissal, on grounds of demand failure, of a shareholder derivative action.

FACT SUMMARY: General Motors (GM) shareholders (P) filed shareholder derivative suits against GM's directors (D), challenging the buy-back of GM stock from Ross Perot (D), its largest shareholder, and others, on the grounds that Perot (D) and the others were wrongfully paid a premium to stop criticizing GM and that the GM directors (D) approving the buy-back could not have acted independently. The Chancery Court dismissed, rejecting the shareholders' (P) claims of demand futility and that the GM directors (D) lacked independence.

🏛 RULE OF LAW

To withstand dismissal of a derivative action, a plaintiff shareholder claiming demand futility or wrongful demand refusal must allege particularized facts that overcome the business judgment rule presumption.

FACTS: Shareholders (P) of the General Motors Corporation (GM) brought several derivative actions involving a transaction by which Ross Perot (D)—a GM director and its largest shareholder—and a few associates sold back to GM their holdings of GM Class E stock in exchange for $743 million. This repurchase was in response to disagreements between Perot (D) and GM senior management concerning the management of GM's EDS subsidiary and its automobile business as well. By the time of the repurchase, GM was in the awkward position of facing Perot's (D) accusations that it sold "second rate cars." A committee of outside directors negotiated the buy-back transaction for GM, which was subsequently approved by the full board at a meeting that Perot (D) did not attend. Perot agreed not to compete with GM and promised not to publicly criticize the company. The derivative suit named all directors (D) and Perot (D) as defendants, and claimed that the transaction paid Perot (D) a premium for his shares for no reason other than stopping his criticisms. The Chancery Court dismissed, rejecting the shareholders' (P) claims of demand futility and wrongful demand refusal and that the GM directors (D) lacked independence. The state's highest court granted review.

ISSUE: To withstand dismissal of a derivative action, must a plaintiff shareholder claiming demand futility or wrongful demand refusal allege particularized facts that overcome the business judgment rule presumption?

HOLDING AND DECISION: (Horsey, J.) Yes. To withstand dismissal of a derivative action, a plaintiff shareholder claiming demand futility or wrongful demand refusal must allege particularized facts that overcome the business judgment rule presumption. The correct application of the business judgment rule is crucial to a determination of the sufficiency of a derivative complaint to withstand dismissal in both a demand excused and a demand refused context. Where demand futility is asserted, two related but distinct questions must be answered: (1) whether threshold presumptions of director disinterest or independence are rebutted by well-pleaded facts; and, if not, (2) whether the complaint pleads particularized facts sufficient to create a reasonable doubt that the challenged transaction was the product of a valid exercise of business judgment. If the plaintiff cannot prove that directors are interested or otherwise not capable of exercising independent business judgment, the plaintiff must plead particularized facts creating a reasonable doubt as to the "soundness" of the challenged transaction sufficient to rebut the presumption that the business judgment rule attaches to the transaction. A showing on either of these prongs permits the plaintiff to proceed with the action. Here, the Chancery Court was correct in limiting its demand futility analysis to the issue of director independence. As to director independence, the record supports the Chancery Court's finding that the shareholders (P) did not plead sufficiently particularized facts to show that the GM outside directors (D) were so manipulated, misinformed and misled that they were subject to management's control and unable to exercise independent judgment, and that a majority of GM's board was independent. The shareholders' (P) allegations more appropriately relate to the issue of director due care and the business judgment rule's application to the challenged transaction—and, in fact, these same allegations are pled for both purposes. Turning to the question of director due care, the finding that the outside directors (D) were not so manipulated, misinformed and misled as to be under management's control means that the shareholders (P) have not pleaded particularized facts sufficient to raise a reasonable doubt that a majority of the GM board acted in so uninformed a manner as to fail to exercise due care. Affirmed.

▶ ANALYSIS

The court also opined that the board's decision to refuse the shareholders' (P) demand was entitled to the business

Continued on next page.

judgment rule presumption, and the burden was on the shareholders (P) to overcome the presumption. For a contrary view, see "Discovery in Federal Demand-Refused Litigation," 105 *Harv. L. Rev.* 1025 (1992).

Quicknotes

BUSINESS JUDGMENT RULE Doctrine relieving corporate directors and/or officers from liability for decisions honestly and rationally made in the corporation's best interests.

DEMAND REFUSED CASE Shareholder derivative suit in which a shareholder complies with the requirement that he make a prior demand for corrective action by the board of directors before commencing the suit, which is rejected by the board.

DUE CARE The degree of care that can be expected from a reasonably prudent person under similar circumstances; synonymous with ordinary care.

SHAREHOLDER DERIVATIVE SUIT Action asserted by a shareholder in order to enforce a cause of action on behalf of the corporation.

Rales v. Blasband

Directors (D) v. Shareholder (P)

Del. Sup. Ct., 634 A.2d 927 (1993).

NATURE OF CASE: Certified question from federal district court relating to demand excusal in shareholder double derivative action.

FACT SUMMARY: Blasband (P), first a shareholder in Easco Hand Tools, Inc. (Easco), and then a shareholder in Danaher Corp. (Danaher), which acquired Easco as a wholly-owned subsidiary, contended that demand was excused in a double derivative action he brought because the Danaher board (D) could not impartially consider the merits of his derivative action (relating to improper use by the Easco board of the proceeds from sales of its senior subordinated notes) without being influenced by improper considerations.

> ## RULE OF LAW
> In a derivative action where demand excusal is asserted against a board that has not made the decision that is the subject of the action, the standard for determining demand excusal is whether the board was capable of impartially considering the action's merits without being influenced by improper considerations.

FACTS: Danaher Corp. (Danaher) acquired Easco Hand Tools, Inc. (Easco), which became Danaher's wholly-owned subsidiary. The two Rales brothers (D) were directors, officers and stockholders of each corporation at all relevant times. Blasband (P) was first an Easco shareholder and then became a Danaher shareholder when Danaher acquired Easco. The Danaher board consisted of eight members (D), including the two Rales brothers (D). Before Danaher acquired Easco, Easco used about $62 million in proceeds from a $100 million sale of senior subordinated notes to invest in highly speculative junk bonds offered through Drexel Burnham Lambert Inc. (Drexel). Blasband (P) brought a double derivative action in federal district court, alleging that this investment was contrary to Easco's prospectus for the sale, which had indicated that the proceeds would be invested in "government and other marketable securities." Blasband (P) alleged that these junk bonds were bought by Easco because of the Rales brothers' (D) desire to help Drexel at a time when it was under investigation and having trouble selling such bonds. Allegedly, Drexel had helped the Rales brothers (D) make a fortune, so they were very loyal to Drexel. He alleged that the investment was made only for the benefit of the Rales brothers (D), rather than for Easco. Furthermore, Blasband (P) alleged that the junk bonds had lost $14 million in value. At the time of the alleged wrongdoing, the Rales brothers (D) and Caplin (D) were members of the boards of Easco and Danaher. Sherman (D), another

director and the President and CEO of Danaher, relied on the Rales brothers (D) for his salary and continued position at the company. Ehrlich (D), another director, was the president of Wabash National Corp. (Wabash). His two brothers were vice presidents at Wabash, in which the Rales brothers (D) held a majority ownership interest. The federal courts concluded that Blasband (P) had pleaded facts raising at least a reasonable doubt that the Easco board's use of proceeds from the note offering was a valid exercise of business judgment. The federal district court certified a question to the Delaware Supreme Court as to whether Blasband (P) had established that demand was excused under the "substantive law of the State of Delaware."

ISSUE: In a derivative action where demand excusal is asserted against a board that has not made the decision that is the subject of the action, is the standard for determining demand excusal, whether the board was capable of impartially considering the action's merits without being influenced by improper considerations?

HOLDING AND DECISION: (Veasey, C.J.) Yes. In a derivative action where demand excusal is asserted against a board that has not made the decision that is the subject of the action, the standard for determining demand excusal is whether the board was capable of impartially considering the action's merits without being influenced by improper considerations. In a double derivative suit a stockholder of a parent corporation seeks recovery for a cause of action belonging to a subsidiary corporation. The business judgment test for demand excusal enunciated in *Aronson v. Lewis*, 473 A.2d 805 (Del. 1984), which assumes that a decision of the board of directors is being challenged in the derivative suit, is inapplicable here since the Danaher board did not make the decision that is being challenged. That is because where there is no conscious decision by directors to act or refrain from acting, the business judgment rule is inapplicable. The appropriate test in such a situation is to examine whether the board that would be addressing the demand can impartially consider its merits without being influenced by improper considerations. Thus, a court must determine whether or not the particularized factual allegations of a derivative stockholder complaint create a reasonable doubt that, as of the time the complaint is filed, the board of directors could have properly exercised its independent and disinterested business judgment in responding to a demand. The defendant directors' (D) argument that this test will fail to discourage "strike suits" is unfounded. First, a plaintiff in a double

Continued on next page.

derivative suit is still required to satisfy the *Aronson* test to establish that demand on the subsidiary's board is futile. Second, requiring demand on the parent board in all double derivative cases, even where a board of directors is interested, would impose an extremely onerous burden to meet at the pleading stage without the benefit of discovery. Applying this test here, i.e., to determine whether the Danaher board could have impartially considered a demand at the time Blasband's (P) original complaint was filed, it is first appropriate to determine the nature of the decision with which the Danaher board would have been confronted. The subject of the demand in this case would be the alleged breaches of fiduciary duty by the Easco board of directors in connection with Easco's investment in Drexel junk bonds. In response to a demand letter, the Danaher board would have to conduct an investigation informing itself of all the facts involved, and then weight its alternatives, including the advisability of implementing internal corrective action and commencing legal proceedings. Directorial interest exists where a corporate decision will have a materially detrimental impact on a director, but not on the corporation and the stockholders. Here, therefore, the Rales brothers (D) and Caplin (D) were "interested" because the federal court had ruled that Blasband (P) had pleaded facts raising at least a reasonable doubt that the Easco board's use of proceeds from the note offering was a valid exercise of business judgment. This raised a substantial likelihood that these three directors (D) could face significant personal liability; the Rales brothers (D) and Caplin (D) have a disqualifying financial interest that disables them from impartially considering a response to a demand by Blasband (P). Because Sherman (D) was Danaher's President and CEO, and because of the Rales brothers' (D) positions on the board (Chairman and Chairman of the Executive Committee), there is a reasonable doubt that Sherman (D) could be expected to act independently considering his substantial financial stake ($1 million annual salary) in maintaining his current offices. There is also a reasonable doubt regarding Ehrlich's (D) ability to act independently since it can be inferred that he is beholden to the Rales brothers (D) in light of his employment, and the employment of his two brothers, at Wabash. Thus, because there is a reasonable doubt that the majority of the Danaher board could have acted impartially, demand is excused.

▌ANALYSIS

The court listed two other situations in which the standard for determining demand excusal set forth in this case (appropriately referred to as the *Rales* standard) would be applicable, and the *Aronson* test would not: (1) where a business decision was made by the board of a company, but a majority of the directors making the decision have

been replaced; and (2) where the subject of the derivative suit is not a business decision of the board.

■■■

Quicknotes

BUSINESS JUDGMENT RULE Doctrine relieving corporate directors and/or officers from liability for decisions honestly and rationally made in the corporation's best interests.

CERTIFIED QUESTION A question that is taken from federal court to the state supreme court so that the court may rule on the issue, or that is taken from a federal court of appeals to the United States Supreme Court.

DEMAND REQUIREMENT Requirement that a shareholder make a demand for corrective action by the board of directors before commencing a derivative suit.

DERIVATIVE SUIT Action asserted by a shareholder in order to enforce a cause of action on behalf of the corporation.

■■■

Zapata Corp. v. Maldonado

Board of directors/corporation (D) v. Shareholder (P)

Del. Sup. Ct., 430 A.2d 779 (1981).

NATURE OF CASE: Interlocutory appeal in a stockholder's derivative suit.

FACT SUMMARY: Maldonado (P) had initiated a derivative suit charging officers and directors of Zapata (D) with breaches of fiduciary duty, but four years later an "Independent Investigation Committee" of two disinterested directors recommended dismissing the action.

🏛 RULE OF LAW
Where the making of a prior demand upon the directors of a corporation to sue is excused and a stockholder initiates a derivative suit on behalf of the corporation, the board of directors or an independent committee appointed by the board can move to dismiss the derivative suit as detrimental to the corporation's best interests, and the court should apply a two-step test to the motion: (1) has the corporation proved independence, good faith, and a reasonable investigation?; and (2) does the court feel, applying its own independent business judgment, that the motion should be granted?

FACTS: At the time Maldonado (P) instituted a derivative suit against Zapata (D), he was excused from making a prior demand on the board of directors because they were all defendants (Maldonado [P] asserting a breach of fiduciary duty on the part of officers and directors of Zapata [D]). The board had changed membership when, four years later, it appointed an "independent investigation committee," composed of two new directors, to investigate the litigation. The committee recommended dismissing the action, calling its continued maintenance "inimical to the company's best interests . . ." In an interlocutory appeal before the Supreme Court of Delaware, the primary focus was on whether or not the aforementioned committee had the power to dismiss the action.

ISSUE: In a case in which a stockholder acted properly in instituting a derivative suit on behalf of the corporation without first making a demand on the board of directors to sue, can the board of directors, or an independent committee appointed by the board move to dismiss the suit as detrimental to the best interests of the corporation?

HOLDING AND DECISION: (Quillen, J.) Yes. Where the making of a prior demand upon the directors of a corporation to sue is excused and a stockholder initiates a derivative suit on behalf of the corporation, the board of directors or an independent committee appointed by the board can move to dismiss the derivative suit as

detrimental to the corporation's best interests and the court should apply a two-step test to the motion: (1) has the corporation proved independence, good faith, and a reasonable investigation?; and (2) does the court feel, applying its own independent business judgment, that the motion should be granted? Where, as in this case, a stockholder acted properly in bringing a derivative suit without first demanding the directors file suit (i.e., where such a demand is "excused"), the board of directors or an independent committee they appoint has the power to choose not to pursue the litigation because such would not be in the best interests of the corporation. The fact that a majority of the board may have been tainted by self-interest is not per se a legal bar to the delegation of the board's power to an independent committee composed of disinterested board members. Thus, a committee, such as that involved in this case, can properly act for the corporation to move to dismiss derivative litigation that is believed to be detrimental to the corporation's best interests. When faced with such a motion, the court should give each side an opportunity to make a record on the motion. The moving party should be prepared to meet the normal burden of showing that there is no genuine issue as to any material fact and that it is entitled to dismiss as a matter of law. The court should apply a two-step test to the motion. First, it should inquire into the independence and good faith of the committee and the bases supporting its conclusions. To aid in such inquiries, limited discovery may be ordered. If the court determines either that the committee is not independent or has not shown reasonable bases for its conclusions, or if the court is not satisfied for other reasons relating to the process, including but not limited to the good faith of the committee, the court shall deny the corporation's motion. It must be remembered that the corporation has the burden of proving independence, good faith, and reasonableness. If the court is satisfied that the committee was independent and showed reasonable bases for good-faith findings and recommendations, the court may proceed, in its discretion, to the second step. This second step provides the essential key in striking the balance between legitimate corporate claims, as expressed in a derivative stockholder suit, and a corporation's best interests, as expressed by an independent investigating committee. The court should determine, applying its own independent business judgment, whether the motion should be granted. This second step is intended to thwart instances where corporation actions meet the criteria of stop one, but the result does not appear to satisfy the spirit, or where corporate actions

Continued on next page.

would simply prematurely terminate a stockholder griev-
ance deserving of further consideration in the corporation's
interest. Of course, the court must carefully consider and
weigh how compelling the corporate interest in dismissal is
when faced with a nonfrivolous lawsuit. It should, when
appropriate, give special consideration to matters of law
and public policy in addition to the corporation's best
interests. If, after all of this, the court's independent business judgment is satisfied, it may proceed to grant the
motion, subject, of course, to any equitable terms or conditions it finds necessary or desirable. Reversed and
remanded.

▶ ANALYSIS

Other courts have chosen to treat this type of situation as
one where the "business judgment rule" is applicable. They
look to see if the committee to whom the board of directors delegated the responsibility of determining the
litigation at issue should be continued was composed of
independent and disinterested members and if it conducted a proper review of the matters before it to reach
a good-faith business judgment concerning whether or not
to continue the litigation. If it did, the committee's decision
stands. This court found that approach too one-sided, as
tending to wrest bona fide derivative actions away from
well-meaning derivative plaintiffs and robbing the shareholders of an effective intracorporate means of policing
boards of directors.

■══■

Quicknotes

BREACH OF FIDUCIARY DUTY The failure of a fiduciary to
observe the standard of care exercised by professionals
of similar education and experience.

BUSINESS JUDGMENT RULE Doctrine relieving corporate
directors and/or officers from liability for decisions honestly and rationally made in the corporation's best
interests.

DERIVATIVE SUIT Action asserted by a shareholder in
order to enforce a cause of action on behalf of the
corporation.

INTERLOCUTORY APPEAL Appeal of an issue that does not
resolve the disposition of the case, but is essential to a
determination of the parties' legal rights.

■══■

In re Oracle Corp. Derivative Litigation

Shareholders (P) v. Directors (D)

Del. Ch. Ct., 824 A.2d 917 (2003).

NATURE OF CASE: Motion to terminate a derivative action.

FACT SUMMARY: Oracle Corp.'s special litigation committee moved to terminate a derivative action brought on Oracle's behalf, claiming it was independent.

🏛 RULE OF LAW

A special litigation committee does not meet its burden of demonstrating the absence of a material dispute of fact about its independence where its members are professors at a university that has ties to the corporation and to the defendants that are the subject of a derivative action that the committee is investigating.

FACTS: Shareholders (P) of Oracle Corp. (Oracle) brought a derivative action asserting insider trading by four members (D) of Oracle's board of directors—Ellison (D), Henley (D), Lucas (D), and Boskin (D). Ellison (D) was Oracle's Chairman and one of the wealthiest men in the world. The suit alleged breaches of fiduciary duty by those directors (D) as well as by the non-trading directors (D), whose indifference according to the plaintiff shareholders (P) amounted to subjective bad faith. Oracle formed a special litigation committee (SLC) to investigate the charges in the derivative action and to determine whether to press the claims raised, terminate the action, or settle. Two Oracle board members, who joined the board after the alleged breaches, were named to the SLC. Both were professors at Stanford University. Both agreed to give up any SLC-related compensation if their compensation was deemed to impair their impartiality. The independence of the SLC's legal and analytic advisors was not challenged. The SLC's investigation was extensive, and the committee produced an extremely lengthy report that concluded that Oracle should not pursue any of the derivative action claims. The SLC based its opinion on Oracle's quarterly earnings cycle, and determined that none of the accused directors had possessed material, non-public information. In its report, the SLC took the position that its members were independent. In this regard, the report pointed out that the SLC members received no compensation from Oracle other than as directors, that neither were on the board at the time of the alleged wrongdoing, that they were willing to return their compensation, and that there were no other material ties between the defendants and the SLC members. However, the report failed to indicate that there were significant ties between Oracle, the trading defendants (D), and Stanford University (Stanford)—namely, in the form of very large donations, or potential donations, of which the SLC members were aware. In addition, one of the SLC members had been taught by one of the trading defendants (D), and the two were both senior fellows and steering committee members of a Stanford research institute. The SLC contended that even together, these facts regarding the ties among Oracle, the trading defendants (D), Stanford, and the SLC members did not impair the SLC's independence. In so arguing, the SLC placed great weight on the fact that none of the trading defendants (D) had the practical ability to deprive either SLC member of their current positions at Stanford. Nor, given their tenure, did Stanford itself have any practical ability to punish them for taking action adverse to Oracle or any of the defendants.

ISSUE: Does a special litigation committee meet its burden of demonstrating the absence of a material dispute of fact about its independence where its members are professors at a university that has ties to the corporation and to the defendants that are the subject of a derivative action that the committee is investigating?

HOLDING AND DECISION: (Strine, V. Chan.) No. A special litigation committee does not meet its burden of demonstrating the absence of a material dispute of fact about its independence where its members are professors at a university that has ties to the corporation and to the defendants that are the subject of a derivative action that the committee is investigating. In analyzing whether the SLC was independent, emphasis should not be placed exclusively on domination and control. Instead, the law should take into account human nature, human motivations, and the social nature of humans. Thus, a court would not only consider greed or avarice, but would also take into account envy, love, friendship, collegiality, and other like motivators. At bottom, the question of independence turns on whether a director is, for any substantial reason, incapable of making a decision with only the best interests of the corporation in mind. Thus, here, the issue is whether the SLC can independently make the difficult decision entrusted to it. In the context of human nature, the SLC has not met its burden to show the absence of a material factual question about its independence. This is the case because the ties among the SLC, the trading defendants (D), and Stanford are so substantial that they cause reasonable doubt about the SLC's ability to impartially consider whether the trading defendants (D) should face suit. The SLC members were already being asked to consider whether the company should level extremely

Continued on next page.

serious accusations of wrongdoing against fellow board members. As to one of the trading defendants (D), Boskin (D), the SLC members faced the additional task of having to determine whether to press serious charges against a fellow professor at their university. Even more daunting was that one of the SLC members had a long history with Boskin (D) and served together with him on a university research institute. That SLC member would find it difficult to assess the Boskin's (D) conduct without pondering his own associations and mutual affiliations with him. This would likewise be true with regard to those trading defendants (D) who were significant university benefactors. In addition, the SLC has not made a convincing argument that tenured faculty are indifferent to large contributors to their institutions, such that a tenured faculty member would not be worried about writing a report finding that a suit by the corporation should proceed against a large contributor and that there was credible evidence that he had engaged in illegal insider trading. To conclude otherwise, would rest on a narrow-minded understanding of the way that collegiality works in institutional settings. Finally, Ellison (D) had publicly indicated that he would make very large contributions to Stanford, and it is implausible that the SLC members were not aware of his intentions. Motion to terminate denied.

▌**ANALYSIS**

The Delaware Supreme Court has reaffirmed that the SLC has the burden of establishing its own independence by a yardstick that must be "like Caesar's wife"—"above reproach." Moreover, unlike the pre-suit demand context, the SLC analysis contemplates not only a shift in the burden of persuasion, but also the availability of discovery into various issues, including independence. Moreover, because the members of an SLC are vested with enormous power to seek dismissal of a derivative suit brought against their director-colleagues in a setting where pre-suit demand is already excused, the Court of Chancery must exercise careful oversight of the members of the SLC and the SLC's process.

■■■■

Quicknotes

BAD FAITH Conduct that is intentionally misleading or deceptive.

BONA FIDE In good faith.

SHAREHOLDER An individual who owns shares of stock in a corporation.

SHAREHOLDER'S DERIVATIVE ACTION Action asserted by a shareholder in order to enforce a cause of action on behalf of the corporation.

■■■■

Joy v. North

[Parties not identified]

692 F.2d 880 (2d Cir. 1982).

NATURE OF CASE: Motion to dismiss a federal diversity derivative action.

FACT SUMMARY: Citytrust's Special Litigation Committee recommended the dismissal of a derivation action brought in federal court under diversity jurisdiction. The federal court determined that under state law it was required to review the committee's decision.

🏛 RULE OF LAW

A special litigation committee's recommendation regarding the termination of derivative litigation must be supported by a demonstration that the derivative action is more likely than not to be against the interests of the corporation.

FACTS: Citytrust's Special Litigation Committee recommended the dismissal of a derivation action brought in federal court under diversity jurisdiction, finding that there was "no reasonable possibility" 23 outside defendants would be held liable. The federal court determined that state law would require judicial review of the committee's decision, and that the committee would bear the burden of proving that continuing with the litigation would more likely than not be against the corporation's interest.

ISSUE: Must a special litigation committee's recommendation regarding the termination of derivative litigation be supported by a demonstration that the derivative action is more likely than not to be against the interests of the corporation?

HOLDING AND DECISION: (Winter, J.) Yes. A special litigation committee's recommendation regarding the termination of derivative litigation must be supported by a demonstration that the derivative action is more likely than not to be against the interests of the corporation. Courts have expertise in determining whether lawsuits should be terminated, so judicial review of such decisions made by special litigation committees is not too difficult or onerous for the courts. Also, the wide discretion afforded directors under the business judgment rule does not apply when a special litigation committee recommends dismissal of a suit. In such cases, the burden is on the moving party—the committee—as in motions for summary judgment generally, to demonstrate that the action is more likely than not to be against the interests of the corporation. This showing is to be based on the underlying data developed in the course of discovery and of the committee's investigation and the committee's reasoning, not simply its naked conclusions. The court's function is to weigh the probability of future benefit to the corporation,

not to decide the underlying litigation on its merits. Factors the court should weigh include attorneys' fees, out-of-pocket expenses, time spent by corporate personnel on the litigation, and non-discretionary indemnification, but not insurance that has already been purchased. If after the court weighs these factors it finds a likely net return to the corporation that is insubstantial relative to shareholder equity, it may take into account two other items as costs. First, it may consider the impact of distraction of key personnel by continued litigation. Second, it may take into account potential lost profits which may result from the publicity of a trial. Motion to dismiss is denied.

DISSENT IN PART: (Cardamone, J.) The majority purports to apply the *Zapata* standard, but goes beyond it. Instead of giving the trial court discretion as to whether to apply its own business judgment, the majority mandates the application of the court's business judgment through an unworkable calculus. The factors listed by the majority are unclear and unquantifiable. They raise more questions than they answer. Even more fundamentally erroneous, however, is the majority's premise that judges are equipped to make business judgments. Such judgments should be left to businessmen, as should the decision whether to pursue litigation, since that decision is a business choice—not a judicial decision. Existing law adequately addresses the situation where a special litigation committee has not acted independently. Thus, there is no need for judicial second-guessing of business decisions rendered by independent special litigation committees.

▶ *ANALYSIS*

Under *Zapata Corp. v. Maldonado*, 430 A.2d 779 (Del. 1981), the SLC must persuade the court that: (1) its members were independent; (2) that they acted in good faith; and (3) that they had reasonable bases for their recommendations. If the SLC meets that burden, the court is free to grant its motion or may, in its discretion, undertake its own examination of whether it would be in the corporation's best interest for the litigation to terminate or advance.

▬▬▬

Quicknotes

BUSINESS JUDGMENT RULE Doctrine relieving corporate directors and/or officers from liability for decisions honestly and rationally made in the corporation's best interests.

Continued on next page.

DIVERSITY JURISDICTION The authority of a federal court to hear and determine cases involving a statutory sum and in which the parties are citizens of different states, or in which one party is an alien.

SHAREHOLDER'S DERIVATIVE ACTION Action asserted by a shareholder in order to enforce a cause of action on behalf of the corporation.

Carlton Investments v. TLC Beatrice International Holdings, Inc.

Shareholder (P) v. Corporation (D)

Del. Ch. Ct., 1997 WL 305829 (May 30, 1997).

NATURE OF CASE: Motion to approve a proposed settlement of a derivative action.

FACT SUMMARY: The Chancery Court reviewed a Special Litigation Committee's (SLC's) proposed settlement of a derivative action on behalf of TLC Beatrice International Holdings, Inc., (TLC Beatrice) (D).

🏛 RULE OF LAW
A proposed settlement negotiated by a Special Litigation Committee (SLC) is to be reviewed under the two-step approach set forth in *Zapata Corp. v. Maldonado*, involving, first, a review of the SLC's independence, good faith, and reasonableness of its decision, and, second, a discretionary business judgment review of the settlement's merits.

FACTS: Carlton Investments (Carlton) (P) brought a derivative action on behalf of TLC Beatrice International Holdings, Inc., (TLC Beatrice) (D) alleging breaches of fiduciary duties and other violations by the company's officers and directors in connection with the compensation package of Lewis, its former chief executive officer (CEO). The case was strongly contested on both sides, and after more than a year of extensive discovery and several contested motions, the company's board unanimously voted to add two new directors and to constitute them as a Special Litigation Committee (SLC), empowering it to investigate the allegations of misconduct and determine the best course of action for the company with regard to the derivative action. After a five-month investigation of eleven principal claims alleged by Carlton (P), the SLC entered into a proposed settlement with Lewis's Estate (Estate). Carlton (P) claimed the settlement was inadequate and opposed it. The SLC moved the Chancery Court to approve the settlement.

ISSUE: Is a proposed settlement negotiated by a Special Litigation Committee (SLC) to be reviewed under the two-step approach set forth in *Zapata Corp. v. Maldonado*, involving, first, a review of the SLC's independence, good faith, and reasonableness of its decision, and, second, a discretionary business judgment review of the settlement's merits?

HOLDING AND DECISION: (Allen, Chan.) Yes. A proposed settlement negotiated by a Special Litigation Committee (SLC) is to be reviewed under the two-step approach set forth in *Zapata Corp. v. Maldonado*, 430 A.2d 779 (Del. 1981), involving, first, a review of the SLC's independence, good faith, and reasonableness of its decision, and, second, a discretionary business judgment

review of the settlement's merits. In general, when reviewing settlements, the court must consider whether the proposed settlement is fair and reasonable in light of the factual support for the alleged claims and defenses in the discovery record before it. The court does not make substantive determinations concerning disputed facts or the merits of the claims alleged. Here, applying the first step of the *Zapata* test, the SLC and its counsel proceeded in good faith throughout the investigation and negotiation of the proposed settlement; the conclusions reached by the SLC, which formed the basis for the amount of the proposed settlement, were well informed by the existing record; and the proposed settlement falls within a range of reasonable solutions to the problem presented. This should be enough to support the settlement, but if undertaking the second *Zapata* step is necessary, with the court exercising its own business judgment of the merits of the settlement, the court's conclusion is that this settlement represents a reasonable compromise of the claims asserted.

▶ ANALYSIS

The court had difficulty with the second *Zapata* step, saying that "As to the conceptually difficult second step of the *Zapata* technique, it is difficult to rationalize in principle; but it must have been designed to offer protection for cases in which, while the court could not consciously determine on the first leg of the analysis that there was no want of independence or good faith, it nevertheless 'felt' that the result reached was 'irrational' or 'egregious' or some other such extreme word." The court indicated that courts ordinarily should not exercise such business judgment except where doing so will protect shareholder welfare.

■▬■

Quicknotes

BREACH OF FIDUCIARY DUTY The failure of a fiduciary to observe the standard of care exercised by professionals of similar education and experience.

BUSINESS JUDGMENT RULE Doctrine relieving corporate directors and/or officers from liability for decisions honestly and rationally made in the corporation's best interests.

SHAREHOLDER'S DERIVATIVE ACTION Action asserted by a shareholder in order to enforce a cause of action on behalf of the corporation.

■▬■

Transactions in Control

Quick Reference Rules of Law

Zetlin v. Hanson Holdings, Inc.

Minority shareholder (P) v. Corporation (D)

N.Y. Ct. App. 397 N.E.2d 387 (1979).

NATURE OF CASE: Appeal from an order in favor of the defendants in an action involving the sale of majority shares of a corporation.

FACT SUMMARY: When Hanson Holdings (D) and the Sylvestri family (D) sold their controlling interest in Gable Industries for a premium price, Zetlin (P), a minority shareholder, brought suit, contending that minority shareholders were entitled to an opportunity to share equally in any premium paid for a controlling interest.

RULE OF LAW

Absent looting of corporate assets, conversion of a corporate opportunity, fraud or other acts of bad faith, a controlling stockholder is free to sell, and a purchaser is free to buy, that controlling interest at a premium price.

FACTS: Zetlin (P) held a two percent interest in Gable Industries (Gable). Hanson Holdings (Hanson) (D) and members of the Sylvestri family (D) owned 44 percent of Gable's shares. After the Sylvestri family (D) and Hanson (D) sold their controlling interest at a premium price per share, Zetlin (P) brought suit, contending that minority stockholders were entitled to an opportunity to share equally in any premium paid for a controlling interest in the corporation. The appellate division disagreed. Zetlin (P) appealed.

ISSUE: Absent looting of corporate assets, conversion of a corporate opportunity, fraud or other acts of bad faith, is a controlling stockholder free to sell, and is a purchaser free to buy, that controlling interest at a premium price?

HOLDING AND DECISION: [Judge not stated in casebook excerpt.] Yes. Absent looting of corporate assets, conversion of a corporate opportunity, fraud or other acts of bad faith, a controlling stockholder is free to sell, and a purchaser is free to buy, that controlling interest at a premium price. Certainly, minority shareholders are entitled to protection against abuse by controlling shareholders. They are not entitled, however, to inhibit the legitimate interests of the other stockholders. It is for this reason that control shares usually command a premium price. The premium is the added amount an investor is willing to pay for the privilege of directly influencing the corporation's affairs. Order affirmed.

ANALYSIS

Zetlin's (P) contention would profoundly affect the manner in which controlling stock interests are now transferred. It would require, essentially, that a controlling interest be transferred only by means of an offer to all stockholders, that is, a tender offer. The New York Court of Appeals declared that this would be contrary to existing law and that the legislature is best suited to make radical changes.

Quicknotes

CONTROLLING SHAREHOLDER A person who has power to vote a majority of the outstanding shares of a corporation, or who is able to direct the management of the corporation with a smaller block of stock because the remaining shares are scattered among small, disorganized holdings.

CORPORATE OPPORTUNITY An opportunity that a fiduciary to a corporation has to take advantage of information acquired by virtue of his or her position for the individual's benefit.

MINORITY SHAREHOLDER A stockholder in a corporation controlling such a small portion of outstanding shares that its votes have no influence in the management of the corporation.

Perlman v. Feldmann

Minority shareholder (P) v. Former controlling shareholder (D)

219 F.2d 173 (2d Cir.), *cert. denied,* 349 U.S. 952 (1955).

NATURE OF CASE: Appeal from a judgment in an action to compel an accounting in the sale of a controlling corporate interest.

FACT SUMMARY: After Feldmann (D) sold his controlling interest in the Newport Steel Corporation, Perlman (P) and other minority stockholders (P) brought a derivative action to compel accounting for, and restitution of, allegedly illegal gains accruing to Feldmann (D) as a result of the sale.

🏛 **RULE OF LAW**
Directors and dominant stockholders stand in a fiduciary relationship to the corporation and to the minority stockholders as beneficiaries thereof.

FACTS: Newport Steel Corporation (Newport) operated mills for the production of steel sheets for sale to manufacturers of steel products. Feldmann (D), the dominant stockholder, chairman of the board of directors, and Newport's president, negotiated a sale of the controlling interest in Newport to a syndicate organized as Wilport Company. A steel shortage existed at the time as a result of demand during the Korean War. Perlman (P) and other minority stockholders (P) brought this derivative action to compel an accounting for, and restitution of, allegedly illegal gains accruing to Feldmann (D) and the other majority stockholders as a result of the sale. The trial court found the share price to be a fair one for a control block of stock. Perlman (P) and the others (P) appealed.

ISSUE: Do directors and dominant stockholders stand in a fiduciary relationship to the corporation and to the minority stockholders as beneficiaries thereof?

HOLDING AND DECISION: (Clark, C.J.) Yes. Directors and dominant stockholders stand in a fiduciary relationship to the corporation and to the minority stockholders as beneficiaries thereof. However, a majority stockholder can dispose of his controlling block of stock to outsiders without having to account to his corporation for profits. But when the sale necessarily results in a sacrifice of an element of corporate good will and consequent unusual profit to the fiduciary who has caused the sacrifice, he should account for his gains. In a time of market shortage, where a call on a corporation's product commands an unusually large premium, a fiduciary may not appropriate to himself the value of this premium. There need not be an absolute certainty that a corporate opportunity is involved; only a possibility of corporate gain is necessary to trigger the fiduciary duty and recovery for breach of that duty. Hence, to the extent that the price

received by Feldmann (D) and the others included such a gain, which rightfully belonged to the corporation, he is accountable to the minority stockholders (P), who are entitled to a recovery in their own right, instead of in the right of Newport Steel. Reversed and remanded.

DISSENT: (Swan, J.) The majority's opinion does not specify exactly the fiduciary duty Feldmann (D) violated, either as a director or as a dominant shareholder. As a dominant shareholder, Feldmann (D) did not have a duty to refrain from selling the stock he controlled. There was also no indication that Wilport would use its newly acquired power to injure Newport, and there is nothing illegal in a dominant shareholder purchasing products made by the company at the same price offered to other customers—which is what the Wilport members did. The majority says that the price paid for the stock included compensation for a "corporate asset," which it describes as "the ability to control the allocation of the corporate product in a time of short supply, through control of the board of directors." If the implication of this is that during tight market conditions a dominant shareholder has a fiduciary duty not to sell his stock to users of the corporation's products who wish to buy a controlling block of stock in order to be able to purchase part of the corporation's output at the same mill list prices as are offered to other customers, such a holding should not stand. Only if Feldmann (D) received value in excess of what his stock was worth, for performing duties he was already under an obligation to perform, should he account for the difference in value. However, the record and trial court findings support that Feldmann (D) did not receive such excess value, since a controlling block of stock is worth significantly more than a block without such control. Finally, the majority is incorrect in holding that the shareholders (P) are entitled to recover in their own right instead of in the corporation's right. This holding contradicts the majority's theory that the price of the stock "included compensation for the sale of a corporate asset." If indeed a corporate asset was sold, then the corporation, not its shareholders, should be entitled to the proceeds from the sale of that asset.

▌ *ANALYSIS*

The court found no fraud, no misuse of confidential information, and no outright looting of a helpless corporation. On the other hand, it did not find compliance with the high standard applied as the rule of law, which other courts have come to expect and demand of corporate fiduciaries.

Continued on next page.

In the words of Judge Cardozo, many forms of conduct permissible in a workaday world for those acting at arm's length are forbidden to those bound by fiduciary ties.

Quicknotes

CORPORATE OPPORTUNITY An opportunity that a fiduciary to a corporation has to take advantage of information acquired by virtue of his or her position for the individual's benefit.

FIDUCIARY DUTY A legal obligation to act for the benefit of another, including subordinating one's personal interests to that of the other person.

MINORITY SHAREHOLDER A stockholder in a corporation controlling such a small portion of outstanding shares that its votes have no influence in the management of the corporation.

RESTITUTION The return or restoration of what the defendant has gained in a transaction to prevent the unjust enrichment of the defendant.

In re Delphi Financial Group Shareholder Litigation

Shareholders (P) v. Board of directors (D)

Del. Ch. Ct., 2012 WL 729232 (Mar. 6, 2012).

NATURE OF CASE: Motion for preliminary injunction.

FACT SUMMARY: After Japanese corporation TMH bid to purchase Delphi Financial Group, Inc. (Delphi), the founder of Delphi (D), Robert Rosenkranz (D) threatened to sour the deal unless his compensation for the deal was considerably higher than all other stockholders, in contravention of the corporate charter. After the board agreed to his demands, the shareholders sought to enjoin the acquisition.

RULE OF LAW

A corporate charter, along with its accompanying bylaws, is a contract between the corporation's stockholders, carrying an inherent implied covenant of good faith and fair dealing.

FACTS: Delphi Financial Group, Inc. (Delphi) is a financial services holding company incorporated in Delaware, and the company's subsidiaries are insurance businesses. Robert Rosenkranz (D), who is Delphi's current chief executive officer (CEO) and chairman, founded Delphi in 1987. Delphi's board consisted of nine directors (D). Seven of the directors (D) are independent and do not hold officer positions within Delphi. After Delphi's initial public offering (IPO) in 1990, the company's ownership was divided between holders of Class A common stock and Class B common stock. Delphi Class A shares were widely held, publicly traded, and entitled to one vote per share. Class B shares were held entirely by Rosenkranz (D) and his affiliates and were entitled to ten votes per share. Although Rosenkranz held 49.9 percent of the Delphi stockholder voting power through his Class B shares, his stock ownership accounted for only around 13 percent of Delphi's equity. In addition, the Delphi corporate charter contained a provision prohibiting disparate consideration between Class A and B stock in the event of a merger. TMH, a Japanese holding company, had no affiliation with Rosenkranz (D), Delphi, or any of the directors or officers (D) when it made an unsolicited offer to buy Delphi. Senior management from Delphi and TMH had general discussions regarding a potential merger, with Rosenkranz (D) representing Delphi. During this time, Rosenkranz (D) considered how he might receive a premium on his Class B shares above what the Class A stockholders would receive in the merger, despite the charter prohibition, and Rosenkranz (D) knew that any premium would require a charter amendment. After much negotiation, TMH offered $45 per share, which at the time was a 106 percent premium over market. Rosenkranz (D) presented TMH's offer to the board (D), acknowledging the offer's substantial premium, but told the board (D) that he nonetheless found it inadequate from his perspective as controlling stockholder, and that he would be unlikely to vote his Class B shares in favor of merger at that price. Because of the conflict of interest Rosenkranz's (D) position created, the board (D) agreed to form a special committee, comprising the Board's seven independent directors to evaluate the proposal from TMH, direct further discussions with TMH, and consider alternatives to the TMH proposal. Simultaneously with the negotiations with TMH, a sub-committee of the special committee negotiated with Rosenkranz (D) regarding whether there would be any disparate allocation of the merger consideration and, if so, what the differential would be. The sub-committee engaged in a back-and-forth with Rosenkranz (D) in the days leading up to an October 14, 2011, meeting with TMH representatives, and neither side wanted to lose momentum in the negotiations with TMH or insult the TMH representatives who were flying in from Japan, and so both sides felt that it was important to keep the October 14th meeting date. With TMH's offer of $46 per share ($45 plus a $1 special dividend for all shareholders) on the table, the sub-committee and Rosenkranz (D) continued their negotiations regarding the division of the merger consideration. Believing the deal to be in jeopardy, the special committee approved a differential of $44.875 for Class A and $53.875 for Class B and accepted TMH's offer. In the merger agreements, one of the key provisions obtained by the special committee was the non-waivable conditioning of the merger on the affirmative vote of a majority of the disinterested Class A stockholders. In addition, since Section Seven of Delphi's Charter prohibits the unequal distribution of merger consideration, the parties agreed to condition the merger on the approval of a charter amendment. The sub-committee found such an amendment to be in the best interests of the Class A stockholders as it was the only way to enable the Class A stockholders to obtain a substantial premium on their shares. Delphi shareholders (P) claimed that the Delphi directors (D) and Rosenkranz (D) breached their fiduciary duties to the Class A stockholders in approving the differential, and that Rosenkranz (D) breached his fiduciary and contractual obligations in seeking such a differential in the first place, because the Delphi charter prohibits the unequal distribution of merger consideration.

ISSUE: Is a corporate charter, along with its accompanying bylaws, a contract between the corporation's

Continued on next page.

stockholders, carrying an inherent implied covenant of good faith and fair dealing?

HOLDING AND DECISION: (Glasscock, V.

Chan.) Yes. A corporate charter, along with its accompanying bylaws, is a contract between the corporation's stockholders carrying an inherent implied covenant of good faith and fair dealing. This implied covenant "embodies the law's expectation that each party to a contract will act with good faith toward the other with respect to the subject matter of the contract." Rosenkranz's (D) argument that under Delaware law, a controlling stockholder is entitled to negotiate a control premium for its shares is correct, and a controlling stockholder is free to consider its interests alone in weighing the decision to sell its shares or evaluating the adequacy of a given price. In addition, the charter provided for its own amendment, so presumably, Rosenkranz (D) could have bought the right to a control premium back from the stockholders through a negotiated vote in favor of a charter amendment. But that doesn't mean that in the midst of merger negotiations, he can coerce such an amendment, because that would render the charter rights illusory. The shareholders' (P) allegations essentially fall under two categories: those attacking the negotiation of the merger price, and those attacking the differential consideration. Their most persuasive argument is that despite a contrary provision in the corporate charter, Rosenkranz (D) sought and obtained a control premium for his shares, an effort that was facilitated by the executive and directors (D), and thereby breached his contractual and fiduciary duties. But whether the rights of the stockholder class (P) sound in breach of contract does not need to be decided at this preliminary stage. The shareholders (P) are reasonably likely to be able to demonstrate at trial that in negotiating for disparate consideration and only agreeing to support the merger if he received it, Rosenkranz (D) violated duties to the stockholders. While the shareholders (P) have shown a reasonable probability of success on the merits, injunctive relief is inappropriate because the threatened harm is largely, if not completely, remediable by damages. It is preferable to allow the stockholders (P) to decide whether they wish to go forward with the merger despite the imperfections of the process leading to its formulation. Preliminary injunction denied.

▶ *ANALYSIS*

In this case, Vice Chancellor Glasscock confirmed that a controlling stockholder is generally permitted to negotiate a control premium, and in doing so to act in his own best interests, without regard to the minority. In this case, however, Rosenkranz (D) already had essentially sold his right to a control premium to the Class A stockholders (P) through the charter prohibition in the IPO. He did that at the time of the IPO presumably to obtain a higher price in the IPO. Allowing a "second" control premium in the TMH transaction would amount to a wrongful transfer of con-

sideration from the Class A stockholders to Rosenkranz (D), and conditioning the merger upon approval of the charter amendment so as to permit disparate consideration was seen by the court as coercive.

◼▬◼▬◼

Quicknotes

BREACH OF FIDUCIARY DUTY The failure of a fiduciary to observe the standard of care exercised by professionals of similar education and experience.

IMPLIED COVENANT OF GOOD FAITH AND FAIR DEALING An implied warranty the parties will deal honestly in the satisfaction of their obligations and without intent to defraud.

INHERENT POWERS Authority possessed absent an express grant; powers derived from the nature of government.

◼▬◼▬◼

Brascan Ltd. v. Edper Equities Ltd.

Corporation (P) v. Purchaser of shares in corporation (D)

477 F. Supp. 773 (S.D.N.Y. 1979).

NATURE OF CASE: Action under § 14(e) of the Williams Act to force divestiture of stock purchases.

FACT SUMMARY: Brascan (P), a Canadian company traded on the American Stock Exchange, contended that Edper (D) violated § 14(e) of the Williams Act when Edper (D) acquired 24 percent of Brascan's (P) stock over two days. Brascan (P) claimed that this acquisition constituted a de facto tender offer and that Edper (D) therefore violated provisions requiring the announcement of further purchases.

> 🏛 **RULE OF LAW**
> The mere acquisition of a large portion of a company's stock by itself does not constitute a tender offer for purposes of § 14(e) of the Williams Act.

FACTS: Over two days, Edper (D) purchased 24 percent of Brascan (P), a Canadian company trading in Canada, in the United Kingdom, and on the American Stock Exchange. Edper (D) already held a 5 percent stake in Brascan (P) and had proposed a friendly acquisition, which Brascan (P) had rejected. Edper (D) then decided to purchase an additional 3 million Brascan (P) shares, and to do so through the American Stock Exchange to avoid Canadian regulations. Edper (D) informed Connacher, president of Gordon Securities Ltd., it might purchase up to three million shares at a premium price if these were available. Gordon Securities contacted between 30 and 50 institutional investors and 10 to 15 individual investors, who held large blocks of Brascan (P) shares, telling them that Edper (D) might be willing to purchase three to four million shares at 22.75 (which was several dollars above the trading price). Edper (D) authorized its broker to purchase 2.5 million shares at 22.75. Edper's (D) broker on the Exchange acquired 2.4 million shares (2 million of which were offered by Gordon Securities on behalf of the shareholders it had just solicited). By the end of the day, Edper (D) had purchased 3.1 million shares. Edper announced, in response to a demand from Canadian officials, that it had no plans to buy any more shares at that time. Nevertheless, the next day, without further public announcement, Edper (D) resumed its buying activity, and Gordon Securities again solicited large holders of Brascan (P). Edper (D) purchased 3.2 million shares at 22.75 or slightly higher, almost half of which came from Gordon Securities or its customers. Brascan (P) sued Edper (D) in federal district court, seeking to require Edper (D) to divest itself of the shares it had bought, claiming that the failure to announce that it was making further purchases violated § 14(e) of the Williams Act.

ISSUE: Does the mere acquisition of a large portion of a company's stock by itself constitute a tender offer for purposes of § 14(e) of the Williams Act?

HOLDING AND DECISION: (Leval, J.) No. The mere acquisition of a large portion of a company's stock by itself does not constitute a tender offer for purposes of § 14(e) of the Williams Act. The conduct Edper (D) engaged in does not constitute what is commonly understood as a tender offer. Edper (D) did not solicit numerous shareholders; its purchasing was not contingent on a minimum fixed number of shares being offered; it did not put out an offer at a fixed price; and the form of the transaction did not provide for tenders by the selling shareholders to be held for some period of time by the purchaser or a depositary. All Edper (D) did was to acquire a large amount of stock in open market purchases. Also, contrary to Brascan's (P) argument, Connacher was not Edper's (D) agent—just its broker. Even if Connacher was deemed to be Edper's (D) agent, Connacher's conduct also did not amount to a tender offer, since Connacher merely scouted between 30 and 50 large institutional holders of Brascan (P) stock, plus about a dozen large individual investors, to collect a large block for Edper (D) to purchase at a price agreeable to both sides of the transaction. This is privately negotiated block trading, which the Williams Act's legislative history indicates was not intended to be covered by the Act, even if such trading is a large accumulation of stock. Finally, Edper's (D) conduct fully meets only one of eight criteria for a tender offer. The first criterion calling for active and widespread solicitation of public shareholders is clearly not met. The second criterion, calling for a large accumulation of stock, is met. The third criterion calling for a premium over the prevailing market price is met, but only to a slight degree. The fourth criterion calling for firm offer terms, rather than negotiable terms, is not met. The fifth criterion, calling for the offer to be contingent on the tender of a fixed minimum number of shares, is met only to a slight degree. The sixth criterion calling for the offer to be open only for a limited period of time is not met. The seventh criterion calling for the offerees to be subjected to pressure to sell their stock was not met. And finally, the eighth criterion calling for public announcements of a purchasing program preceding or accompanying a rapid accumulation was not met. Therefore, Edper (D) did not violate § 14(e) of the Williams Act. Judgment on this issue for defendant.

Continued on next page.

▶ *ANALYSIS*

The Williams Act, passed in 1967, sought to provide share-holders sufficient time and information to make an informed decision about tendering their shares and to warn the market about an impending offer. Arguably, it was also intended to assure shareholders an equal opportunity to participate in offer premia and to discourage hostile tender offers on the margin. The Williams Act, however, does not define "tender offer." While a small number of cases have held that the Williams Act applies to large accumulations such as the one that is the subject of this case, most courts have rejected such an interpretation of the Act, since the consequence of bringing such large scale open market and privately negotiated purchases within the scope of the Williams Act would be to rule, in effect, that no large scale acquisition program may be lawfully accomplished except in the manner of a conventional tender offer—a consequence not supported by the Act's legislative history.

Quicknotes

AGENT An individual who has the authority to act on behalf of another.

DE FACTO STATUS In fact; something that is recognized by virtue of its existence in reality, but is illegal for failure to comply with statutory requirements.

TENDER OFFER An offer made by one corporation to the shareholders of a target corporation to purchase their shares subject to number, time, and price specifications.

Fundamental Transactions:
Mergers and Acquisitions

Quick Reference Rules of Law

Katz v. Bregman

Shareholder (P) v. Chief executive officer (P)

Del. Ch. Ct., 431 A.2d 1274 (1981).

NATURE OF CASE: Action to enjoin proposed sale of corporate assets.

FACT SUMMARY: In Katz's (P) action against Bregman (D), the chief executive officer of Plant Industries (Plant), to enjoin the proposed sale of the Canadian assets of Plant, Katz (P), a Plant shareholder, contended that a sale of substantially all the assets of a corporation required the unanimous vote of the stockholders.

🏛 RULE OF LAW
Under Delaware law the decision of a corporation to sell all or substantially all of its property and assets requires not only the approval of the corporation's board of directors, but also a resolution adopted by a majority of the outstanding stockholders of the corporation entitled to vote.

FACTS: Katz (P) was the owner of approximately 170,000 shares of common stock of Plant Industries (Plant), which had operations in the United States and Canada. After selling off Plant's unprofitable U.S. operations, Bregman (D), Plant's chief executive officer (CEO), embarked on a course of action designed to dispose of Plant's Canadian assets, which allegedly constituted Plant's only income producing facility during the four years prior to the proposed sale. The purpose of the sale, which would have disposed of around 51 percent of Plant's total assets, which produced 45 percent of its income, was to improve Plant's balance sheet. Plant entered into a firm bid with Vulcan, which was later matched and then topped by Universal. Katz (P) then brought an action to enjoin the sale of the Canadian assets, contending that a sale of all or substantially all the assets of a corporation required the unanimous vote of the shareholders.

ISSUE: Under Delaware law, does the decision of a corporation to sell all or substantially all of its property and assets require the approval not only of the corporation's board of directors, but also a resolution adopted by a majority of the outstanding shareholders of the corporation entitled to vote?

HOLDING AND DECISION: (Marvel, Chan.) Yes. Under Delaware law, the decision of a corporation to sell all or substantially all of its property and assets requires not only the approval of the corporation's board of directors, but also a resolution adopted by a majority of the outstanding stockholders of the corporation entitled to vote. Katz (P), in his bid for relief sought, relied on the fact that the board studiously refused to consider a potentially higher bid for the assets in question. Here, the proposed sale of Plant's Canadian operations would, if consummated, constitute a sale of substantially all of the assets of Plant Industries as presently constituted. Thus, under the law of the State of Delaware, an injunction should issue preventing the consummation of such sale at least until it has been approved by a majority of the outstanding stockholders of Plant, entitled to vote at a meeting duly called on at least 20 days' notice. A preliminary injunction against the consummation of such transaction, at least until stockholder approval is obtained, will be granted.

▶ ANALYSIS

At common law, it is generally accepted that a sale of substantially all assets of a corporation required unanimous shareholder approval. This is based on the theory that such a sale breached an implied contract among the shareholders to further the corporate enterprise. The case law has held that a sale of substantially all assets in the ordinary course of business does not require shareholder approval on the theory that such a sale does not prevent furtherance of the corporate enterprise.

■—■

Quicknotes

SUBSIDIARY A company a majority of whose shares are owned by another corporation and which is subject to that corporation's control.

■—■

Hariton v. Arco Electronics, Inc.

Shareholder (P) v. Corporation (D)

Del. Ch. Ct., 182 A.2d 22 (1962), *aff'd*, 188 A.2d 123 (1963).

NATURE OF CASE: Action to declare sale of corporate assets void.

FACT SUMMARY: Arco Electronics, Inc. (Arco) (D) sold all of its assets to Loral Corporation in exchange for Loral common stock. Hariton (P), a shareholder in Arco (D), challenged the transaction as a de facto merger.

🏛 RULE OF LAW
A corporation may sell its assets to another corporation even if the result is the same as a merger without following the statutory merger requirements.

FACTS: Arco Electronics, Inc. (Arco) (D) was an electronics distributor and Loral an electronics producer. Arco (D) had outstanding 486,500 shares of Class A common stock and 362,500 shares of Class B common stock. The rights of the holders of the Class A and Class B common stock differed only as to preferences in dividends. Arco's (D) balance sheet showed total assets of $3,013,642. Its net income for the preceding year was $273,466. Loral had total assets of $16,453,479. Its net income for the year was $1,301,618. After two rejected offers, Loral offered a purchase price based on the ratio of one share of Loral common stock for three shares of Arco (D) common stock. Arco (D) accepted this offer. The transaction was structured so that Arco (D) would convey and transfer to Loral all of its assets and property of every kind, tangible and intangible, and would grant to Loral the use of its name and slogans. Loral would assume and pay all of Arco's (D) debts and liabilities, and would issue to Arco (D) 283,000 shares of its common stock. Upon the closing of the transaction, Arco (D) would dissolve and distribute to its shareholders, pro rata, shares of the common stock of Loral. Arco (D) called a special meeting, at which the shareholders present voted unanimously in favor of the sale. After the transaction was carried out, Hariton (P), an Arco (D) shareholder, challenged the action as a de facto merger and sued to have it set aside since the statutory merger provisions were not complied with. Arco (D) argued that it had engaged in a legal sale of corporate assets and had complied with all the applicable provisions.

ISSUE: If a transaction is in the form of a sale of corporate assets but has the same effect as if a merger had been undertaken, must the formalities of a merger be followed?

HOLDING AND DECISION: (Short, V. Chan.) No. The statutes dealing with merger and sale of corporate assets may be overlapping in the sense that they may be used to achieve similar results, but the two procedures are subject to equal dignity. If all of the applicable provisions are complied with, a corporation may achieve a result in a manner that would be illegal under another statute. In other words, there is no interaction between these statutes, and since the sale of corporate assets statute was followed correctly, the provisions of the merger statute are of no relevance. The theory of de facto merger can only be introduced by the legislature, not the courts. Also, it is impossible to differentiate this transaction from one in which no dissolution of the selling corporation is required by the agreement since Arco (D) continued in existence after the sale, even though only to distribute the Loral stock to its shareholders. Therefore, Arco (D) didn't immediately cease to exist as it would have in an actual merger. Finally, the rationale of de facto merger that is based upon the theory that a shareholder shouldn't be forced to accept a new investment in a different corporation fails in this case. In Delaware, there is no right of appraisal for a sale of corporate assets, so Hariton (P) knew when he purchased the Arco (D) stock that Arco (D) might at any time sell all of its assets for stock in another corporation. Affirmed.

▶ *ANALYSIS*

The *Hariton* decision rejects the de facto merger doctrine set forth in *Farris v. Glen Alden Corp.*, 393 Pa. 427, 143 A.2d 25 (1958). The reason for the *Hariton* holding is a desire to give corporations greater freedom of reorganization than is given under the restrictive merger statutes. The court mentions the fact that no appraisal right is given for a sale of corporate assets is a possible indication of legislative sympathy for corporate freedom. The *Hariton* result is the minority rule and has been criticized for its emphasis on the form rather than the substance of the transaction in question. Since the merger procedure is authorized to achieve the result sought by Arco (D), it seems unfair to allow the use of another device to obtain the same result indirectly in order to deny the protections given to minority shareholders under the more direct approach.

Quicknotes

DE FACTO MERGER The acquisition of one company by another without compliance with the requirements of a statutory merger but treated by the courts as such.

DISSOLUTION Annulment or termination of a formal or legal bond, tie or contract.

Kahn v. Lynch Communication Systems, Inc.

Minority shareholder (P) v. Corporation (D)

Del. Sup. Ct., 638 A.2d 1110 (1994).

NATURE OF CASE: Appeal from judgment in a shareholder class action seeking monetary damages and seeking to enjoin a cash-out merger.

FACT SUMMARY: After the board of Lynch Communication Systems, Inc. (D) board approved a controlling shareholder's per share tender offer for its minority shares, Kahn (P) sought to enjoin the cash-out merger and to recover monetary damages.

🏛 RULE OF LAW
A shareholder owes a fiduciary duty if it owns a majority interest in or exercises control over the business affairs of the corporation.

FACTS: Alcatel (D), a subsidiary of a French corporation, acquired a large block of Lynch Communication Systems, Inc.'s (Lynch's) (D) common stock pursuant to a stock purchase agreement that also required an 80 percent affirmative vote of Lynch's (D) shareholders in the future for approval of any business combination. Alcatel (D) later opposed Lynch's (D) intention to acquire Telco, proposing instead that Lynch (D) acquire Celwave, an indirect subsidiary of Alcatel's (D) parent company. After an independent committee opposed that proposal, Alcatel (D) offered to acquire the entire equity interest in Lynch (D). When Alcatel's (D) offers were rejected as insufficient, it made a final offer, indicating it was ready to proceed with an unfriendly tender if its final offer was not approved. The offer was approved. Kahn (P), a minority shareholder, brought this class-action suit. The court upheld the board's action. Kahn (P) appealed.

ISSUE: Does a shareholder owe a fiduciary duty if it owns a majority interest in or exercises control over the business affairs of the corporation?

HOLDING AND DECISION: (Holland, J.) Yes. A shareholder owes a fiduciary duty if it owns a majority interest in or exercises control over the business affairs of the corporation. Despite its 43.3 percent minority shareholder interest, Alcatel (D) exercised control over Lynch (D) by dominating its corporate affairs. A controlling or dominating shareholder standing on both sides of a transaction bears the burden of proving its entire fairness, which can be established by showing that negotiations were conducted at arm's length and that there was no compulsion to reach an agreement. The Court of Chancery's determination that such was the case here is not supported by the record. Under the circumstances, the Court of Chancery erred in then shifting the burden of proof with regard to entire fairness to Kahn (P). Any semblance here of arm's length bargaining ended when the independent committee surrendered to the ultimatum accompanying Alcatel's (D) final offer. Reversed and remanded.

▶ ANALYSIS

The controlling stockholder relationship has the potential to influence, however subtly, the vote of minority stockholders in a manner that is not likely to occur in a transaction with a noncontrolling party. Even where no coercion is intended, shareholders might perceive that their disapproval could risk retaliation of some kind by the controlling stockholder. In this case, Lynch (D) was not in a position to shop for other acquirers, since Alcatel (D) could block any alternative transaction.

━━━

Quicknotes

CASH OUT MERGER Occurs when a merging company prematurely redeems the securities of a holder as part of the merger.

FIDUCIARY DUTY A legal obligation to act for the benefit of another, including subordinating one's personal interests to that of the other person.

TENDER OFFER An offer made by one corporation to the shareholders of a target corporation to purchase their shares subject to number, time, and price specifications.

━━━

Kahn v. M&F Worldwide Corp. et al.

Minority shareholder (P) v. Corporation (D)

Del. Sup. Ct., 88 A.3d 635 (2014) (*en banc*).

NATURE OF CASE: Appeal from judgment for defendants in action challenging a going private transaction.

FACT SUMMARY: Kahn (P) and other minority shareholders (P) of M&F Worldwide Corp. (MFW) (D) challenged a going private, controller buyout merger by MacAndrews & Forbes (M & F) (D), asserting that the appropriate standard of review should be entire fairness, rather than business judgment, notwithstanding that the transaction was conditioned on approval by an independent special committee and a vote of a majority of the minority shareholders. Kahn (P) also asserted that there were triable issues of fact as to the independence of some of the members of the special committee that approved the merger.

🏛 RULE OF LAW

A going private, controller buyout merger will be reviewed under the business judgment standard of review if, and only if: (i) the controller conditions the procession of the transaction on the approval of both a special committee and a majority of the minority stockholders; (ii) the special committee is independent; (iii) the special committee is empowered to freely select its own advisors and to say no definitively; (iv) the special committee meets its duty of care in negotiating a fair price; (v) the vote of the minority is informed; and (vi) there is no coercion of the minority.

FACTS: MacAndrews & Forbes (M & F) (D), which owned 43 percent of M&F Worldwide Corp. (MFW) (D), sought to take MFW (D) private in a merger initially valued at $24 per share. The merger was conditioned on approval by an independent special committee and a vote of the majority-of-the-minority stockholders. The MFW (D) board formed an independent special committee to negotiate with M & F (D). The special committee, comprised of four members, selected its own legal and financial advisors, met several times over several months, and negotiated vigorously with M & F (D). As a result of the negotiations, the special committee obtained an offer of $25 per share. In a vote of shareholders excluding M & F (D), 65.4 percent of the shares voted in favor of the transaction, and the transaction was consummated. Kahn (P) and other MFW minority shareholders (P) brought suit in the Delaware Chancery Court challenging the transaction. The Chancery Court ruled that the appropriate standard of review was business judgment, rather than entire fairness, where the controller buyout was conditioned on both the

approval of an independent special committee and a vote of a majority of the minority. Kahn (P) appealed, maintaining that notwithstanding the dual deal protections, the appropriate standard of review should be entire fairness, and that, in any event, three of the four special committee members were not independent. In this regard, Kahn (P) claimed that these three members (Webb (D), Dinh (D) and Byorum (D)) were beholden to Perelman (D), the owner of M & F (D), and a director of MFW (D), because of their prior business and/or social dealings with Perelman (D) or Perelman-related entities. As to Webb (D), Kahn (P) claimed he was not independent because he and Perelman (D) had shared a lucrative business partnership nine years earlier. As to Dinh (D), an attorney and law professor, Kahn (P) adduced evidence that Dinh's (D) law firm had advised M & F (D) and its affiliates, but such engagements were inactive by the time the merger was announced, and they had been disclosed to the special committee. Kahn (P) also claimed that Dinh (D) was influenced by another board member of M & F (D), Schwartz (D), who sat on the board of Dinh's (D) law school. However, at the time of the merger, Dinh (D) was fully tenured, and had been so even before he ever knew Schwartz (D). Schwartz (D) invited Dinh (D) to join the board of another company after the merger, which Kahn (P) alleged showed an ongoing relationship between Dinh (D) and Schwartz (D). Finally, as to Byorum (D), Kahn (D) adduced evidence that she had had prior dealings with Perelman (D), but failed to show there was an ongoing economic relationship with Perelman (D) that was material to her in any way. Advisory work she had done years prior to the merger for an M & F (D) affiliate had also been fully disclosed to the special committee. The Delaware Supreme Court granted review.

ISSUE: Will a going private, controller buyout merger be reviewed under the business judgment standard of review if, and only if: (i) the controller conditions the procession of the transaction on the approval of both a special committee and a majority of the minority stockholders; (ii) the special committee is independent; (iii) the special committee is empowered to freely select its own advisors and to say no definitively; (iv) the special committee meets its duty of care in negotiating a fair price; (v) the vote of the minority is informed; and (vi) there is no coercion of the minority?

HOLDING AND DECISION: (Holland, J.) Yes. A going private, controller buyout merger will be reviewed

Continued on next page.

under the business judgment standard of review if, and only if: (i) the controller conditions the procession of the transaction on the approval of both a special committee and a majority of the minority stockholders; (ii) the special committee is independent; (iii) the special committee is empowered to freely select its own advisors and to say no definitively; (iv) the special committee meets its duty of care in negotiating a fair price; (v) the vote of the minority is informed; and (vi) there is no coercion of the minority. This case presents an issue of first impression: what should be the standard of review for a merger between a controlling stockholder and its subsidiary, where the merger is conditioned ab initio upon the approval of both an independent, adequately empowered special committee that fulfills its duty of care, and the uncoerced, informed vote of a majority of the minority stockholders. The Court of Chancery reasoned that by giving controlling stockholders the opportunity to have a going private transaction reviewed under the business judgment rule, a strong incentive is created to give minority stockholders both procedural protections. Having both protections is critically different than a structure that uses only one of the procedural protections, as the "both" structure effects arm's-length merger steps by requiring two independent approvals. Nevertheless, Kahn (P) argues that neither procedural protection is adequate to protect minority stockholders, because possible ineptitude and timidity of directors may undermine the special committee protection, and because majority-of-the-minority votes may be unduly influenced by arbitrageurs that have an institutional bias to approve virtually any transaction that offers a market premium, however insubstantial it may be. Such a skeptical view is rejected, because independent directors are viewed largely as being effective at protecting public stockholders—and it is the exception when an independent director has little regard for her or his duties. Also, regarding the majority-of-the-minority vote, Kahn (P) is not saying that minority stockholders will vote against a going private transaction because of fear of retribution, but merely that investors like a premium and will tend to vote for a deal that delivers one. Thus, the standard adopted by the Chancery Court is affirmed. Where the controller irrevocably and publicly disables itself from using its control to dictate the outcome of the negotiations and the shareholder vote, the controlled merger then acquires the shareholder-protective characteristics of third-party, arm's-length mergers, which are reviewed under the business judgment standard. Also, the dual procedural protection merger structure optimally protects the minority stockholders in controller buyouts. Finally, applying the business judgment standard to the dual protection merger structure is consistent with the central tradition of Delaware law, which defers to the informed decisions of impartial directors, especially when those decisions have been approved by the disinterested stockholders on full information and without coercion. Such a structure is in the best interests of the minority shareholders and enables

them to get the best price, which typically is the preponderant merger consideration for an investor. A controller that uses only one of the dual procedural protections continues to receive burden shifting within the entire fairness standard of review framework. At this point, having set forth the standard for business judgment review of a controlled merger, it must be determined whether the standard has been met in this case. Kahn (P) claims three of the four special committee members were not independent, but the Chancery Court correctly ruled that he failed to adduce sufficient evidence that they were so beholden, or so controlled by, Perelman (D) that they would not be able to make independent decisions regarding the merger. The mere fact that Webb (D) engaged in business dealings with Perelman (D) nine years earlier did not raise a triable fact issue regarding his ability to evaluate the merger impartially. As to Dinh (D), the fees that his law firm obtained from its engagements with M & F (D) and its affiliates was de minimis and would not have influenced his decisionmaking with respect to the M & F (D) proposal. The relationship between Dinh (D) M & F's (D) Schwartz (D) also did not create a triable issue of fact as to Dinh's independence, since Schwartz (D) could not influence Dinh's (D) tenure, and Schwartz's (D) invitation to Dinh (D) to join the board of another company came months after the merger was consummated. Finally, as to Byorum (D), the evidence presented similarly did not create a triable issue of fact as to her independence, since no evidence was presented that she had an ongoing economic relationship with Perelman (D) that was material to her in any way. Additionally, any moneys she received while advising an affiliate of M & F (D) were not material to her, and no evidence to the contrary was presented. In sum, it is well established that bare allegations that directors are friendly with, travel in the same social circles as, or have past business relationships with the proponent of a transaction or the person they are investigating are not enough to rebut the presumption of independence. Here, there was insufficient evidence, applying a subjective standard, that the directors' ties with Perelman (D) or M & F (D) and its affiliates were material, in the sense that the alleged ties could have affected the impartiality of any individual director. Accordingly, the special committee was independent. The committee was also empowered to hire its own advisors, and to negotiate with M & F (D) over the deal terms. The committee also had the power to reject the deal outright if it believed the deal was not in the minority shareholders' best interests. Although the committee did not have the authority to sell MFW (D) to buyers other than M & F (D), the committee nevertheless explored other sales options that might have generated more value for the shareholders. The committee also exercised due care, meeting often, and reviewing a rich body of financial information relevant to whether and at what price a

Continued on next page.

going private transaction was advisable. Finally, it was undisputed that the majority-of-the-minority vote was informed and uncoerced. Therefore, all conditions under the standard are met. Affirmed.

▶ ANALYSIS

If a plaintiff such as Kahn (P) were able to plead a reasonably conceivable set of facts showing that any or all of the enumerated conditions set forth in the Court's holding did not exist, that complaint would state a claim for relief that would entitle the plaintiff to proceed and conduct discovery. If, after discovery, triable issues of fact remained about whether either or both of the dual procedural protections were established, or if established were effective, the case would proceed to a trial in which the court would conduct an entire fairness review. Here, because Kahn (P) was unable to convince the Court that any of the conditions for business judgment review were not met, Kahn (P) was unable to advance his case.

■■■

Quicknotes

AB INITIO From its inception or beginning.

BUSINESS JUDGMENT RULE Doctrine relieving corporate directors and/or officers from liability for decisions honestly and rationally made in the corporation's best interests.

DE MINIMIS Insignificant; trivial; not of sufficient significance to require legal action.

DUTY OF CARE Duty that an officer or director owes to the corporation, by virtue of his fiduciary relationship, to act for the benefit of the corporation.

ENTIRE FAIRNESS A defense to a claim that a director engaged in an interested director transaction by showing the transaction's fairness to the corporation.

■■■

In re CNX Gas Corporation Shareholders Litigation

Shareholders (P) v. Corporation (D)

Del. Ch. Ct., 2010 WL 2291842 (May 25, 2010).

NATURE OF CASE: Motion for a preliminary injunction.

FACT SUMMARY: CONSOL Energy, Inc., the controlling stockholder of CNX Gas Corporation (D), attempted a two-step freeze-out of the minority shareholders (P) of CNX.

RULE OF LAW

The "entire fairness standard" applies to a controlling stockholder tender offer that lacks a special committee recommendation.

FACTS: CONSOL Energy, Inc. (CONSOL) (D) is a coal and gas production-company and the controlling stockholder of CNX Gas Corporation (CNX) (D). CONSOL (D) wanted to acquire the shares of CNX (D) that it did not already own, and in April 2010, CONSOL (D) announced that it had entered into a purchase agreement with T. Rowe Price Associates, Inc., which was the second-largest stockholder of CNX (D) and a significant stockholder of CONSOL (D). Under the agreement, CONSOL (D) agreed to begin a tender offer at a price of $38.25, and T. Rowe Price agreed to tender all of its shares. The board of directors of CNX (D) formed a special committee that consisted of its only independent director and authorized the special committee to determine CNX's (D) position with respect to the tender offer and make a recommendation to stockholders. The special committee received the opinion from its independent financial advisor that the tender offer was fair to CNX's (D) unaffiliated stockholders (P) from a financial point of view; but the committee declined to offer to CNX (D) an opinion about the tender offer, remaining neutral because of its concerns about the process by which CONSOL (D) determined the offer price and the special committee's view that CONSOL (D) was unwilling to negotiate the offer price with the special committee. Several CNX stockholders (P) filed lawsuits challenging the tender offer and asked the court to enjoin the tender offer on the ground that it was subject to judicial review for entire fairness and failed that test. The plaintiffs also argued that CONSOL (D) and the special committee (D) had failed to disclose all material facts to CNX stockholders (P).

ISSUE: Does the "entire fairness standard" apply to a controlling stockholder tender offer that lacks a special committee recommendation?

HOLDING AND DECISION: (Laster, V. Chan.) Yes. The "entire fairness standard" applies to a controlling stockholder tender offer that lacks a special committee

recommendation. The business judgment rule applies both to a freeze-out merger and a freeze-out tender offer only if the transaction is (1) negotiated and approved by a special committee of independent directors and (2) conditioned on the affirmative vote (or tender) of a majority of the minority shares. In this case, the special committee did not affirmatively recommend the controlling stockholder's proposal, and the two-step freeze-out therefore cannot be evaluated under the business judgment rule. Instead, it is appropriate here to apply the "entire fairness" standard for reviewing controlling stockholder freeze-outs described in *In re Cox Communications Shareholders Litigation*, 879 A.2d 604 (Del. Ch. 2005). This standard is "unified" in the sense that it applies both to controlling stockholder mergers negotiated between the controlling stockholder and the subsidiary and to controlling stockholder tender offers, where previously two different standards had applied. Under *Kahn v. Lynch Communications Systems*, 638 A.2d 1110 (Del. 1994), a negotiated merger between a controlling stockholder and its subsidiary is reviewed for entire fairness. But under *In re Siliconix Inc. Shareholders Litigation*, 2001 WL 716787 (Del. Ch. June 19, 2001), a controller's unilateral tender offer followed by a short-form merger is reviewed under an evolving standard far less onerous than *Lynch*. The tender offer in this case was not subject to the business judgment rule because the special committee did not make a recommendation in favor of the transaction, and that fact alone is enough to end the analysis and impose an obligation on CONSOL (D) to pay a fair price. The special committee was not provided with authority comparable to what a board would possess in a third-party transaction, including the ability to seek alternative transactions and to adopt a rights plan to provide the subsidiary with time to respond, negotiate and develop alternatives. In addition, the CNX shareholders (P) raised questions about the role of T. Rowe Price to undercut the effectiveness of the tender condition. In particular, because T. Rowe Price owned 6.5 percent of CONSOL's (D) outstanding stock and 6.3 percent of CNX's (D) outstanding stock and had negotiated the tender offer price with CONSOL (D), it had materially different incentives with respect to the tender offer than a holder of CNX stock, thereby calling into question the effectiveness of the majority-of-the-minority condition. Despite the fact that the CNX shareholders (P) have established a reasonable likelihood of success on the merits of their substantive claims, the tender offer will not be enjoined because the CNX shareholders (P) failed to

Continued on next page.

show that an award of money damages would not provide an adequate remedy.

▶ *ANALYSIS*

Since *In re Siliconix*, the Delaware courts have applied different standards of legal review to acquisitions of a target company by a controlling stockholder (commonly known as "freeze-outs") based on how the transaction is structured. For those transactions structured as one-step freeze-out mergers, the standard of review is entire fairness; for those transactions structured as a tender offer followed by a short-form merger—a two-step freeze-out— the standard of review has been the more deferential business judgment rule standard. The CNX decision holds that entire fairness is the appropriate standard for review of a two-step freeze-out, thus creating a "unified standard for reviewing controlling stockholder freeze-outs" that was previously proposed in *In re Cox Communications*.

■■■■

Quicknotes

BUSINESS JUDGMENT RULE Doctrine relieving corporate directors and/or officers from liability for decisions honestly and rationally made in the corporation's best interests.

ENTIRE FAIRNESS A defense to a claim that a director engaged in an interested director transaction by showing the transaction's fairness to the corporation.

FREEZE-OUT Merger whereby the majority shareholder forces minority shareholders into the sale of their securities.

TENDER OFFER An offer made by one corporation to the shareholders of a target corporation to purchase their shares subject to number, time, and price specifications.

■■■■

CHAPTER 13

Public Contests for Corporate Control

Quick Reference Rules of Law

Unocal Corp. v. Mesa Petroleum Co.

Corporation (D) v. Shareholder company (P)

Del. Sup. Ct., 493 A.2d 946 (1985).

NATURE OF CASE: Interlocutory appeal from a temporary restraining order.

FACT SUMMARY: Mesa Petroleum Co. (Mesa) (P), which was a stockholder in Unocal Corp. (D), was attempting a takeover that Unocal's (D) directors tried to fight by making an exchange offer from which Mesa (P) was excluded.

🏛 RULE OF LAW
A court will not substitute its own judgment for that of the board of directors of a corporation that has decided to fight a takeover attempt by one of the shareholders in the absence of a showing that the decision was primarily based on some breach of the directors' duty.

FACTS: Mesa Petroleum Co. (Mesa) (P), a 13 percent shareholder in Unocal Corp. (D), made a two-tier "front loaded" cash tender offer for 64 million shares, or approximately 37 percent, of Unocal's outstanding stock at a price of $54 per share. The "back-end" of the proposed deal was designed to eliminate the remaining publicly held shares by an exchange of securities purportedly worth $54 per share. The securities offered in the second-step merger would be highly subordinated, i.e., "junk bonds." Unocal's (D) board consisted of eight outsiders and six insiders. At a lengthy board meeting at which 13 directors were present (one of the insiders did not attend), and at which presentations were made by reputable legal and financial advisors, the board of directors of Unocal (D) determined that the consideration for the proposed takeover was wholly inadequate. It also decided to respond with a self-tender by Unocal (D) for its own stock, at $72 per share. This offer would cause Unocal (D) to incur $6.1-6.5 billion of additional debt. The self-tender conditions required that if Mesa (P) acquired 64 million shares of Unocal stock through its own offer (the Mesa Purchase Condition), Unocal (D) would buy the remaining 49 percent outstanding for an exchange of debt securities having an aggregate par value of $72 per share. This Mesa Purchase Condition was later dropped as to 50 million shares (roughly 30 percent of outstanding shares). The self-tender effectively excluded Mesa (P) from the offer. Mesa (P) sought and obtained a preliminary injunction preventing Unocal (D) from proceeding with the exchange offer unless it included Mesa (P). This was based on the trial court's conclusion a corporation may not discriminate in this fashion against one shareholder. One of the main issues when the matter was heard via an interlocutory appeal was whether or not the action taken by the board was covered by the business judgment rule.

ISSUE: Will a court substitute its own judgment for that of the board of directors of a corporation that has decided to fight a takeover attempt by one of the shareholders in the absence of a showing that the decision was primarily based on some breach of the directors' duty?

HOLDING AND DECISION: (Moore, J.) No. A court will not substitute its own judgment for that of the board of directors of a corporation that has decided to fight a takeover attempt by one of the shareholders in the absence of a showing that the decision was primarily based on some breach of the directors' duty. There is no duty owed to a stockholder in a corporation that would preclude the directors from fighting a takeover bid by the stockholder if the board determines that the takeover is not in the best interests of the corporation. If such a decision is made, the court will not substitute its judgment for that of the board unless it is shown by a preponderance of the evidence that the directors' decision was primarily based on perpetuating themselves in office or some other breach of fiduciary duty, such as fraud, overreaching, lack of good faith, or being uninformed. The restriction placed upon a selective stock repurchase is that the directors may not have acted solely or primarily out of a desire to perpetuate themselves in office or to take inequitable action. A further aspect is the element of balance, requiring that, if a defensive measure is to come within the ambit of the business judgment rule, it must be reasonable in relation to the threat posed. Here, the Mesa (P) offer was a classic coercive measure designed to stampede shareholders into tendering at the first tier, even if the price is inadequate, out of fear of what they will receive at the back end of the transaction. Wholly beyond the coercive aspect of an inadequate two-tier tender offer, the threat was posed by a corporate raider with a national reputation as a "greenmailer." In adopting the selective exchange offer, the board stated that its objective was either to defeat the inadequate Mesa (P) offer or, should the offer still succeed, to provide the 49 percent of its stockholders, who would otherwise be forced to accept "junk bonds" with $72 worth of senior debt. Both these purposes are valid. Moreover, such efforts would have been thwarted by Mesa's (P) participation in the exchange offer, since if Mesa (P) could tender its shares, Unocal (D) would effectively be subsidizing Mesa's (P) continuing effort to buy Unocal (D) stock at $54 per share. Second, Mesa (P) could

Continued on next page.

not, by definition, fit within the class of shareholders being protected from its own coercive and inadequate tender offer. Thus, the selective exchange offer was reasonably related to the threats posed (inadequate and coercive two-tier tender offer) and fit within the directors' duty to ensure that the minority stockholders receive equal value for their shares. Although Mesa (P) argues correctly that no case previously ever sanctioned a device that precludes a raider from sharing in a benefit available to all other stockholders, given the nature of the threat posed here the response is neither unlawful nor unreasonable. If, as here, the board of directors is disinterested, has acted in good faith and with due care, its decision in the absence of an abuse of discretion will be upheld as a proper exercise of business judgment. Reversed.

▶ *ANALYSIS*

The business judgment rule protects only those actions by directors that are reasonable in relation to the threat posed. Among the considerations the courts have held are appropriate concerns of the board of directors in taking "defensive" actions are the impact on "constituencies" other than shareholders (such as creditors, customers, employees, and maybe even the community generally) and, also, the risk of nonconsummation.

Quicknotes

BREACH OF FIDUCIARY DUTY The failure of a fiduciary to observe the standard of care exercised by professionals of similar education and experience.

BUSINESS JUDGMENT RULE Doctrine relieving corporate directors and/or officers from liability for decisions honestly and rationally made in the corporation's best interests.

COERCION The overcoming of a person's free will as a result of threats, promises, or undue influence.

INTERLOCUTORY APPEAL Appeal of an issue that does not resolve the disposition of the case, but is essential to a determination of the parties' legal rights.

TEMPORARY RESTRAINING ORDER A court order preserving the status quo pending a hearing regarding injunctive relief.

Smith v. Van Gorkom

Shareholder (P) v. Chief executive officer (D)

Del. Sup. Ct., 488 A.2d 858 (1985).

NATURE OF CASE: Appeal from defense verdict in a class action suit brought by a corporation's shareholders against its board of directors.

FACT SUMMARY: The board of directors (D) of Trans Union Corporation (D) voted to approve a merger agreement based solely on the representations of Van Gorkom (D), one of its directors.

> ## 🏛 RULE OF LAW
> The business judgment rule shields directors or officers of a corporation from liability only if, in reaching a business decision, the directors or officers acted on an informed basis, availing themselves of all material information reasonably available.

FACTS: Van Gorkom (D), chief executive officer (CEO) and director of Trans Union Corporation (D), approached Pritzker, a corporate takeover specialist, to stage a leveraged buy-out at a proposed per share price of $55. Van Gorkom (D) consulted no other board members except Petersen, the company's controller, for help in calculating the feasibility of such a takeover. On September 18, 1980, Van Gorkom (D) met with Pritzker, who demanded that Trans Union (D) respond to his offer within three days. Van Gorkom (D) called a special meeting of the company's senior management and of the board (D) for the next day. Despite senior management's adverse reaction to the proposed merger, the board of directors (D) approved the agreement based on Van Gorkom's (D) twenty-minute oral presentation. The board (D) did not have sufficient time to study the merger documents, nor did Van Gorkom (D) substantiate the $55 per share price. Without reviewing its contents, Van Gorkom (D) executed the merger agreement on September 22. Smith (P) and other stockholders (P) subsequently filed a class action suit against Trans Union (D) and the board of directors (D). On February 10, 1981, however, the shareholders voted to approve the merger. The Court of Chancery found the board's (D) actions shielded by the business judgment rule.

ISSUE: Is a director or officer of a corporation shielded by the business judgment rule when he relies on the representations of other directors or officers?

HOLDING AND DECISION: (Horsey, J.) No. The business judgment rule shields directors or officers of a corporation from liability only, if in reaching a business decision, the directors or officers acted on an informed basis, availing themselves of all material information reasonably available. The director has a duty to the corporation's shareholders to make an informed business decision regarding a proposed merger before it is subjected to shareholder approval. Subsequent shareholder ratification does not relieve the director from this duty, unless their approval is also based on an informed decision. In this case, the directors (D) breached their duty of care by failing to conduct further investigation as to the proposed merger, and by submitting the proposal for shareholder approval without providing them with the relevant facts necessary to make an educated decision. Reversed.

▶ ANALYSIS

A director or officer may not passively rely on information provided by other directors or officers, outside advisers, or authorized committees. The director may only rely on credible information provided by competent individuals, after taking reasonable measures to substantiate it.

■━■

Quicknotes

BUSINESS JUDGMENT RULE Doctrine relieving corporate directors and/or officers from liability for decisions honestly and rationally made in the corporation's best interests.

CLASS ACTION A suit commenced by a representative on behalf of an ascertainable group that is too large to appear in court, who shares a commonality of interests and who will benefit from a successful result.

DUTY OF CARE Duty that an officer or director owes to the corporation, by virtue of his fiduciary relationship, to act for the benefit of the corporation.

■━■

Revlon, Inc. v. MacAndrews and Forbes Holdings, Inc.

Takeover target (D) v. Suitor (P)

Del. Sup. Ct., 506 A.2d 173 (1986).

NATURE OF CASE: Appeal of injunction prohibiting exercise of certain options.

FACT SUMMARY: Solely to prevent a hostile takeover, the board of Revlon, Inc. (D) granted Forstmann (D) certain lock-up options.

🏛 RULE OF LAW
A board of directors cannot grant lock-up options solely to prevent competitive bidding for a corporation.

FACTS: Pantry Pride (P) instituted a tender offer for Revlon, Inc. (D) stock at a price of $47.50. Revlon's (D) board took certain defensive measures. Pantry Pride (P) upped its offer to $53. At this point, Revlon's (D) directorate negotiated a leveraged buyout by Forstmann Little, Inc. (D). When Pantry Pride's (P) offer had increased to $56.25 and Forstmann's (D) offer increased to $57.25, Revlon's (D) directors executed certain "lock-up" options, granting financial favors to Forstmann (D) if its buyout did not occur and effectively making acquisition by Pantry Pride (P) financially impracticable. Pantry Pride (P) brought an action seeking to enjoin the lock-ups. The Chancery Court issued such an injunction, and Revlon (D) appealed.

ISSUE: Can a board of directors grant lock-up options solely to prevent competitive bidding for a corporation?

HOLDING AND DECISION: (Moore, J.) No. A board of directors cannot grant lock-up options solely to prevent competitive bidding for a corporation. When it appears that an active bidding contest for a corporation is underway, the board of directors, whose primary duty is to the shareholders, is under an obligation to do what it can to maximize the sale price for the benefit of the stockholders. A lock-up is not necessarily illegal, and when it is done to prevent a takeover that would be detrimental to shareholders, it may be employed. Where, however, the lock-up has no effect other than to prevent competitive bidding, thus depressing the stock's price, the lock-up works not to benefit the shareholders, but rather it burdens them. Here, it has not been shown that the lock-ups were designed to do anything other than stifle competition, and this was improper. Affirmed.

▶ ANALYSIS

Pantry Pride's (P) original tender offer, $47.50, was considered by the board to be too low. This was verifiable, based on expert opinion. The court did not argue with the board's early defensive measures. These measures drove up the price of the stock. In doing this, the court felt, the board properly discharged its duties.

Quicknotes

INJUNCTION A court order requiring a person to do or prohibiting that person from doing a specific act.

LEVERAGED BUYOUT A transaction whereby corporate outsiders purchase the outstanding shares of a publicly held corporation mostly with borrowed funds.

LOCK-UP OPTION A defensive strategy to a takeover attempt whereby a target corporation sets aside a specified portion of the company's shares for purchase by a friendly investor.

Paramount Communications, Inc. v. Time, Inc.

Corporation (P) v. Corporation (D)

Del. Sup. Ct., 571 A.2d 1140 (1989).

NATURE OF CASE: Appeal from judgment upholding corporate antitakeover actions.

FACT SUMMARY: Paramount Communications, Inc. (Paramount) (P) contended that antitakeover measures enacted by Time, Inc.'s (D) directors in response to its tender offer were invalid because Paramount's (P) per-share offer amount was fair market value.

RULE OF LAW

A board of directors' efforts to prevent a takeover via tender offer will not be invalid merely because the takeover offer constituted fair market value.

FACTS: Time, Inc.'s (D) board was considering an acquisition-merger with Warner Communications, Inc. (Warner). Time's (D) board had been considering a merger with an entertainment company for some time and decided that a merger with Warner presented the best prospects for long-term enrichment, as well as preservation of Time's (D) corporate climate. A deal was struck with Warner's management wherein Time (D) would acquire Warner, Warner's shareholders would receive 62 percent of the new company, and the two company's directorates would share control. A proxy statement urging shareholder approval was sent to Time's (D) shareholders. However, before the vote, Paramount Communications, Inc. (Paramount) (P) announced a $175 per-share tender offer for Time (D) stock, which was then selling for $126 per share. Time's (D) board concluded that: (1) the $48 per-share premium was insufficient consideration for control and (2) the Warner deal presented a better long-term opportunity for preservation of corporate climate than did Paramount's (P) proposed acquisition. Time (D) instituted certain antitakeover measures. Paramount (P) sued to enjoin the measures. The Chancery Court upheld the measures. Paramount (P) appealed.

ISSUE: Will a board of directors' efforts to prevent a takeover via tender offer be invalid merely because the offer constituted fair market value?

HOLDING AND DECISION: (Horsey, J.) No. A board of directors' efforts to prevent a takeover via tender offer will not be invalid merely because the offer constituted fair market value. Under *Revlon, Inc. v. MacAndrews and Forbes Holdings, Inc.*, 506 A.2d 173 (Del. 1986), a directorate is under a duty to maximize shareholder prices only when it is clear that a corporation is "on the block," that is, when a sale is a foregone conclusion. Here, it is asserted (by the shareholders) that *Revlon* duties were triggered since

the Time-Warner agreement effectively put Time (D) up for sale and erected barriers to further bids. This assertion is based on the fact that Warner shareholders would receive 62 percent of the combined company and that Time's (D) board adopted various defensive measures. However, Time (D) was not up for sale; Warner was not a suitor, even though its shareholders would eventually own a majority of the new corporation's stock. Also, in negotiating with Warner, the Time (D) board did not make the dissolution or breakup of the corporate entity inevitable, as was the case in *Revlon*. Consequently, Time (D) was not the object of a bidding war, and was not effectively up for sale, which would have triggered a duty under *Revlon* on the part of Time's (D) directors to maximize per-share value. This being so, for the business judgment rule to attach, the rule under *Unocal Corp. v. Mesa Petroleum Co.*, 493 A.2d 946 (Del. 1985), is that a directorate may oppose a takeover if: (1) there are reasonable grounds for believing that a danger to corporate effectiveness and policy exist and (2) the defensive measures adopted are reasonable. Paramount (P) first argues that since its tender offer was more valuable to shareholders than shares in the new corporation would have been, no danger to Time (D) existed, and the Time (D) board had no reasonable ground to believe that Paramount (P) posed both a legally cognizable threat to Time shareholders and a danger to Time's corporate policy and effectiveness. Instead, Paramount (P) contends, the underlying motivation for Time's (D) defensive measures was its desire to entrench themselves. The Chancery Court framed the issue as short-term versus long-term corporate strategy. However, short-term dollar value is not the only factor here. The question of "long-term" versus "short-term" values is largely irrelevant because directors, generally, are obliged to charter a course for a corporation that is in its best interest without regard to a fixed investment horizon. Second, absent a limited set of circumstances as defined under *Revlon*, a board of directors, while always required to act in an informed manner, is not under any per se duty to maximize shareholder value in the short term, even in the context of a takeover. A court should not, under *Unocal*, substitute its judgment for that of the corporation's as to what is a "better" deal. In fact, the policies underlying the business judgment rule militate against a court's engaging in the process of attempting to appraise and evaluate the relative merits of a long-term versus a short-term investment goal for shareholders. Here, Time's (D) board had decided, after long deliberation, that the Warner deal was in the best long-term interests of the corporation. The

Continued on next page.

board reasonably determined that inadequate value was not the only legally cognizable threat that Paramount's (P) all-cash, all-shares offer could present, but that another threat was that Time (D) shareholders might elect to tender into Paramount's (P) cash offer in ignorance or a mistaken belief of the strategic benefit which a business combination with Warner might produce. Finally, under the second part of the *Unocal* analysis, Time's (D) response to the threat was reasonable. It was not a cram-down on its shareholders of a management-sponsored plan, but was designed to carry forward a pre-existing transaction in an altered form. The revised agreement and its accompanying safety devices did not preclude Paramount (P) from making an offer for the combined Time-Warner company or from changing the conditions of its offer so as not to make the offer dependent upon the nullification of the Time-Warner agreement. Thus, the response was proportionate. For these reasons, Time's (D) defensive measures, which frustrated Paramount's (P) tender offer, were reasonable and entitled to business judgment rule protection. Affirmed.

▶ ANALYSIS

When a corporation becomes a target in a bidding war, the discretion of the target's directorate becomes severely limited. All it can do is try to get the shareholders the best deal possible. Ironically, Paramount (P) itself became the subject of such a bidding war in its highly publicized 1994 takeover by Viacom, Inc., after a long bidding war with QVC.

▬▬▬

Quicknotes

BUSINESS JUDGMENT RULE Doctrine relieving corporate directors and/or officers from liability for decisions honestly and rationally made in the corporation's best interests.

TENDER OFFER An offer made by one corporation to the shareholders of a target corporation to purchase their shares subject to number, time, and price specifications.

▬▬▬

Paramount Communications, Inc. v. QVC Network, Inc.

Corporation (D) v. Corporation (P)

Del. Sup. Ct., 637 A.2d 34 (1994).

NATURE OF CASE: Appellate review of preliminary injunction.

FACT SUMMARY: The Paramount Communications, Inc. (Paramount) (D) board approved unusually restrictive contractual provisions to prevent unsolicited tender offers from interfering with their intention to transfer control of Paramount (D) to Viacom, Inc.

RULE OF LAW

(1) A change of corporate control or a breakup of the corporation subjects directors to enhanced scrutiny and requires them to pursue a transaction that will produce the best value for stockholders.

(2) A board of directors breaches its fiduciary duty if it contractually restricts its right to consider competing merger bids.

FACTS: Paramount Communications, Inc. (Paramount) (D) is a Delaware corporation that had over 100 million shares outstanding as of early 1993. Viacom is a Delaware corporation that is controlled by Sumner Redstone. QVC (P) is a Delaware corporation with several large stockholders. In the late 1980s, Paramount (D) began exploring acquisition of or merger with, companies in the entertainment industry. In April, 1993, Paramount (D) met with Viacom to discuss a merger. The discussions broke down, but reopened when Davis, chairman of Paramount (D), learned of QVC's (P) possible interest in Paramount. On September 12, 1993, the Paramount (D) board unanimously approved the original merger agreement whereby Paramount (D) would merge into Viacom. The Paramount (D) shareholders were to receive primarily nonvoting shares in the new company. Additionally, the merger agreement included numerous provisions pertaining to Paramount's (D) activities with other potential bidders. First, under the no-shop provision, the Paramount (D) board would not engage in any way with a competing transaction unless: (1) a third party makes an unsolicited proposal not subject to any material financing contingencies; and (2) the Paramount (D) board determines that negotiations with the third party are necessary for the Paramount (D) board to comply with its fiduciary duties. Second, under the termination fee provision, Viacom would receive a $100 million fee if a competing transaction was responsible for a termination of the original merger agreement, a recommendation by the board of Paramount (D) of a competing transaction ended the negotiations, or the stockholders of Paramount (D) did not approve the merger. The third, and most significant provision, was the stock option agreement. The provision gave Viacom the option to purchase 19.9 percent of Paramount's (D) outstanding common stock for $69.14 per share if any of the termination fee triggering events occurred. The payment clause was not capped at a maximum dollar value. On September 20, 1993, QVC (P) sent a merger proposal letter to Davis at Paramount (D), offering $80 per share and later publicly announced an $80 cash tender offer. On November 6, 1993, Viacom unilaterally raised its tender offer price to $85 per share. QVC (P) responded by upping its offer to $90 per share. At its November 15 meeting, the Paramount (D) board determined that the QVC (P) offer was not in the best interest of the shareholders. QVC (P) filed suit to preliminarily enjoin the defensive measures of the original and amended agreements promulgated by the Paramount (D) board. The Court of Chancery's preliminary injunction was then heard in an expedited interlocutory appeal.

ISSUE:

(1) Is a change of corporate control or a breakup of the corporation required before directors are subject to enhanced scrutiny and required to pursue a transaction that will produce the best value for stockholders?

(2) Has a board of directors breached its fiduciary duty if it contractually restricts its right to consider competing merger bids?

HOLDING AND DECISION: (Veasey, C.J.)

(1) No. Either a change of corporate control or a breakup of the corporation will subject directors to enhanced scrutiny and require them to pursue a transaction that will produce the best value for stockholders. In general, the board of directors in a corporation is given broad discretion to run the corporation. However, when the board undertakes actions that strike at the heart of the corporate entity, certain safeguards to protect the shareholders are activated. In situations where the shareholders' power is substantially changed, such as a sale of control of the corporation to another entity, or a threatened loss of majority status of existing shareholders, board action is subject to enhanced scrutiny. A judicial determination must be made as to whether the board's decision-making process was reasonable, and whether the board's actions were reasonable given the existing circumstances. By selling a controlling interest in Paramount (D) to Viacom, the majority shareholders in Paramount (D) would lose the ability to guide the corporation through the selection of directors. The very contemplation of a change in corporate control is a significant action. Therefore, the fiduciary

Continued on next page.

duties of the directors require that they endeavor to assure that the shareholders receive the greatest possible value for their interests. Enhanced judicial review is appropriate when either a change of corporate control or a corporate breakup is contemplated.

(2) Yes. A board of directors has breached its fiduciary duty if it contractually restricts its right to consider competing merger bids. In this case, the board of Paramount (D) is subject to enhanced judicial scrutiny by its consideration of a change in corporate control. Solicitation of competing bids for the corporation is a reasonable method to ensure that shareholder interests are properly valued. In this case, the Paramount (D) board entered into highly restrictive contracts that prevented it from considering other offers. The board had several meetings at which the value of the QVC (P) offers could have been explored in detail. Although the board of Paramount (D) suggested that the merger with Viacom met their long-term strategic plans more effectively, this argument overlooks the fact that the board was essentially giving control of the corporation to one individual. Thus, after the merger, the strategic goals of the Paramount (D) board would become highly moot. The disparity between the competing offers could have given the board tremendous negotiation leverage had it permitted itself to consider it. The board was under a duty to inform itself of all realistic options that might maximize the position of the shareholders. The Paramount (D) board failed in its fiduciary duties. Affirmed and remanded for further proceedings.

▶ ANALYSIS

After *Paramount Communications, Inc. v. QVC Network, Inc.*, stock option lockups are seen as being legally too risky. Termination fees are still considered acceptable as a price for canceling a major negotiation. The reasonableness of different termination fee sizes has not yet been tested clearly.

■=■

Quicknotes

FIDUCIARY DUTY A legal obligation to act for the benefit of another, including subordinating one's personal interests to that of the other person.

INTERLOCUTORY APPEAL Appeal of an issue that does not resolve the disposition of the case, but is essential to a determination of the parties' legal rights.

PRELIMINARY INJUNCTION A judicial mandate issued to require or restrain a party from certain conduct; used to preserve a trial's subject matter or to prevent threatened injury.

TENDER OFFER An offer made by one corporation to the shareholders of a target corporation to purchase their shares subject to number, time, and price specifications.

■=■

Lyondell Chemical Co. v. Ryan

Shareholders (P) v. Corporate directors (D)

Del. Sup. Ct., 970 A.2d 235 (2009).

NATURE OF CASE: Interlocutory appeal during shareholder class action lawsuit.

FACT SUMMARY: Shareholders (P) brought a class action lawsuit against the directors (D) of their corporation, arguing that the sale process was tainted by the directors' self-interest, and that the directors (D) thereby breached their fiduciary duties.

RULE OF LAW
There are no legally prescribed steps that directors must follow to satisfy their *Revlon* duties, such that failure to take those steps during the sale of their company demonstrates a conscious disregard of their duties.

FACTS: Leonard Blavatnik, who controlled Basell AF through a controlling interest in Access Industries, made an oral offer to buy Lyondell Chemical Co. (Lyondell) for $48 per share. Dan Smith, Lyondell's chairman and chief executive officer, responded to the offer by calling a special meeting of Lyondell's board (D) the next day in order to consider Basell's offer. The board (D) agreed to request a written offer and additional financial details from Basell. After a short period of additional negotiation, which resulted in a $15 million reduction in the deal's $400 million break-up fee, and receiving the advice of legal and financial advisers, Lyondell's board (D) agreed to approve the merger and recommended it to the company's shareholders. The merger was eventually approved by over 99 percent of the voted shares for approximately $13 billion. Despite the overwhelming approval of the merger, some shareholders (P) alleged that the directors (D) only looked out for their own self-interest and that the process by which the merger was approved and recommended was flawed. The Chancery Court denied summary judgment for the directors (D), finding that the $48 per share price received by the shareholders was a fair one and may have been the best that could reasonably have been obtained in that market or any market since then. The Chancery Court held that when control of the corporation is at stake, however, directors (D) are expected to take context-appropriate steps to assure themselves and, thus, their shareholders (P) that the price to be paid is the best price reasonably available, as required by *Revlon Inc. v. MacAndrews & Forbes Holdings Inc.*, 506 A.2d 173 (Del. 1986).

ISSUE: Are there legally prescribed steps that directors must follow to satisfy their *Revlon* duties, such that failure to take those steps during the sale of their company demonstrates a conscious disregard of their duties?

HOLDING AND DECISION: (Berger, J.) No. There are no legally prescribed steps that directors must follow to satisfy their *Revlon* duties, such that failure to take those steps during the sale of their company demonstrates a conscious disregard of their duties. Directors are required to act reasonably, not perfectly, and the state's Chancery Court erred in denying summary judgment to the directors (D) of Lyondell Chemical. The Chancery Court acted under a mistaken view of the applicable law. First, the Chancery Court imposed *Revlon* duties on the Lyondell directors (D) before they either had decided to sell, or before the sale had become inevitable. Second, the court read *Revlon* and its progeny as creating a set of requirements that must be satisfied during the sale process. Third, the Chancery Court equated an arguably imperfect attempt to carry out *Revlon* duties with a knowing disregard of one's duties that constitutes bad faith. But there is only one *Revlon* duty—to get the best price for the stockholders at the sale of the company. Moreover, courts cannot dictate how directors reach that goal, because they will be facing a unique combination of circumstances, many of which will be outside their control. The directors' (D) failure to take any specific steps during the sale process could not have demonstrated a conscious disregard of their duties. There is a vast difference between an inadequate or flawed effort to carry out fiduciary duties and a conscious disregard for those duties. The trial court approached the record from the wrong perspective. Instead of questioning whether disinterested, independent directors did everything that they (arguably) should have done to obtain the best sale price, the inquiry should have been whether those directors utterly failed to attempt to obtain the best sale price. Reversed and remanded.

ANALYSIS

The director who is conscious of her fiduciary duties, and who makes a good faith effort to fulfill them, does not breach them even if her effort to carry them out is flawed, or the net result of her actions are not beneficial to the shareholders. Remember in your analysis to distinguish between the director's consciousness of duty and her methods for executing them.

Quicknotes

FIDUCIARY DUTY A legal obligation to act for the benefit of another, including subordinating one's personal interests to that of the other person.

C&J Energy Services, Inc. v. City of Miami General Employees and Sanitation Employees Retirement Trust

Corporation (D) v. Shareholder (P)

Del. Sup. Ct., 107 A.3rd 1049 (2014).

NATURE OF CASE: Appeal from preliminary injunction granted to plaintiff in class action challenging a merger.

FACT SUMMARY: C&J Energy Services, Inc. (C&J) (D), which was to merge with a subsidiary of Nabors, Inc., challenged a preliminary injunction issued by the Delaware Court of Chancery that enjoined the shareholder vote on the merger and that required C&J (D) to shop itself in violation of the merger agreement between C&J (D) and Nabors, which prohibited C&J (D) from soliciting other bids.

⚖ RULE OF LAW

(1) A company's board may fulfill its *Revlon* duties without shopping itself, so that a mandatory injunction ordering the company to shop itself may be set aside where the board has likely fulfilled its *Revlon* duties by exercising its judgment in good faith, testing the transaction through a viable passive market check, and giving its stockholders a fully informed, uncoerced opportunity to vote to accept the deal.

(2) It is not an appropriate exercise of a court's equitable authority to issue a preliminary injunction that strips an innocent third party of its contractual rights while simultaneously binding that party to consummate a merger transaction in the absence of findings that there has been any wrongdoing by any party to that transaction.

FACTS: C&J Energy Services, Inc. (C&J) (D), a U.S. corporation, entered into a merger agreement with Nabors, Inc., a Bermuda corporation, to acquire a Nabors subsidiary. Upon completion of the merger, Nabors would retain a majority of the equity in the surviving company. To obtain more favorable tax rates, the surviving entity, C&J Energy Services, Ltd. ("New C&J"), was to be based in Bermuda. The agreement included certain protections. First, a bylaw guaranteed that all stockholders would share pro rata in any future sale of New C&J, which bylaw could only be repealed by a unanimous stockholder vote. C&J (D) also bargained for a "fiduciary out" if a superior proposal was to emerge during a lengthy passive market check, during which a potential competing bidder faced only modest deal protection barriers. An institutional C&J shareholder (P) challenged the merger and sought to preliminarily enjoin it. The Delaware Court of Chancery

determined there was a "plausible" violation of the board's duties under *Revlon v. MacAndrews & Forbes Holdings, Inc.*, 506 A.2d 173 (Del. 1986), because the board did not affirmatively shop the company either before or after signing. On that basis, the Chancery Court enjoined the stockholder vote for 30 days, and it ordered C&J (D) to shop itself in violation of the merger agreement. The order dealt with this issue by stating "[t]he solicitation of proposals consistent with this Order and any subsequent negotiations of any alternative proposal that emerges will not constitute a breach of the Merger Agreement in any respect." C&J (D) appealed, and the Delaware Supreme Court granted review.

ISSUE:
(1) May a company's board fulfill its *Revlon* duties without shopping itself, so that a mandatory injunction ordering the company to shop itself may be set aside where the board has likely fulfilled its *Revlon* duties by exercising its judgment in good faith, testing the transaction through a viable passive market check, and giving its stockholders a fully informed, uncoerced opportunity to vote to accept the deal?

(2) Is it an appropriate exercise of a court's equitable authority to issue a preliminary injunction that strips an innocent third party of its contractual rights while simultaneously binding that party to consummate a merger transaction in the absence of findings that there has been any wrongdoing by any party to that transaction?

HOLDING AND DECISION: (Strine, C.J.)
(1) Yes. A company's board may fulfill its *Revlon* duties without shopping itself, so that a mandatory injunction ordering the company to shop itself may be set aside where the board has likely fulfilled its *Revlon* duties by exercising its judgment in good faith, testing the transaction through a viable passive market check, and giving its stockholders a fully informed, uncoerced opportunity to vote to accept the deal. First, a preliminary injunction must be supported by a finding that the plaintiffs have demonstrated a reasonable probability of success on the merits, but the Court of Chancery made no such finding here, and the analysis that it conducted rested on the erroneous proposition that a company selling itself in a change of control transaction is required to shop itself to fulfill its duty to seek the highest immediate value. However, *Revlon* and its progeny do not set out a specific route a board must follow when

Continued on next page.

fulfilling its fiduciary duties, and an independent board is entitled to use its business judgment to decide to enter into a strategic transaction that promises great benefit, even when it creates certain risks. Here, it was undisputed that a deal with Nabors made strategic business sense and offered substantial benefits for C&J's (D) stockholders, and it was clear that the shareholders would be able to determine for themselves whether to accept the deal through a fully informed, uncoerced vote. Accordingly, the Chancery Court's order requiring C&J (D) to shop itself in order to fulfill its *Revlon* duties was erroneous, and the injunction cannot stand.

(2) No. It is not an appropriate exercise of a court's equitable authority to issue a preliminary injunction that strips an innocent third party of its contractual rights while simultaneously binding that party to consummate a merger transaction in the absence of findings that there has been any wrongdoing by any party to that transaction. First, a mandatory injunction should only issue with the confidence of findings made after a trial or on undisputed facts. To blue-pencil a contract as the Court of Chancery did here is not an appropriate exercise of equitable authority in a preliminary injunction order. That is especially true because the Court of Chancery made no finding that Nabors had aided and abetted any breach of fiduciary duty, and the Court of Chancery could not even find that it was reasonably likely such a breach by C&J's (D) board would be found after trial. Reversed.

▌ *ANALYSIS*

Revlon and its progeny primarily involved board resistance to a competing bid after the board had agreed to a change of control, which threatened to impede the emergence of another higher-priced deal. In those cases, therefore, it was appropriate to require that the company shop itself. Here, however, there was no hint of such a defensive, entrenching motive, which was another reason the Delaware Supreme Court concluded that ordering C&J (D) to shop itself was erroneous.

▬▬

Quicknotes

BREACH OF FIDUCIARY DUTY The failure of a fiduciary to observe the standard of care exercised by professionals of similar education and experience.

▬▬

Omnicare, Inc. v. NCS Healthcare, Inc.

Acquiring corporation (P) v. Target corporation (D)

Del. Sup. Ct., 818 A.2d 914 (2003).

NATURE OF CASE: Appeal from decision holding that lockup deal protection measures were reasonable.

FACT SUMMARY: Omnicare, Inc. (Omnicare) (P) sought to acquire NCS Healthcare, Inc. (NCS) (D). Genesis Health Ventures, Inc. (Genesis) had made a competing bid for NCS (D) that the NCS board had originally recommended, but the NCS board withdrew its recommendation and instead recommended that stockholders accept the Omnicare (P) offer, which was worth more than twice the Genesis offer. However, the agreement between Genesis and NCS (D) contained a provision that the agreement be placed before the NCS (D) shareholders for a vote, even if the board no longer recommended it. There was also no fiduciary out clause in the agreement. Pursuant to voting agreements, two NCS shareholders who held a majority of the voting power agreed unconditionally to vote all their shares in favor of the Genesis merger, thus assuring that the Genesis transaction would prevail. Omnicare (P) challenged the defensive measures that were part of the Genesis transaction.

🏛 RULE OF LAW
Lock-up deal protection devices, which when operating in concert are coercive and preclusive, are invalid and unenforceable in the absence of a fiduciary out clause.

FACTS: In late 1999, NCS Healthcare, Inc. (NCS) (D) began to experience serious liquidity problems that led to a precipitous decline in the market value of its stock. As a result, it began to explore strategic alternatives to address its situation. In the summer of 2001, Omnicare, Inc. (Omnicare) (P), a NCS (D) competitor, made a series of offers to acquire NCS's (D) assets in a bankruptcy sale—at less than face value of NCS's (D) outstanding debts, and with no recovery for NCS stockholders. NCS (D) rejected Omnicare's (P) offers. By early 2002, NCS's (D) financial condition was improving, and the NCS board began to believe it might be able to realize some value for its shareholders. An Ad Hoc Committee of NCS (D) creditors contacted Genesis Health Ventures, Inc. (Genesis), an Omnicare (P) competitor, and Genesis expressed interest in bidding on NCS (D). Genesis made it clear that it did not want to be a "stalking horse" for NCS (D) and demanded an exclusivity agreement. After Genesis steadily increased its offers, NCS (D) granted Genesis the exclusivity it sought. The NCS board consisted of Outcalt and Shaw, who together controlled more than 65 percent of voting power in NCS (D), and Sells and Osborne, both of whom

were disinterested, outside directors. In its negotiations, Genesis sought an agreement that would require, as permitted by Delaware General Corporation Law (DGCL) § 251(c), NCS (D) to submit the merger to NCS stockholders regardless of whether the NCS Board recommended the merger; an agreement by Outcalt and Shaw to vote their NCS stock in favor of the merger; and omission of any effective fiduciary out clause from the agreement. Meanwhile, Omnicare (P) learned that NCS (D) was negotiating with Genesis and made a proposed bid for a transaction in which all of NCS's (D) debt would be paid off and NCS stockholders would receive greater value than offered by Genesis. This offer was conditioned on satisfactory completion of due diligence. Fearing that Genesis might abandon its offer, NCS (D) refused to negotiate with Omnicare (P), but used Omnicare's (P) proposal to negotiate for improved terms with Genesis, which Genesis provided. However, in exchange, Genesis conditioned its offer on approval the next day. The NCS board gave such approval to the merger, in which NCS stockholders would receive Genesis stock and all NCS (D) debt would be paid off. The merger transaction included the provisions that Genesis had sought during negotiations, as well as the voting agreements with Outcalt and Shaw. Thus, the combined terms of the merger agreement and voting agreement guaranteed that the transaction proposed by Genesis would be approved by the NCS stockholders. Omnicare (P) filed suit to enjoin the merger and then launched a tender offer for all NCS (D) stock at a value of more than twice the then current market value of the shares to be received in the Genesis transaction. Otherwise, its offer equaled that of Genesis. Several months later, but before the NCS stockholders were to vote on the Genesis merger, as a result of Omnicare (P) irrevocably committing itself to its offer, the NCS board withdrew its recommendation of the Genesis merger and recommended, instead, that NCS shareholders vote for the Omnicare (P) merger because it was a superior proposal. The Chancery Court ruled that the voting agreements with Outcalt and Shaw, combined with the provision requiring a stockholder vote regardless of board recommendation, constituted defensive measures, but found that, under the enhanced judicial scrutiny standard of *Unocal Corp. v. Mesa Petroleum Co.*, 493 A.2d 946 (Del. 1985), these measures were reasonable. The Delaware Supreme Court granted review.

ISSUE: Are lock-up deal protection devices, which when operating in concert are coercive and preclusive,

Continued on next page.

invalid and unenforceable in the absence of a fiduciary out clause?

HOLDING AND DECISION: (Holland, J.) Yes.
Lock-up deal protection devices, which when operating in concert are coercive and preclusive, are invalid and unenforceable in the absence of a fiduciary out clause. The Chancery Court concluded that because the Genesis transaction did not result in a change of control, the transaction would be reviewed under the business judgment rule standard. Under this standard, the Chancery Court concluded that the NCS board had not breached its duty of care in approving the transaction. The Chancery Court's decision to use the business judgment rule standard, rather than enhanced scrutiny, is not outcome-determinative and this court will assume that the NCS board exercised due care when it approved the Genesis transaction. However, as to the defensive measures, enhanced scrutiny is required because of the inherent potential conflict of interest between a board's interest in protecting a merger transaction it has approved and the shareholders' statutory right to make the final decision to either approve or not approve a merger. This requires a threshold determination that the board approved defensive measures comport with the directors' fiduciary duties. In applying enhanced judicial scrutiny to defensive measures designed to protect a merger agreement, a court must first determine that those measures are not preclusive or coercive before its focus shifts to a "range of reasonableness" proportionality determination. When the focus shifts to the range of reasonableness, *Unocal* requires that any devices must be proportionate to the perceived threat to the corporation and its stockholders if the merger transaction is not consummated. Here, the voting agreements were inextricably intertwined with the defensive aspects of the Genesis merger agreement, and, under *Unocal*, the defensive measures require special scrutiny. Under such scrutiny, these measures were neither reasonable nor proportionate to the threat NCS (D) perceived from the potential loss of the Genesis transaction. The threat identified by NCS (D) was the possibility of losing the Genesis offer and being left with no comparable alternative transaction. The second part of the *Unocal* analysis requires the NCS directors to demonstrate that their defensive response was reasonable in response to the threat posed. This inquiry itself involves a two-step analysis. The NCS directors must first establish that the deal protection devices adopted in response to the threat were not "coercive" or "preclusive," and then must demonstrate that their response was within a "range of reasonable responses" to the threat perceived. Here, the defensive measures were both preclusive and coercive, and, therefore, draconian and impermissible. That is because any stockholder vote would be "robbed of its effectiveness" by the impermissible coercion that predetermined the outcome of the merger without regard to the merits of the Genesis transaction at the time the vote was scheduled to take place. They were also preclusive because they accomplished a fait accompli.

Accordingly, the defensive measures are unenforceable. They are alternatively unenforceable because the merger agreement completely prevented the board from discharging its fiduciary responsibilities to the minority stockholders when Omnicare (P) presented its superior transaction. Here, the NCS board could not abdicate its fiduciary duties to the minority by leaving it to the stockholders alone to approve or disapprove the merger because Outcalt and Shaw had combined to establish a majority of the voting power that made the outcome of the stockholder vote a foregone conclusion. Thus, the NCS board did not have authority to accede to the Genesis demand for an absolute "lock-up." Instead, it was required to negotiate a fiduciary out clause to protect the NCS shareholders if the Genesis transaction became an inferior offer. Therefore, the defensive measures—the voting agreements and the provision requiring a shareholder vote regardless of board recommendation—when combined to operate in concert in the absence of an effective fiduciary out clause are invalid and unenforceable.

DISSENT: (Veasey, C.J.) The NCS board's actions should have been evaluated based on the circumstances present at the time the Genesis merger agreement was entered into—before the emergence of a subsequent transaction offering greater value to the stockholders. The lock-ups were reached at the conclusion of a lengthy search and intense negotiation process in the context of insolvency, at a time when Genesis was the only viable bidder. Under these facts the NCS board's action before the emergence of the Omnicare (P) offer, reflected the actions of "a quintessential, disinterested, and informed board" made in good faith, and was within the bounds of its fiduciary duties and should be upheld. Moreover, situations arise where business realities demand a lock-up so that wealth enhancing transactions may go forward. Accordingly, any bright-line rule prohibiting lock-ups, such as the one put forth by the majority, could, in circumstances such as those faced by the NCS board, chill otherwise permissible conduct. Here, the deal protection measures were not preclusive or coercive in the context of what they were intended for. They were not adopted to fend off a hostile takeover, but were adopted so that Genesis—the "only game in town"—would save NCS (D), its creditors, and stockholders. Still, here there was no meaningful minority stockholder vote to coerce, given Outcalt and Shaw's majority position, so that the "preclusive" label has no application. Thus, giving Genesis an absolute lock-up under the circumstances, by agreeing to omit a fiduciary out clause, was not a per se violation of fiduciary duty. Hopefully, the rule announced by the majority will be interpreted narrowly and will be seen as sui generis.

Continued on next page.

▌ *ANALYSIS*

One of the primary troubling aspects of the majority opinion, as voiced by the dissent, is the majority's suggestion that it can make a *Unocal* determination after-the-fact with a view to the superiority of a competing proposal that may subsequently emerge. Many commentators agree with the dissent that the lock-ups in this case should not have been reviewed in a vacuum. In a separate dissent, Justice Steele argued that when a board agrees rationally, in good faith, without conflict and with reasonable care to include provisions in a contract to preserve a deal in the absence of a better one, their business judgment should not be second-guessed in order to invalidate or declare unenforceable an otherwise valid merger agreement. Given the tension between the majority's and dissenters' positions, the full impact of the court's decision will need to await further judicial development.

■■■

Quicknotes

FIDUCIARY DUTY A legal obligation to act for the benefit of another, including subordinating one's personal interests to that of the other person.

LOCK-UP OPTION A defensive strategy to a takeover attempt whereby a target corporation sets aside a specified portion of the company's shares for purchase by a friendly investor.

SUI GENERIS Peculiar to its own type or class.

■■■

Blasius Industries, Inc. v. Atlas Corp.

Corporation (P) v. Takeover target (D)

Del. Ch. Ct., 564 A.2d 651 (1988).

NATURE OF CASE: Action seeking to invalidate action by corporate directors.

FACT SUMMARY: The board of directors of Atlas Corp. (the "board") (D) sought to prevent Blasius Industries, Inc. (P) from obtaining shareholder approval of its plan to enlarge the board (D) by voting to expand the board (D), and placing persons of its own choosing in the new seats.

🏛 RULE OF LAW

A board of directors may not enlarge the size of the board for the purpose of preventing a majority of shareholders from voting to expand the board to give control to an insurgent group.

FACTS: Blasius Industries, Inc. (Blasius) (P) acquired roughly nine percent of the voting stock of Atlas Corp. (D). Blasius (P) presented the board of directors of Atlas (the "board" or the "directors") (D) with a restructuring proposal that would have left Atlas (D) highly leveraged. The directors (D) did not approve the proposal, considering it potentially damaging to the company. At this point, Blasius (P) began soliciting shareholders for approval of a proposal to expand the board from seven to fifteen members and to fill the eight new seats with persons of its choosing. This would have given control to Blasius (P). The board (D) responded by voting to enlarge the board to nine members and choosing the persons to fill the new seats. Blasius (P) filed a lawsuit to invalidate the board's (D) action, alleging breach of fiduciary duty.

ISSUE: May a board of directors enlarge the size of the board for the purpose of preventing a majority of shareholders from voting to expand the board to give control to an insurgent group?

HOLDING AND DECISION: (Allen, Chan.) No. A board of directors may not enlarge the size of the board for the purpose of preventing a majority of shareholders from voting to expand the board to give control to an insurgent group. Shareholder franchise is the ideological basis for directorial power. The only legitimate reason why a select group of persons can control assets not belonging to them is a mandate from those who do control the assets. Consequently, any effort by the directors to frustrate the will of the majority, even if taken for the most unselfish of reasons, must fail. Directors are agents of shareholders, not their philosopher-kings. The business judgment rule simply does not apply in this context. Any attempt to frustrate shareholder voting cannot stand up to a challenge. Here, the board (D) clearly based its action on a desire to prevent shareholder approval of a plan to give control to an insurgent group. Even though it was apparently taken by the board (D) out of concerns for the welfare of the corporation, it was an invalid attempt to thwart shareholder voting power, and the action must therefore be voided.

▶ ANALYSIS

Corporate directors, by virtue of their position, have a decided advantage with respect to corporate control. They have the power to set the corporate agenda and to time shareholder meetings. As the present case shows, however, this power is not unlimited. Courts will restrain overreaching by directors.

Quicknotes

BUSINESS JUDGMENT RULE Doctrine relieving corporate directors and/or officers from liability for decisions honestly and rationally made in the corporation's best interests.

RECAPITALIZATION The restructuring of the capital of a corporation.

CHAPTER 14

Trading in the Corporation's Securities

Quick Reference Rules of Law

Goodwin v. Agassiz

Former shareholder (P) v. Corporate director (D)

Mass. Sup. Jud. Ct., 186 N.E. 659 (1933).

NATURE OF CASE: Action for rescission of sale of stock.

FACT SUMMARY: Agassiz (D) and another, president and directors of the corporation, purchased stock of Goodwin (P) in the corporation (through a stock exchange) without disclosing inside information which turned out to be important.

🏛 RULE OF LAW
A director of a corporation may not personally seek out a stockholder for the purpose of buying his shares without disclosing material facts within his peculiar knowledge as a director and not within reach of the stockholder; but, the fiduciary obligations of directors are not so onerous as to preclude all dealing in the corporation's stock where there is no evidence of fraud.

FACTS: Agassiz (D) and another, president and directors of the Cliff Mining Co., purchased Goodwin's (P) stock in that corporation through a broker on the Boston Stock Exchange. Prior to the sale, certain corporate property had been explored for mineral deposits, unsuccessfully. The director and president, however, had knowledge of a geological theory by which they expected to discover minerals on that land. They decided not to disclose it publicly, however, so that another mining company, in which they were also stockholders, could acquire options on adjacent land. Goodwin (P) sued to force a rescission of the stock sale on the grounds that the director and president had breached their fiduciary duties by failing to disclose the geological theory, their belief in it, and its subsequent successful testing. From a dismissal of the complaint, Goodwin (P) appealed.

ISSUE: May a director of a corporation deal in the corporation's shares where his action is based upon inside knowledge?

HOLDING AND DECISION: (Rugg, C.J.) Yes. A director of a corporation may not personally seek out a stockholder for the purpose of buying his shares without disclosing material facts within his peculiar knowledge as a director and not within reach of the stockholder, but the fiduciary obligations of directors are not so onerous as to preclude all dealing in the corporation's stock where there is no evidence of fraud. Business must be governed by practical rules. An honest director would be in a difficult situation if he could neither buy nor sell stock in his own corporation without seeking out the other actual ultimate party to such transaction. Absent fraud, he must be per-

mitted to deal. Here, there is no evidence of any fraud: (1) Agassiz (D) did not personally solicit Goodwin (P) to sell his stock; (2) Agassiz (D) was an experienced stock dealer who made a voluntary decision to sell; (3) at the time of sale, the undisclosed theory had not yet been proven; and, (4) had the director and president disclosed it prematurely, they would have exposed themselves to litigation if it proved to be false. The judgment below must be affirmed.

▶ ANALYSIS

Prior to the Securities Exchange Act of 1934, this case pointed up the general standard for "insider" liability: fraud. The use of inside information by corporate officers to gain personal profit could be proscribed only if some showing of fraud could be made. Note that this is consistent with the general common-law caveat emptor approach to the relationship between shareholders and management. At common law, it was held that no fiduciary relationship existed between management and shareholders, so, by caveat emptor, any trading done by either was legal unless provably fraudulent. Note, finally, that even where a common-law duty was found to exist, it was always limited to direct dealings between directors and shareholders. Shareholders selling to or buying from third parties were never protected.

Quicknotes

CAVEAT EMPTOR Let the buyer beware; doctrine that a buyer purchases at his own risk.

FIDUCIARY DUTY A legal obligation to act for the benefit of another.

MATERIALITY Importance; the degree of relevance or necessity to the particular matter.

RESCISSION The canceling of an agreement and the return of the parties to their positions prior to the formation of the contract.

Freeman v. Decio

Shareholder (P) v. Corporate directors/officers (D)

584 F.2d 186 (7th Cir. 1978).

NATURE OF CASE: Derivative action for damages for fraud based on insider trading.

FACT SUMMARY: Freeman (P) alleged in a derivative action that Decio (D) and other insiders (D) sold stock of the Skyline Corporation on the basis of material inside information and demanded disgorgement to the corporation of the insiders' (D) profits.

🏛 RULE OF LAW
Insider trading on the basis of material inside information does not constitute a breach of a fiduciary duty to the corporation.

FACTS: For many years, Skyline Corporation experienced continual growth and reported in 1971 that over the previous five years sales had increased at a 40 percent average compound rate and that net income had grown at a 64 percent rate. Then in the last quarter of 1972, the company reported a significant drop in earnings and the New York Stock Exchange (NYSE) suspended trading in its stock. Trading resumed a few days later at 30 percent lower than previous trading. Freeman (P), a Skyline shareholder, brought a derivative action alleging that Decio (D), Skyline's largest shareholder, its chairman of the board, and its president, as well as other insiders (D), breached their fiduciary duty to the corporation by having sold stock on the basis of material inside information. Freeman (P) alleged that the insiders knew that results for the previous quarter understated material costs and overstated earnings, and that they made significant sales of Skyline stock based on this information. She also asserted that Decio (D) and other insiders (D) made gifts and sales of Skyline stock while knowing that reported earnings for the last quarter of 1972 would decline significantly. Her suit demanded disgorgement to the corporation of the insiders' (D) profits. The district court held for the insiders (D), and the court of appeals granted review.

ISSUE: Does insider trading on the basis of material inside information constitute a breach of a fiduciary duty to the corporation?

HOLDING AND DECISION: (Wood, Jr., J.) No. Insider trading on the basis of material inside information does not constitute a breach of a fiduciary duty to the corporation. The issue is raised by the holding in *Diamond v. Oreamuno*, 248 N.E.2d 910 (1969), which reached the opposite result. However, it is clear that the remedies for insider trading under the federal securities laws now constitute a more effective deterrent than they did when

Diamond was decided because the Rule 10b-5 class action has made substantial advances as a remedy. Affirmed.

▶ ANALYSIS

The Seventh Circuit, in rejecting the holding of *Diamond* in the decision above, concluded with the following comment: "although the court [in *Diamond*] sought to ground its ruling in accepted principles of corporate common law, that decision can best be understood as an example of judicial securities regulation. Although the question is a close one, we believe that were the issue to be presented to the Indiana courts at the present time, they would most likely . . . [refuse] to adopt the New York court's innovative ruling." In another case, tipper and tippee activity was involved. It was held that the cause was not a corporate one. This result affirmed the district court's holding. *Schein v. Chasen*, 519 F.2d 453 (2d Cir. 1975), 313 So. 2d 739 (1975); 478 F.2d 817 (2d Cir. 1973); *Lehman Brothers v. Schein*, 416 U.S. 386 (1974).

▬▬■

Quicknotes

BREACH OF FIDUCIARY DUTY The failure of a fiduciary to observe the standard of care exercised by professionals of similar education and experience.

DERIVATIVE CLAIM Action asserted by a shareholder in order to enforce a cause of action on behalf of the corporation.

INSIDER INFORMATION Information regarding the corporation that is available only to insiders.

RULE 10b-5 It is unlawful to defend or make untrue statements in connection with purchase or sale of securities.

▬▬■

SEC v. Texas Gulf Sulphur Co.

Government regulatory agency (P) v. Corporation (D)

401 F.2d 833 (2d Cir. 1968) (*en banc*).

NATURE OF CASE: Appeal from judgment in an action to compel rescission of securities transactions made in violation of federal securities law.

FACT SUMMARY: The Securities and Exchange Commission (SEC) (P) brought this action based on insider trading after certain employees and officers of Texas Gulf Sulphur Co. (TGS) (D) purchased shares and options of TGS (D) stock before knowledge of a rich ore strike became public.

🏛 RULE OF LAW
Anyone in possession of material inside information must either disclose it to the investing public, or, if ordered not to disclose it to protect a corporate confidence, abstain from trading in the securities concerned while such inside information remains undisclosed.

FACTS: Employees of Texas Gulf Sulphur (TGS) (D), doing exploratory drilling in Canada, discovered unusually rich ore deposits. To facilitate purchase of all the land containing those deposits, Stephens, president of TGS (D), instructed the exploratory team not to disclose the results of their drilling to anyone else, including other TGS employees, directors and officers, and drilling ceased. During a period of about four months, some of those with knowledge of the drilling results purchased TGS (D) stock or calls thereon. Also during this period, TGS (D) issued stock options to 26 of its officers and employees whose salaries exceeded a specified amount, five of whom knew or had some knowledge of the drilling results. At this point, neither the board nor the compensation committee knew of the drilling results. Drilling then resumed, and rumors began to circulate in the press of a rich ore strike. TGS (D) issued a press release to downplay these rumors and stated that the work done to date was not sufficient to reach definite conclusions as to the size and grade of any ore discovered. The TGS (D) official who issued the press release knew of the developments to date. Four days later, TGS (D) officially announced a major strike. During those four days, certain TGS (D) employees and officers who knew about the strike purchased substantial amounts of TGS (D) stock and call options. After the strike announcement, the price of TGS (D) stock increased dramatically. The Securities and Exchange Commission (SEC) (P) sued, alleging that TGS's (D) conduct constituted insider trading in violation of § 10(b) of the Securities Exchange Act and SEC Rule 10b-5. It sought to compel the rescission of those securities transactions which violated the Act. The trial court concluded that the results of the first drill core were too remote to be deemed material or to have had any significant impact on the market. The SEC (P) appealed.

ISSUE: Must anyone in possession of material inside information either disclose it to the investing public, or, if ordered not to disclose it to protect a corporate confidence, abstain from trading in the securities concerned while such inside information remains undisclosed?

HOLDING AND DECISION: (Waterman, J.) Yes. Anyone in possession of material inside information must either disclose it to the investing public, or, if ordered not to disclose it to protect a corporate confidence, abstain from trading in the securities concerned while such inside information remains undisclosed. Material facts include those that may affect the desire of investors to buy, sell, or hold the company's securities. Here, knowledge of the possible existence of a remarkably rich drill core would certainly have been an important fact to a reasonable investor in deciding whether he should buy, sell, or hold. A survey of the facts found by the trial court conclusively establishes that knowledge of the results of the discovery hole constituted material information. Therefore, all transactions in TGS (D) stock by individuals apprised of the drilling results were made in violation of SEC Rule 10b-5. Reversed.

▶ ANALYSIS

Whether facts are material within SEC Rule 10b-5 will depend upon a balancing of both the indicated probability that an event will occur and the anticipated magnitude of the event in light of the totality of the company activity. The court of appeals' disagreement with the district judge on the issue of materiality did not go to his findings of basic fact but to his understanding of the legal standard applicable to them. One TGS (D) officer was absolved by the trial court because his telephone order was placed shortly after a press release announcing the strike. However, the court of appeals stated that, at the minimum, the officer should have waited until the news could reasonably have been expected to appear over the media of widest circulation, the Dow Jones broad tape.

■■■

Quicknotes

INSIDER TRADING Trading accomplished by any person within a corporation who has access to information not available to the public.

Continued on next page.

MATERIAL FACT A fact without the existence of which a contract would not have been entered.

RESCISSION The canceling of an agreement and the return of the parties to their positions prior to the formation of the contract.

RULE 10b-5 It is unlawful to defend or make untrue statements in connection with purchase or sale of securities.

Santa Fe Industries Inc. v. Green

Corporation (D) v. Shareholder (P)

430 U.S. 462 (1977).

NATURE OF CASE: Appeal from motion to dismiss for violation of § 10(b) of the Securities Exchange Act of 1934 and Rule 10b-5.

FACT SUMMARY: Santa Fe Industries (D) merged with Kirby Lumber for the sole purpose of eliminating minority shareholders.

RULE OF LAW

Before a claim of fraud or breach of fiduciary duty may be maintained under § 10(b) of the Securities Exchange Act of 1934 or Rule 10b-5, there must first be a showing of manipulation or deception.

FACTS: Santa Fe Industries (Santa Fe) (D) owned 90 percent of Kirby Lumber's (Kirby's) stock. Under Delaware law, a parent could merge with a subsidiary without prior notice to minority shareholders and could pay them the fair market value of the stock. Solely to eliminate these minority shareholders, Santa Fe (D) merged with Kirby. A complete audit was run of the business and shareholders were sent an offer of $150 a share plus the asset appraisal report and an opinion letter that the shares were worth $125. Green (P) and other shareholders did not appeal the price offered them as provided by state law. Instead, they initiated suit under § 10(b) of the Securities Exchange Act of 1934 and Rule 10b-5. Green (P) alleged that the merger had not been made for a business purpose and no prior notice was given shareholders. Green (P) further alleged that the value of the stock as disclosed in the appraisal should have been $722 per share based on the assets of Kirby divided by the number of shares. The court held that the merger was valid under state law which did not require a business purpose or prior notice for such mergers. The court held there was no misrepresentation, manipulation, or deception as to the value of the shares since all relevant information appeared in the appraisal report. The court of appeals reversed, finding a breach of fiduciary duty to the minority shareholders and no business purpose or notice.

ISSUE: Is breach of duty alone, without a showing of deception or manipulation grounds for a § 10(b) or Rule 10b-5 action?

HOLDING AND DECISION: (White, J.) No. Before any action may be brought under § 10(b) or Rule 10b-5, there must be a showing of manipulation or deception. The Act and Rule speak plainly in these terms. Not every act by a corporation or its officers was intended to be actionable under § 10(b) or Rule 10b-5. Here, there was full disclosure. If the minority shareholders were dissatisfied they could seek a court appraisal under the state statute. Neither notice nor a business purpose is required under state law. If minority shareholders feel aggrieved they must pursue state remedies since no private right of action has even been granted under § 10(b) or Rule 10b-5 in cases such as this one. Ample state remedies exist for breach of fiduciary duty actions and for appraisals. Reversed.

ANALYSIS

In *Blue Chip Stamps v. Manor Drug Stores*, 421 U.S. 723 (1975), the Court also held that mere negligence is not grounds for an action under § 10(b) and Rule 10b-5. In *Ernst & Ernst v. Hochfelder*, 425 U.S. 185 (1976), the Court held that the SEC could not enact rules which conflicted with plain expressions of congressional intent. Hence, Rule 10b-5 could not be more restrictive in nature than could actions under § 10(b) of the Securities Act of 1934.

Quicknotes

FAIR MARKET VALUE The price of particular property or goods that a buyer would offer and a seller accept in the open market, following full disclosure.

FIDUCIARY DUTY A legal obligation to act for the benefit of another.

MINORITY SHAREHOLDER A stockholder in a corporation controlling such a small portion of outstanding shares that its votes have no influence in the management of the corporation.

RULE 10b-5 It is unlawful to defend or make untrue statements in connection with purchase or sale of securities.

SECURITIES EXCHANGE ACT § 10(b) Makes it unlawful for any person to use manipulation or deception in the buying or selling of securities.

Chiarella v. United States

Printer (D) v. Federal government (P)

445 U.S. 222 (1980).

NATURE OF CASE: Appeal from conviction for violating federal securities law.

FACT SUMMARY: While employed as a printer, Chiarella (D) saw information that one corporation was planning to attempt to secure control of another, and he used this information to make a profit from trading the stock of the corporations.

🏛 **RULE OF LAW**
A purchaser of stock who has no duty to a prospective seller because he is neither an insider nor a fiduciary has no obligation to disclose material information he has acquired, and his failure to disclose such information does not, therefore, constitute a violation of § 10(b) of the Securities Exchange Act of 1934.

FACTS: In the course of his job as a printer at Pandick Press, Chiarella (D) was exposed to documents of one corporation revealing its plan to attempt to secure control of a second corporation. Although the identities of the corporations were concealed by blank spaces or false names until the true names were sent over on the night of the final printing, Chiarella (D) had deduced the names of the target companies beforehand from other information contained in the documents. Without revealing any of this information to the prospective sellers, he went about purchasing shares in the target corporations. He sold them after the takeover attempts were made public, thus realizing a gain of more than $30,000 in the course of 14 months. The Securities and Exchange Commission (SEC) began an investigation, which culminated in Chiarella's (D) entering into a consent decree agreeing to return his profits to the sellers of the shares. He was, that same day, fired by Pandick Press. Eight months later, he was indicted and convicted on 17 counts of violating § 10(b) of the Securities Exchange Act of 1934 and SEC Rule 10b-5. The court of appeals affirmed, and the United States Supreme Court granted certiorari.

ISSUE: If a stockholder owed no duty of disclosure to the party from whom he purchased securities, does his failure to disclose to the seller material information he has acquired constitute a violation of § 10(b) of the Securities Exchange Act of 1934?

HOLDING AND DECISION: (Powell, J.) No. If one who purchases stock is neither an insider nor a fiduciary, and thus owes no duty to the prospective seller, his failure to disclose inside material information he has acquired does not constitute a fraud in violation of § 10(b) of

the Securities Exchange Act of 1934. Administrative and judicial interpretations have established that silence in connection with the purchase or sale of securities may operate as a fraud actionable under § 10(b) despite the absence of statutory language or legislative history specifically addressing the legality of nondisclosures. However, such liability is premised upon a duty to disclose arising from a relationship of trust and confidence between parties to a transaction. In this case, the charges of the lower courts did not reflect his duty requirement adequately. Furthermore, both courts failed to identify a relationship between Chiarella (D) and the sellers that could give rise to a duty and thus provide a basis for his conviction under § 10(b) for failure to disclose the information he had. It may well be that he breached a duty to the acquiring corporation when he acted upon information he obtained by virtue of his position as an employee of the printer employed by the corporation. Whether this breach of duty would support a conviction under § 10(b) for fraud need not be decided, for this theory was not presented to the jury. Reversed.

DISSENT: (Burger, C.J.) Section 10(b) and Rule 10b-5 mean that a person who has misappropriated nonpublic information has an absolute duty to disclose that information or to refrain from trading. The broad language of the statute and Congress's intent to use it as an elastic "catch-all" provision to protect the uninitiated investor from misbehavior, evidences the propriety of such an interpretation.

▶ *ANALYSIS*

The SEC has not made a practice of challenging trading by noninsiders on the basis of undisclosed market information. In fact, it has generally pointed to some fiduciary duty or special relationship between the purchase or seller and the outsider trader as a basis for such challenges. For example, in *SEC v. Campbell*, [993 F.2d 878 (3d Cir. 1993)], the writer of a financial column engaged in "scalping," i.e., purchasing stocks shortly before recommending them in his column and then selling them when the price rose after the recommendation was published. The SEC went to great lengths to equate his relationship with his readers to that of an adviser's relationship with his clients.

▪━▪━▪

Quicknotes

CERTIORARI A discretionary writ issued by a superior court to an inferior court in order to review the lower

Continued on next page.

court's decisions; the Supreme Court's writ ordering such review.

RULE 10b-5 Unlawful to defend or make untrue statements in connection with purchase or sale of securities.

SECURITIES EXCHANGE ACT § 10(b) Makes it unlawful for any person to use manipulation or deception in the buying or selling of securities.

Dirks v. SEC

Broker (D) v. Government regulatory agency (P)

463 U.S. 646 (1983).

NATURE OF CASE: SEC action for violation of § 10(b).

FACT SUMMARY: Dirks (D), based on some nonpublic information he received and a subsequent investigation, aided the Securities and Exchange Commission (SEC) (P) in convicting Equity Funding of America (EFA) for corporate fraud and was then sued by the SEC (P) for violating § 10(b) because he openly disclosed the nonpublic information to investors.

🏛 RULE OF LAW
A tippee will be held liable for openly disclosing nonpublic information received from an insider, if the tippee knows or should know that the insider will benefit in some fashion from disclosing the information to the tippee.

FACTS: Dirks (D), officer of a brokerage firm, was told by Secrist, the insider, Equity Funding of America (EFA) was engaging in corporate fraud. Dirks (D) then investigated EFA to verify Secrist's information. Neither Dirks (D) nor his firm owned or traded EFA stock. However, during Dirks's (D) investigation, he openly revealed the information to investors and caused many of them to sell their EFA stock. Consequently, the price of EFA stock dropped from $26 to $15. However, largely due to Dirks's (D) investigation, the Securities and Exchange Commission (SEC) (P) was able to convict the officers of EFA for corporate fraud. Still, the SEC (P) sued and reprimanded Dirks (D) for his disclosure of the nonpublic information to the investors. The court of appeals affirmed. Dirks (D), then applied for and was granted certiorari by the United States Supreme Court.

ISSUE: Will a tippee automatically be liable for openly disclosing nonpublic information received from an insider?

HOLDING AND DECISION: (Powell, J.) No. A tippee will be held liable for openly disclosing nonpublic information received from an insider if the tippee knows or should know that the insider will benefit in some fashion for disclosing the information to the tippee. Mere receipt of nonpublic information by a tippee from an insider does not automatically carry with it the fiduciary duty of an insider. In this case, Secrist, the insider, did not receive a benefit for his disclosure. He disclosed the information to Dirks (D), the tippee, solely to help expose the fraud being perpetrated by the officers of EFA. Therefore, since Secrist, the insider, did not receive a benefit for his disclosure of nonpublic information to Dirks (D), the tippee, Secrist did not breach his fiduciary duty to the shareholders. Conse-

quently, since Secrist, the insider, did not breach his duty to the shareholders, there was no derivative breach by Dirks (D) when he passed on the nonpublic information to investors. Reversed.

DISSENT: (Blackmun, J.) It is not necessary that an insider receive a benefit from his disclosure of nonpublic information before a court can hold he breached his duty to the shareholders. All that is necessary is that the shareholders suffer an injury. Here Secrist's disclosure to Dirks (D) resulted in Dirks's (D) clients trading on the information. Consequently, Secrist, the insider, breached his duty, and therefore Dirks (D), as tippee, derivatively breached. Thus, Dirks (D) violated § 10(b).

▌ ANALYSIS

This case is consistent with the Court's decision in *Chiarella v. United States*, (445 U.S. 222 [1980]), where the Court found that there is no general duty to disclose before trading on material nonpublic information and held that a duty to disclose under § 10(b) does not arise from mere possession of nonpublic market information. Rather, such a duty, the Court found, arises from the existence of a fiduciary relationship.

■■■

Quicknotes

FIDUCIARY DUTY A legal obligation to act for the benefit of another.

FRAUD A false representation of facts with the intent that another will rely on the misrepresentation to his detriment.

RULE 10b-5 It is unlawful to defend or make untrue statements in connection with purchase or sale of securities.

SECURITIES EXCHANGE ACT § 10(b) Makes it unlawful for any person to use manipulation or deception in the buying or selling of securities.

■■■

United States v. Newman

Federal government (P) v. Convicted inside trader (D)

773 F.3d 438 (2d Cir. 2014).

NATURE OF CASE: Appeal from conviction of securities fraud and conspiracy to commit securities fraud.

FACT SUMMARY: Newman (D) and Chiasson (D), who had been convicted of securities fraud and conspiracy to commit securities fraud, contended their convictions should be set aside because the district court erred in failing to instruct the jury it had to find a tippee knew the insider disclosed confidential information in exchange for a personal benefit, and because the Government's (P) evidence of any personal benefit received by the alleged insiders was insufficient, as was evidence Newman (D) and Chiasson (D) knew they were trading on information obtained from insiders in violation of those insiders' fiduciary duties.

RULE OF LAW

(1) To prevail on charges of securities fraud based on insider trading, the government must prove beyond a reasonable doubt that a tippee knew of the personal benefit received by the insider in exchange for the disclosure.

(2) In an action for securities fraud based on insider trading, where the evidence that an insider received a personal benefit in exchange for disclosure, or that the disclosure constituted a breach of confidentiality, is so scant that it gives equal or nearly equal circumstantial support to a theory of guilt and a theory of innocence, a reasonable jury cannot find beyond a reasonable doubt that a tippee knew of the insider's benefit or that the disclosure was in breach of fiduciary duties.

FACTS: Newman (D) and Chiasson (D) were portfolio managers at two separate, unrelated hedge funds. The Government (P) charged them with committing securities fraud and conspiracy to commit securities fraud. The Government (P) based these charges on allegations that a group of financial analysts exchanged information they obtained from company insiders, both directly and more often indirectly. Specifically, the Government (P) alleged that these analysts received information from insiders at Dell and NVIDIA disclosing those companies' earnings numbers before they were publicly released in Dell's May 2008 and August 2008 earnings announcements and NVIDIA's May 2008 earnings announcement. These analysts then passed the inside information to their portfolio managers, including Newman (D) and Chiasson (D), who, in turn, executed trades in Dell and NVIDIA stock, earning approximately $4 million and $68 million, respectively, in profits for their

respective funds. Newman (D) and Chiasson (D) were several steps removed from the corporate insiders and there was no evidence that either was aware of the source of the inside information. With respect to the Dell tipping chain, the evidence established that a Dell insider (Ray) tipped information regarding Dell's consolidated earnings numbers to an analyst (Goyal) who in turn gave the information to an analyst at Newman's (D) fund, who in turn passed the information on to Newman (D), as well as to an analyst at Chiasson's (D) fund, who passed the information on to Chiasson (D). Thus, Newman (D) and Chiasson (D) were three and four levels removed from the Dell inside tipper, Ray, respectively. With respect to the NVIDIA tipping chain, an NVIDIA insider (Choi) tipped information to a church acquaintance (Lim) who in turn passed the information to an analyst, who in turn passed the information to several analyst friends, including analysts, respectively, at Newman's (D) fund and Chiasson's (D) fund. Thus, Newman (D) and Chiasson (D) were four levels removed from the NVIDIA inside tipper, Choi. At the close of evidence, Newman (D) and Chiasson (D) moved for a judgment of acquittal, arguing there was no evidence the corporate insiders provided inside information in exchange for a personal benefit which is required to establish tipper liability under *Dirks v. S.E.C.,* 463 U.S. 646 (1983). Newman (D) and Chiasson (D) also argued that, even if the corporate insiders had received a personal benefit in exchange for the inside information, there was no evidence they knew about any such benefit, and that the district court should have instructed the jury that before it could convict them, the jury had to find that as tippees, Newman (D) and Chiasson (D) knew the insiders had disclosed confidential information in exchange for a personal benefit. The district court denied their motion, and did not give the requested jury instruction. The jury convicted them on all counts. The court of appeals granted review.

ISSUE:

(1) To prevail on charges of securities fraud based on insider trading, must the government prove beyond a reasonable doubt that a tippee knew of the personal benefit received by the insider in exchange for the disclosure?

(2) In an action for securities fraud based on insider trading, where the evidence that an insider received a personal benefit in exchange for disclosure, or that the disclosure constituted a breach of confidentiality, is so scant that it gives equal or nearly equal circumstantial support to a theory of guilt and a theory of

Continued on next page.

innocence, can a reasonable jury find beyond a reasonable doubt that a tippee knew of the insider's benefit or that the disclosure was in breach of fiduciary duties?

HOLDING AND DECISION: (Parker, J.)

(1) Yes. To prevail on charges of securities fraud based on insider trading, the government must prove beyond a reasonable doubt that a tippee knew of the personal benefit received by the insider in exchange for the disclosure. Insider trading liability reaches situations where the insider or misappropriator in possession of material nonpublic information (the "tipper") does not himself trade but discloses the information to an outsider (a "tippee") who then trades on the basis of the information before it is publicly disclosed. Here, Newman (D) and Chiasson (D) are tippees. In *Dirks v. S.E.C.*, 463 U.S. 646 (1983), the Supreme Court rejected the SEC's theory that a tippee must refrain from trading whenever he receives inside information from an insider. Instead, the Court held that the tippee's duty to disclose or abstain is derivative from that of the insider's duty. Because the tipper's breach of fiduciary duty requires that he personally will benefit, directly or indirectly, from his disclosure, a tippee may not be held liable in the absence of such benefit. Moreover, the Supreme Court held a that tippee may be found liable only when the tippee knows or should know that there has been a breach by the insider. It thus follows that without establishing that the tippee knows of the personal benefit received by the insider in exchange for the disclosure, the Government (P) cannot meet its burden of showing that the tippee knew of a breach. Further, there is no support for the Government's (P) contention that knowledge of a breach of the duty of confidentiality without knowledge of the personal benefit is sufficient to impose criminal liability. This conclusion comports with the judgment of every district court (other than the one below) that has considered the question, and it comports with the mens rea requirement in criminal law, which requires that it be proved that the accused knew the facts that made his conduct illegal. This is also a statutory requirement, because only "willful" violations are subject to criminal provision. For these reasons, the challenged jury instruction was erroneous, since the district court was required to instruct the jury that the Government (P) had to prove beyond a reasonable doubt that Newman (D) and Chiasson (D) knew that the tippers received a personal benefit for their disclosure, and the district court failed to do so. Judgment for Newman (D) and Chiasson (D) as to this issue.

(2) No. In an action for securities fraud based on insider trading, where the evidence that an insider received a personal benefit in exchange for disclosure, or that the disclosure constituted a breach of confidentiality, is so scant that it gives equal or nearly equal circumstantial support to a theory of guilt and a theory of innocence, a

reasonable jury cannot find beyond a reasonable doubt that a tippee knew of the insider's benefit or that the disclosure was in breach of fiduciary duties. If the evidence of a crime is nonexistent or so meager, such that it gives equal or nearly equal circumstantial support to a theory of guilt and a theory of innocence, then a reasonable jury must necessarily entertain a reasonable doubt. Here, even when viewed in the light most favorable to the Government (P), the circumstantial evidence in this case was simply too thin to warrant the inference that the corporate insiders received any personal benefit in exchange for their tips. As to the Dell tips, the insider (Ray) and the first-level tippee/tipper (Goyal) had known each other for many years, having gone to the same business school, and having worked at Dell together, although they were not close friends. Ray had sought career advice from Goyal on becoming an analyst. Goyal had provided Ray advice on different subjects, and had done so for over a year before Ray had provided Goyal with any tips. As to the NVIDIA tips, the insider (Choi) and the first-level tippee/tipper (Lim) were church acquaintances and Choi did not even know that Lim was trading in stocks (which he was not at the time of the disclosures). To permissibly infer a personal benefit from a personal relationship between the tipper and tippee, where the tippee's trades resemble trading by the insider himself followed by a gift of the profits to the recipient, there must be proof of a meaningfully close personal relationship that generates an exchange that is objective, consequential, and represents at least a potential gain of a pecuniary or similarly valuable nature. Here, such personal benefit may not be inferred as to either the Dell tips or the NVIDIA tips. The career advice given by Goyal to Ray was the kind of encouragement a fellow alum or casual acquaintance might give, and Goyal testified that he would have given Ray advice without receiving information because he routinely did so for industry colleagues. Moreover, this advice giving started a year before Ray provided Goyal with insider information. For these reasons, it would not be possible under the circumstances for a jury in a criminal trial to find beyond a reasonable doubt that Ray received a personal benefit in exchange for the disclosure of confidential information. The evidence of personal benefit was even more scant in the NVIDIA chain. Choi and Lim were merely casual acquaintances. The evidence did not establish a history of loans or personal favors between the two. During cross examination, Lim testified that he did not provide anything of value to Choi in exchange for the information. Because Choi did not know that Lim was trading NVIDIA stock, this undermines any inference that Choi intended to make a "gift" of the profits earned on any transaction based on confidential

Continued on next page.

information. Even assuming, arguendo, that it could be inferred that the insiders derived a personal benefit from their disclosures, the Government (P) failed to present any evidence that Newman (D) and Chiasson (D) knew that they were trading on information obtained from insiders, or that those insiders received any benefit in exchange for such disclosures, or even that Newman (D) and Chiasson (D) consciously avoided learning of these facts. In fact, their tippers also disavowed such knowledge. Also rejected is the Government's (P) argument that the specificity, timing, and frequency of the updates provided to Newman (D) and Chiasson (D) about Dell and NVIDIA were so "overwhelmingly suspicious" that they warranted various material inferences that could support a guilty verdict. Such inferences must be rejected in the face of evidence that analysts at hedge funds routinely estimate metrics such as revenue, gross margin, operating margin, and earnings per share through legitimate financial modeling using publicly available information and educated assumptions about industry and company trends. Also weighing heavily against such inferences is the fact that NVIDIA and Dell's investor relations personnel routinely "leaked" earnings data in advance of quarterly earnings. Such information was arguably similar to the information disclosed by Ray and Choi. Accordingly, no reasonable jury could have found beyond a reasonable doubt that Newman (D) and Chiasson (D) knew, or deliberately avoided knowing, that the information originated with corporate insiders. In sum, the facts adduced by the Government (P) are as consistent with an inference of innocence as one of guilt. Where the evidence viewed in the light most favorable to the prosecution gives equal or nearly equal circumstantial support to a theory of innocence as a theory of guilt, that evidence necessarily fails to establish guilt beyond a reasonable doubt. [The convictions are vacated.]

▌ *ANALYSIS*

Under *Newman*, to sustain an insider trading conviction against a tippee, the Government (P) must prove each of the following elements beyond a reasonable doubt that: (1) the corporate insider was entrusted with a fiduciary duty; (2) the corporate insider breached his fiduciary duty by (a) disclosing confidential information to a tippee (b) in exchange for a personal benefit; (3) the tippee knew of the tipper's breach, that is, he knew the information was confidential and divulged for personal benefit; and (4) the tippee still used that information to trade in a security or tip another individual for personal benefit.

Quicknotes

BREACH OF FIDUCIARY DUTY The failure of a fiduciary to observe the standard of care exercised by professionals of similar education and experience.

INSIDER INFORMATION Information regarding a corporation that is available only to insiders.

United States v. O'Hagan

Federal government (P) v. Attorney (D)

521 U.S. 642 (1997).

NATURE OF CASE: Appeal of the reversal of convictions for violations of § 10(b) and § 14(e) of the Securities Exchange Act.

FACT SUMMARY: O'Hagan (D) began purchasing call options on Pillsbury stock when his law firm was retained to handle a potential tender offer by Grand Met for Pillsbury stock. When the tender offer was announced, O'Hagan (D) sold his options, profiting by more than $4.3 million.

🏛 RULE OF LAW

(1) A person who trades in securities for personal profit by using confidential information misappropriated in breach of a fiduciary duty to the source of the information is guilty of violating Securities Exchange Act § 10(b) and Rule 10b-5.

(2) The Securities and Exchange Commission (SEC) did not exceed its rulemaking authority by adopting Rule 14e-3(a), which proscribes trading on undisclosed information in the tender offer setting, even in the absence of a duty to disclose.

FACTS: O'Hagan (D) was a partner in the law firm of Dorsey & Whitney. Grand Met retained the law firm to represent Grand Met regarding a potential tender offer for the common stock of Pillsbury Company. O'Hagan (D) did no work on the representation in the firm. He did, however, buy 2,500 Pillsbury options. When Grand Met announced its tender offer, O'Hagan (D) sold his call options, making a profit of more than $4.3 million. The SEC (P) investigated O'Hagan's (D) transactions, eventually issuing a fifty-seven-count indictment, including violations of § 10(b), § 14(e), Rule 10b-5, and Rule 14e-3(a). O'Hagan (D) was convicted on all fifty-seven counts and received a forty-one-month term of imprisonment. He appealed, and all the convictions were reversed when the court reasoned that a "misappropriation theory" was not a proper basis for securities fraud and that Rule 14e-3(a) exceeded SEC (P) rulemaking authority. The SEC (P) appealed.

ISSUE:

(1) Is a person who trades in securities for personal profit by using confidential information misappropriated in breach of a fiduciary duty to the source of the information guilty of violating Securities Exchange Act § 10(b) and Rule 10b-5?

(2) Did the Securities and Exchange Commission (SEC) exceed its rulemaking authority by adopting Rule 14e-3(a), which proscribes trading on undisclosed information in the tender offer setting, even in the absence of a duty to disclose?

HOLDING AND DECISION: (Ginsburg, J.)

(1) Yes. A person who trades in securities for personal profit by using confidential information misappropriated in breach of a fiduciary duty to the source of the information is guilty of violating Securities Exchange Act § 10(b) and Rule 10b-5. A fiduciary's undisclosed, self-serving use of a principal's information to purchase or sell securities, in breach of a duty of loyalty and confidentiality, defrauds the principal of the exclusive use of that information. In this case, O'Hagan (D) owed a duty of loyalty and confidentiality to his law firm and the firm's client. O'Hagan (D) took information that was the exclusive property of the client and used it to make securities trades. His actions fall squarely within behaviors that the Exchange Act sought to eliminate to "insure the maintenance of fair and honest markets." While prior cases have held that there is no general duty to disclose between members of the marketplace, when a special relationship exists, misappropriation is a sufficient basis upon which to rest a conviction for violations of § 10(b) and Rule 10b-5. Reversed.

(2) No. The Securities and Exchange Commission (SEC) (P) did not exceed its rulemaking authority by adopting Rule14e-3(a), which proscribes trading on undisclosed information in the tender offer setting, even in the absence of a duty to disclose. Rule 14e-3(a) is reasonably designed to prevent fraud in tender offers and therefore qualifies under § 14(e)'s rulemaking authority. The SEC (P) has broad latitude under § 14(e), so that under that section, it may prohibit acts, not themselves fraudulent under the common law or § 10(b), if doing so will prevent fraudulent acts or practices. Moreover, the SEC's (P) assessment that Rule 14e-3(a) is reasonably designed to prevent fraudulent acts is not arbitrary, capricious, or manifestly contrary to the statute, so this assessment is controlling. Reversed.

▶ ANALYSIS

Chiarella v. United States, 445 U.S. 222 (1980), which involved securities trades by a printer privy to corporate takeover plans, left open the questions posed in this case. In *Chiarella*, the Court held that there was no general duty between all participants in market transactions to forgo action based on material, nonpublic information.

Continued on next page.

The Court suggested that a special relationship was necessary to give rise to a duty to disclose or abstain from trading. However, the Court did not specify whether the only relationship prompting liability was the relationship between a corporation's insiders and shareholders. Another issue left undecided until this case was whether misappropriation of information could be a basis for criminal liability.

Quicknotes

BREACH OF FIDUCIARY DUTY The failure of a fiduciary to observe the standard of care exercised by professionals of similar education and experience.

PRINCIPAL A person or entity who authorizes another (the agent) to act on its behalf and subject to its authority to the extent that the principal may be held liable for the actions of the agent.

RULE 10b-5 It is unlawful to defend or make untrue statements in connection with purchase or sale of securities.

Elkind v. Liggett & Myers, Inc.

Shareholders (P) v. Corporation (D)

635 F.2d 156 (2d Cir. 1980).

NATURE OF CASE: Appeal of award of damages in class action for violation of insider trading laws.

FACT SUMMARY: Shareholders (P) of Liggett & Myers, Inc. (Liggett) (D) brought an action against Liggett (D) for wrongfully tipping certain individuals information concerning a soon-to-be-disclosed earnings decline. A key issue was the measure of damages in a private Rule 10b-5 insider trading class action.

🏛 RULE OF LAW
The preferred measure of damages available when inside information indicating a stock price decline is involved is the decline in the purchaser's stock up to the amount of the tippee's realized benefit.

FACTS: Shareholders of Liggett & Myers, Inc. (D) were informed that Liggett (D) would soon announce an earnings decline. These shareholders then sold their shares. When the decline was made public, the stock value fell. Specifically, there was tippee trading of 1,800 Liggett shares on the afternoon of July 17, 1972. The actual preliminary Liggett earnings were released publicly at 2:15 P.M. on July 18 and were effectively disseminated in a Wall Street Journal article published on the morning of July 19. The market price of Liggett stock opened on July 17, 1972, at $55.625, and remained at substantially the same price on that date, closing at $55.25. By the close of the market on July 18 the price declined to $52.50 per share. By the close of the market on July 19 the market price had declined to $46.375 per share. Purchasing shareholders (P) brought a class action against the selling shareholders, contending that the sellers had benefited from inside information. A district court awarded damages based on the difference between the price paid and the value of the stock had the information been available to all investors. The court of appeals granted review.

ISSUE: Is the preferred measure of damages available when inside information indicating a stock decline is involved equal to the decline in the purchaser's stock up to the amount of the tippee's realized benefit?

HOLDING AND DECISION: (Mansfield, J.) Yes. The preferred measure of damages available when inside information indicating a stock decline is involved is the decline in the purchaser's stock up to the amount of the tippee's realized benefit. The measure used by the district court is the "out-of-pocket" measure, which consists of the difference between the price paid and the "value" of the stock when bought. This measure, which is used where a buyer is induced to purchase stock by materially misleading statements or omissions, is inapposite here since uninformed traders on an open, impersonal market are not induced by representations on the part of the tipper or tippee to buy or sell. Also inappropriate is the nunc pro tunc "value" method, which rests on the fundamental assumptions (1) that the tipped information is substantially the same as that later disclosed publicly, and (2) that one can determine how the market would have reacted to the public release of the tipped information at an earlier time by its reaction to that information at a later, proximate time. This theory depends on the parity of the "tip" and the "disclosure." When they differ, however, the basis of the damage calculation evaporates. This measure also risks imposing exorbitant damages that are not proportionate to the wrong committed. Another measure would compensate an uninformed investor for the loss in market value that he suffers as a direct result of the tippee's conduct, assuming the impact of such conduct is measurable. An advantage of this method is that it avoids windfall recoveries by investors at the expense of stockholders other than the tippee trader. However, a disadvantage of this measure is that it does not permit recovery for the tippee's violation of his duty to disclose the inside information before trading. Another difficulty with this measure is that it could be very difficult, as an evidentiary matter, to prove when the market was actually affected by the tippee's conduct. Yet another measure is the decline in the purchaser's stock up to the amount of the tippee's realized benefit. This measure, called the disgorgement measure, has several advantages. On the one hand, it deters tipping by making tippers and tippees liable up to the amount of their gain. On the other hand, by limiting recovery up to the amount of the ill-gotten gains, the measure bars windfall recoveries. Also, the proof required by such a measure does not present the difficulties that some of the alternative measures that exist do. A plaintiff would simply be required to prove (1) the time, amount, and price per share of his purchase, (2) that a reasonable investor would not have paid as high a price or made the purchase at all if he had had the information in the tippee's possession, and (3) the price to which the security had declined by the time he learned the tipped information or at a reasonable time after it became public, whichever event first occurred. Although this method also has its disadvantages—it modifies the principle that ordinarily gain to the wrongdoer should not be a prerequisite to liability for violation of Rule 10b-5, and in some instances the total claims could exceed the wrongdoer's gain, or the cost of recovery might be

Continued on next page.

inadequate for making a class action worthwhile—among all the methods reviewed, this is the one best suited for achieving an equitable result in this case. Applying this disgorgement method, any member of the class who bought Liggett shares during the period from the afternoon of July 17 to the close of the market on July 18 and met the reasonable investor requirement would be entitled to claim a pro rata portion of the tippee's gain, based on the difference between their purchase price and the price to which the market price declined within a reasonable time after the morning of July 19. The total recovery thus would be limited to the gain realized by the tippee from the inside information, i.e., 1,800 shares multiplied by approximately $9.35 per share. Reversed.

▶ ANALYSIS

The damages measure adopted in this case has become the standard measure of damages in private Rule 10b-5 insider trading cases.

Quicknotes

INSIDER TRADING Trading accomplished by any person within a corporation who has access to information not available to the public.

RULE 10b-5 It is unlawful to defend or make untrue statements in connection with purchase or sale of securities.

Basic Inc. v. Levinson

Company directors (P) v. Shareholders (D)

485 U.S. 224 (1988).

NATURE OF CASE: Appeal from circuit court decision in a class action suit.

FACT SUMMARY: Levinson (P) and other shareholders of Basic Incorporated (D) brought a class action against the company (D) and its directors (D), alleging they suffered injuries from selling their shares at depressed prices, in reliance on materially misleading statements issued by Basic (D) in violation of the Securities and Exchange Act of 1934 and Rule 10b-5.

RULE OF LAW
Reliance on materially misleading statements by a corporation will be presumed for a class action plaintiff asserting a Rule 10b-5 claim where he relied instead on the integrity of the price set by the market in trading.

FACTS: Basic Incorporated (D) was a publicly traded company engaged in the business of manufacturing for the steel industry. Another company, Combustion Engineering, Inc. met with Basic directors (D) concerning the possibility of a merger. Basic (D) made three public statements denying that it was engaged in merger discussions. Levinson (P) and other shareholders (P) sold their stock after these denials. Basics (D) board subsequently endorsed Combustion's offer and publicly announced its merger approval. Levinson (P) and the shareholders then brought a class action suit, asserting that Basic (D) issued misleading public statements in violation of Rule 10b-5.

ISSUE: Can reliance on materially misleading statements by a corporation be presumed for a class action plaintiff asserting a Rule 10b-5 claim where he relied instead on the integrity of the price set by the market in trading?

HOLDING AND DECISION: (Blackmun, J.) Yes. Reliance on materially misleading statements by a corporation will be presumed for a class action plaintiff asserting a Rule 10b-5 claim where he relied instead on the integrity of the price set by the market in trading. The "fraud-on-the-market" theory is based on the premise that misleading material information in the open market will affect the price of a company's stock, whether or not the individual investor relied on the misrepresentation. The lower courts applied a rebuttable presumption of reliance. Levinson (P) argued that the shareholders sold their stock in Basic (D) based on the depressed price created by Basic's (D) misrepresentation. If a court required proof of each individual shareholder's reliance in a class action, such proof would prevent the case from going forward since

the individual issues would overwhelm issues common to the class. Basic (D) contended that a claim under Rule 10b-5 requires proof of reliance and that, in applying the fraud-on-the-market theory the court effectively eliminated that requirement. While reliance is an element of a Rule 10b-5 cause of action, there are other ways of demonstrating a causal connection between the company's misrepresentations and the shareholder's injury. This Court has held that the causal connection has been demonstrated where a duty to disclose material information was breached or material omissions or misstatements were made in connection with a proxy solicitation. The Court's interpretation on Rule 10b-5 must take into consideration the conditions of modern securities markets, in which millions of shares are traded daily. Presumptions allow the Court to manage such circumstances in which direct proof is difficult to obtain. Here, the lower courts accepted a presumption that the individual shareholders traded in reliance on Basic's (D) depressed price and that because of the company's (D) material misrepresentations that price was fraudulently depressed. Requiring each individual shareholder to demonstrate reliance would impose an unrealistic burden on the shareholder who traded on the open market. The presumption is consistent with Congress's intent in enacting the 1934 Act to facilitate investors' reliance on the integrity of the market any information provided in relation thereto, as well as with common sense. Most courts have held that where misleading statements have been issued, reliance of individual shareholders on the integrity of the market price may be presumed. Since an investor buys or sells stock based on the integrity of that price, it may be presumed for Rule 10b-5 purposes that the investor also relied on the public material misrepresentation as reflected in the market price. The court of appeals found that Basic (D) made public material misrepresentations and sold its shares in the open market. Since the shareholders (P) established their loss, the burden shifted to Basic (D) to rebut the elements giving rise to the presumption. Basic (D) failed to rebut the presumption.

CONCURRENCE AND DISSENT: (White, J.) Even as the Court attempts to limit the fraud-on-the-market theory it endorses today, the pitfalls in its approach are revealed by previous uses by the lower courts of the broader versions of the theory. Confusion and contradiction in court rulings are inevitable when traditional legal analysis is replaced with economic theorization by the federal courts. While the economists' theories which

Continued on next page.

underpin the fraud-on-the-market presumption may have the appeal of mathematical exactitude and scientific certainty, they are nothing more than theories which may or may not prove accurate upon further consideration. Thus, while the majority states that, for purposes of reaching its result, it need only make modest assumptions about the way in which "market professionals generally" do their jobs and about how the conduct of market professionals affects stock prices, it is doubtful that the court is in much of a position to assess which theories aptly describe the functioning of the securities industry. Consequently, the majority errs in its effort to reconfigure the securities laws, based on recent economic theories, to better fit what it perceives to be the new realities of financial markets. This task should be left to others more equipped for the job than the court. Although the law should not retreat from the many protections that § 10(b) and Rule 10b-5, as interpreted in the Court's prior cases, provide to investors, any extension of these laws, to approach something closer to an investor insurance scheme, should come from Congress, and not from the courts.

▶ ANALYSIS

Early cases involving Rule 10b-5 involved face-to-face transactions in which plaintiffs were required to demonstrate their reliance on the defendant's misrepresentation and that such reliance caused their losses. The development of the modern securities exchange eliminated this personal interaction, thus making it difficult or impossible to prove the element of reliance in order to establish the causal connection. The fraud-on-the-market theory eliminates the necessity of the plaintiffs demonstrating reliance on the alleged misstatement or omission, or that the plaintiff was privy to the misleading information.

■■■■■

Quicknotes

FRAUD A false representation of facts with the intent that another will rely on the misrepresentation to his detriment.

MISREPRESENTATION A statement or conduct by one party to another that constitutes a false representation of fact.

RELIANCE Dependence on a fact, that causes a party to act or refrain from acting.

RULE 10b-5 Unlawful to defend or make untrue statements in connection with purchase or sale of securities.

■■■■■

Glossary

Common Latin Words and Phrases Encountered in the Law

A FORTIORI: Because one fact exists or has been proven, therefore a second fact that is related to the first fact must also exist.

A PRIORI: From the cause to the effect. A term of logic used to denote that when one generally accepted truth is shown to be a cause, another particular effect must necessarily follow.

AB INITIO: From the beginning; a condition which has existed throughout, as in a marriage which was void ab initio.

ACTUS REUS: The wrongful act; in criminal law, such action sufficient to trigger criminal liability.

AD VALOREM: According to value; an ad valorem tax is imposed upon an item located within the taxing jurisdiction calculated by the value of such item.

AMICUS CURIAE: Friend of the court. Its most common usage takes the form of an amicus curiae brief, filed by a person who is not a party to an action but is nonetheless allowed to offer an argument supporting his legal interests.

ARGUENDO: In arguing. A statement, possibly hypothetical, made for the purpose of argument, is one made arguendo.

BILL QUIA TIMET: A bill to quiet title (establish ownership) to real property.

BONA FIDE: True, honest, or genuine. May refer to a person's legal position based on good faith or lacking notice of fraud (such as a bona fide purchaser for value) or to the authenticity of a particular document (such as a bona fide last will and testament).

CAUSA MORTIS: With approaching death in mind. A gift causa mortis is a gift given by a party who feels certain that death is imminent.

CAVEAT EMPTOR: Let the buyer beware. This maxim is reflected in the rule of law that a buyer purchases at his own risk because it is his responsibility to examine, judge, test, and otherwise inspect what he is buying.

CERTIORARI: A writ of review. Petitions for review of a case by the United States Supreme Court are most often done by means of a writ of certiorari.

CONTRA: On the other hand. Opposite. Contrary to.

CORAM NOBIS: Before us; writs of error directed to the court that originally rendered the judgment.

CORAM VOBIS: Before you; writs of error directed by an appellate court to a lower court to correct a factual error.

CORPUS DELICTI: The body of the crime; the requisite elements of a crime amounting to objective proof that a crime has been committed.

CUM TESTAMENTO ANNEXO, ADMINISTRATOR (ADMINISTRATOR C.T.A.): With will annexed; an administrator c.t.a. settles an estate pursuant to a will in which he is not appointed.

DE BONIS NON, ADMINISTRATOR (ADMINISTRATOR D.B.N.): Of goods not administered; an administrator d.b.n. settles a partially settled estate.

DE FACTO: In fact; in reality; actually. Existing in fact but not officially approved or engendered.

DE JURE: By right; lawful. Describes a condition that is legitimate "as a matter of law," in contrast to the term "de facto," which connotes something existing in fact but not legally sanctioned or authorized. For example, de facto segregation refers to segregation brought about by housing patterns, etc., whereas de jure segregation refers to segregation created by law.

DE MINIMIS: Of minimal importance; insignificant; a trifle; not worth bothering about.

DE NOVO: Anew; a second time; afresh. A trial de novo is a new trial held at the appellate level as if the case originated there and the trial at a lower level had not taken place.

DICTA: Generally used as an abbreviated form of obiter dicta, a term describing those portions of a judicial opinion incidental or not necessary to resolution of the specific question before the court. Such nonessential statements and remarks are not considered to be binding precedent.

DUCES TECUM: Refers to a particular type of writ or subpoena requesting a party or organization to produce certain documents in their possession.

EN BANC: Full bench. Where a court sits with all justices present rather than the usual quorum.

EX PARTE: For one side or one party only. An ex parte proceeding is one undertaken for the benefit of only one party, without notice to, or an appearance by, an adverse party.

EX POST FACTO: After the fact. An ex post facto law is a law that retroactively changes the consequences of a prior act.

EX REL.: Abbreviated form of the term "ex relatione," meaning upon relation or information. When the state brings an action in which it has no interest against an individual at the instigation of one who has a private interest in the matter.

FORUM NON CONVENIENS: Inconvenient forum. Although a court may have jurisdiction over the case, the action should be tried in a more conveniently located court, one to which parties and witnesses may more easily travel, for example.

GUARDIAN AD LITEM: A guardian of an infant as to litigation, appointed to represent the infant and pursue his/her rights.

HABEAS CORPUS: You have the body. The modern writ of habeas corpus is a writ directing that a person (body) being detained (such as a prisoner) be brought before the court so that the legality of his detention can be judicially ascertained.

IN CAMERA: In private, in chambers. When a hearing is held before a judge in his chambers or when all spectators are excluded from the courtroom.

IN FORMA PAUPERIS: In the manner of a pauper. A party who proceeds in forma pauperis because of his poverty is one who is allowed to bring suit without liability for costs.

INFRA: Below, under. A word referring the reader to a later part of a book. (The opposite of supra.)

IN LOCO PARENTIS: In the place of a parent.

IN PARI DELICTO: Equally wrong; a court of equity will not grant requested relief to an applicant who is in pari delicto, or as much at fault in the transactions giving rise to the controversy as is the opponent of the applicant.

IN PARI MATERIA: On like subject matter or upon the same matter. Statutes relating to the same person or things are said to be in pari materia. It is a general rule of statutory construction that such statutes should be construed together, i.e., looked at as if they together constituted one law.

IN PERSONAM: Against the person. Jurisdiction over the person of an individual.

IN RE: In the matter of. Used to designate a proceeding involving an estate or other property.

IN REM: A term that signifies an action against the res, or thing. An action in rem is basically one that is taken directly against property, as distinguished from an action in personam, i.e., against the person.

INTER ALIA: Among other things. Used to show that the whole of a statement, pleading, list, statute, etc., has not been set forth in its entirety.

INTER PARTES: Between the parties. May refer to contracts, conveyances or other transactions having legal significance.

INTER VIVOS: Between the living. An inter vivos gift is a gift made by a living grantor, as distinguished from bequests contained in a will, which pass upon the death of the testator.

IPSO FACTO: By the mere fact itself.

JUS: Law or the entire body of law.

LEX LOCI: The law of the place; the notion that the rights of parties to a legal proceeding are governed by the law of the place where those rights arose.

MALUM IN SE: Evil or wrong in and of itself; inherently wrong. This term describes an act that is wrong by its very nature, as opposed to one which would not be wrong but for the fact that there is a specific legal prohibition against it (malum prohibitum).

MALUM PROHIBITUM: Wrong because prohibited, but not inherently evil. Used to describe something that is wrong because it is expressly forbidden by law but that is not in and of itself evil, e.g., speeding.

MANDAMUS: We command. A writ directing an official to take a certain action.

MENS REA: A guilty mind; a criminal intent. A term used to signify the mental state that accompanies a crime or other prohibited act. Some crimes require only a general mens rea (general intent to do the prohibited act), but others, like assault with intent to murder, require the existence of a specific mens rea.

MODUS OPERANDI: Method of operating; generally refers to the manner or style of a criminal in committing crimes, admissible in appropriate cases as evidence of the identity of a defendant.

NEXUS: A connection to.

NISI PRIUS: A court of first impression. A nisi prius court is one where issues of fact are tried before a judge or jury.

N.O.V. (NON OBSTANTE VEREDICTO): Notwithstanding the verdict. A judgment n.o.v. is a judgment given in favor of one party despite the fact that a verdict was returned in favor of the other party, the justification being that the verdict either had no reasonable support in fact or was contrary to law.

NUNC PRO TUNC: Now for then. This phrase refers to actions that may be taken and will then have full retroactive effect.

PENDENTE LITE: Pending the suit; pending litigation under way.

PER CAPITA: By head; beneficiaries of an estate, if they take in equal shares, take per capita.

PER CURIAM: By the court; signifies an opinion ostensibly written "by the whole court" and with no identified author.

PER SE: By itself, in itself; inherently.

PER STIRPES: By representation. Used primarily in the law of wills to describe the method of distribution where a person, generally because of death, is unable to take that which is left to him by the will of another, and therefore his heirs divide such property between them rather than take under the will individually.

PRIMA FACIE: On its face, at first sight. A prima facie case is one that is sufficient on its face, meaning that the evidence supporting it is adequate to establish the case until contradicted or overcome by other evidence.

PRO TANTO: For so much; as far as it goes. Often used in eminent domain cases when a property owner receives partial payment for his land without prejudice to his right to bring suit for the full amount he claims his land to be worth.

QUANTUM MERUIT: As much as he deserves. Refers to recovery based on the doctrine of unjust enrichment in those cases in which a party has rendered valuable services or furnished materials that were accepted and enjoyed by another under circumstances that would reasonably notify the recipient that the rendering party expected to be paid. In essence, the law implies a contract to pay the reasonable value of the services or materials furnished.

QUASI: Almost like; as if; nearly. This term is essentially used to signify that one subject or thing is almost analogous to another but that material differences between them do exist. For example, a quasi-criminal proceeding is one that is not strictly criminal but shares enough of the same characteristics to require some of the same safeguards (e.g., procedural due process must be followed in a parole hearing).

QUID PRO QUO: Something for something. In contract law, the consideration, something of value, passed between the parties to render the contract binding.

RES GESTAE: Things done; in evidence law, this principle justifies the admission of a statement that would otherwise be hearsay when it is made so closely to the event in question as to be said to be a part of it, or with such spontaneity as not to have the possibility of falsehood.

RES IPSA LOQUITUR: The thing speaks for itself. This doctrine gives rise to a rebuttable presumption of negligence when the instrumentality causing the injury was within the exclusive control of the defendant, and the injury was one that does not normally occur unless a person has been negligent.

RES JUDICATA: A matter adjudged. Doctrine which provides that once a court of competent jurisdiction has rendered a final judgment or decree on the merits, that judgment or decree is conclusive upon the parties to the case and prevents them from engaging in any other litigation on the points and issues determined therein.

RESPONDEAT SUPERIOR: Let the master reply. This doctrine holds the master liable for the wrongful acts of his servant (or the principal for his agent) in those cases in which the servant (or agent) was acting within the scope of his authority at the time of the injury.

STARE DECISIS: To stand by or adhere to that which has been decided. The common law doctrine of stare decisis attempts to give security and certainty to the law by following the policy that once a principle of law as applicable to a certain set of facts has been set forth in a decision, it forms a precedent which will subsequently be followed, even though a different decision might be made were it the first time the question had arisen. Of course, stare decisis is not an inviolable principle and is departed from in instances where there is good cause (e.g., considerations of public policy led the Supreme Court to disregard prior decisions sanctioning segregation).

SUPRA: Above. A word referring a reader to an earlier part of a book.

ULTRA VIRES: Beyond the power. This phrase is most commonly used to refer to actions taken by a corporation that are beyond the power or legal authority of the corporation.

Addendum of French Derivatives

IN PAIS: Not pursuant to legal proceedings.

CHATTEL: Tangible personal property.

CY PRES: Doctrine permitting courts to apply trust funds to purposes not expressed in the trust but necessary to carry out the settlor's intent.

PER AUTRE VIE: For another's life; during another's life. In property law, an estate may be granted that will terminate upon the death of someone other than the grantee.

PROFIT A PRENDRE: A license to remove minerals or other produce from land.

VOIR DIRE: Process of questioning jurors as to their predispositions about the case or parties to a proceeding in order to identify those jurors displaying bias or prejudice.